Marilyn M-P
April 2017

JAMESTOWN, THE TRUTH REVEALED

JAMES

TOWN

THE TRUTH REVEALED

William M. Kelso

UNIVERSITY OF VIRGINIA PRESS
Charlottesville and London

University of Virginia Press
© 2017 William M. Kelso
All rights reserved
Printed in the United States of America on acid-free paper

First published 2017

9 8 7 6 5 4 3 2 1

LIBRARY OF CONGRESS CATALOGING-IN-PUBLICATION DATA

Names: Kelso, William M., author.
Title: Jamestown, the truth revealed / William M. Kelso.
Description: Charlottesville : University of Virginia Press, 2017. | Includes biblio-
    graphical references and index.
Identifiers: LCCN 2017001103 | ISBN 9780813939933 (cloth : alk. paper) | ISBN
    9780813939940 (e-book)
Subjects: LCSH: Jamestown (Va.)—History. | Jamestown (Va.)—Antiquities. | Excava-
    tions (Archaeology)—Virginia—Jamestown. | Colonial National Historical Park
    (Va.)—Antiquities.
Classification: LCC F234.J3 K47 2017 | DDC 975.5/4251—dc23 LC record available at
    https://lccn.loc.gov/2017001103

Cover art: Forensic sculpture reconstruction of Jane's face on a digital resin copy of her skull (Studio EIS); John Smith's map of Virginia (courtesy of the Library of Virginia)

For Ellen
and my mentors
Ivor Noël Hume
J. C. Harrington
Stanley South
John L. Cotter

CONTENTS

Acknowledgments

The achievements of the Jamestown Rediscovery® project at Historic James-towne®, Virginia, are due in large measure to the many individuals and organizations who have provided leadership, generous financial support, scholarly advice, and expertise.

Among the hundreds who could be acknowledged, I highlight a few here for special recognition: The Jamestown Rediscovery National Advisory Board, especially chairman Dr. Warren M. Billings, Dennis B. Blanton, Dr. Edward Bond, Dr. Jeffrey P. Brain, Dr. Cary Carson, Dr. Kathleen Dea-gan, Dr. Rex M. Ellis, Dr. Alaric Faulkner, Frederick Faust, Dr. William W. Fitzhugh, Ms. Roxanne Gilmore, Ms. Camille Hedrick, Dr. James Horn, Dr. Carter L. Hudgins, Dr. Jon Kukla, Dr. Henry Miller, Dr. David Orr, Dr. Douglas Owsley, Mr. Oliver Perry, Dr. Carmel Schrire, Dr. George Stuart, Dr. Sandra Treadway, Dr. Edwin Randolph Turner, Mr. Robert Wharton; APVA Preservation Virginia's Trustees, especially Presidents Peter I. C. Knowles II, Ivor Massey Jr., William B. Kerkam III, and John Guy IV; Executive Director Elizabeth S. Kostelny, and the staff and membership for the constant interest and support; and our special partner, the National Park Service. Many of the new discoveries happened during a collaborative program with the Colonial Williamsburg Foundation, which had been art-fully managed by Dr. James Horn, Colonial Williamsburg's Vice President of Research and Interpretation. There have been numerous generous bene-factors during the twenty-year (1994–2014) Rediscovery Project, including the U.S. Congress, the Commonwealth of Virginia, National Geographic Society, National Endowment for the Humanities, Virginia Foundation for the Humanities, James City County, City of Williamsburg, the Mellon Foundation, the Mary Morton Parsons Foundation, Jessie Ball DuPont Fund, 1772 Foundation, the Morgan Foundation, an anonymous Richmond foundation, the Garden Club of Virginia, the William Byrd and Colonial Capital Branches of the APVA, the Beirne Carter Foundation, Anheuser-Busch, Dominion Resources, Universal Leaf Corporation, Wachovia, and Verizon. My most sincere gratitude to the Anonymous Donor, Roy Hock and Margaret Fowler, and Forrest Mars and the Mars Foundation, and also for the generosity of Don and Elaine Bogus for funding this publication, Mark and Loretta Roman, Martha R. Rittenhouse, the William M. Grover Jr. Family, Mr. Ivor Massey Jr., Mr. and Mrs. Peter I. C. Knowles II, Mr. and Mrs. John H. Guy IV, Mr. and Mrs. D. Anderson Williams, Mr. and Mrs. John A. Prince, the Alan M. Voorhees Family, Mrs. T. Eugene Worrell, the Edward Maria Wingfield Family Society, the Fontaine C. Stanton Estate, William G. Beville, Mr. and Mrs. John H. Van Landingham III, Mr. and Mrs. Martin Kirwan King, and Mr. and Mrs. William Garbee. I am especially grateful to Patricia Cornwell for her timely support and enthusiastic encouragement, and to many other generous individuals.

The project has been very much a staff team effort from the start and is now very much an experienced team effort. With an open mind to ways of improving the process, over the twenty years of the project the staff has had an opportunity to fine-tune the way things have been done. I am especially grateful for their ability to decipher together the ever-widening archaeological story at Historic Jamestowne. I am indebted to senior curator Bly Straube for her unequaled and ever-expanding understanding of postmedieval material culture and for her disciplined and insightful reading of seventeenth-century Jamestown documents; curator of collections Merry Outlaw for her long-standing interest and knowledge of colonial material culture and collection organization skills; former senior staff archaeologist Eric Deetz for his growing mastery of fieldwork, insight into postmedieval vernacular architecture, and education of students and visitors; senior staff archaeologist Danny Schmidt for his insightful directing of the fieldwork, interpreting the fine signs in the earth, his visitor tours and reporting of field discoveries; senior archaeologist and graphic artist Jamie May for her skillful fieldwork, her exceptional artistic eye on the computer and extraordinary ability to research the Internet, and for organizing and creating the images for this publication; senior staff archaeologist and information technologist Dave Givens for creating our GIS archives, and for his vast field experience, for his insight into Virginia Indian archaeology, and for his many and varied mechanical skills; and staff archaeologists Mary Anna

Richardson for her fine excavation and data organization skills and public interpretation; the late staff archaeologist Daniel Boyd Smith for his tenacious field, computer, and historical research work, and for his undivided love of Jamestown; Don Warmke for his tireless excavation and conservation ethic; and Dr. Carter C. Hudgins for his field skills, interpretive insight, and commitment to the archives and historical research; Dr. Douglas W. Owsley, Curator and Division Head of Physical Anthropology, Smithsonian Institution, for teaching me about forensic science and its tremendous contribution to understanding the people of Jamestown and for the extraordinary scientific scholarship of his assistant, Kari Bruwelheide; Ashley McKeown for her dedication, insight, and ability to unravel the art and mystery of Historic Jamestowne's skeletal biology; conservator/photographer Michael Lavin for his uniquely experienced conservation touches and photographic eye; Dan Gamble for his ever-diligent and talented conservation work; Caroline Taylor for her careful artifact processing; Catherine Correll-Walls for accumulating the insightful Early Jamestown Biographies database; and to the many, many skilled archaeologists along the way, for their diligent and talented fieldwork, especially Nick Luccketti, Luke Peccarero, Seth Mallios, Sarah Stroud, Heather Lapham, Elliott Jordan, and the very many others who served on the staff. The efforts of twenty seasons of University of Virginia annual field schools are especially recognized and appreciated, as are the public relations work of Paula Neely; the diligent administrative work of Bonnie Lent; the managerial talent of program coordinator Ann Berry; and Sheryl Mays for her multitude of administrative successes. I also want to acknowledge the talented and instructive editing of this volume by Kenny Marotta and my 2004 Virginia Foundation for the Humanities fellowship, which gave me some much-needed writing time in Charlottesville. I am especially grateful for the stalwart and always encouraging corps of Historic Jamestowne interpreters and the field and lab volunteers. Andrew Scott, James Halsall, and Edward and Joanna Martin made the Gosnold DNA study in England possible.

And I am forever indebted to Ivor Noël Hume for first revealing to me the rigorous process of historical archaeology, the thrill of archaeological discovery, and the archaeological possibilities at Jamestown. Without the original support of past APVA president Mary Douthat Higgins and Shirley Van Landingham, Jamestown Rediscovery archaeology at APVA Jamestown would never have happened. Deep appreciation, too, to Carter L. Hudgins and Henry Miller for unselfishly sharing their ever-helpful interpretations of seventeenth-century Chesapeake historical archaeology.

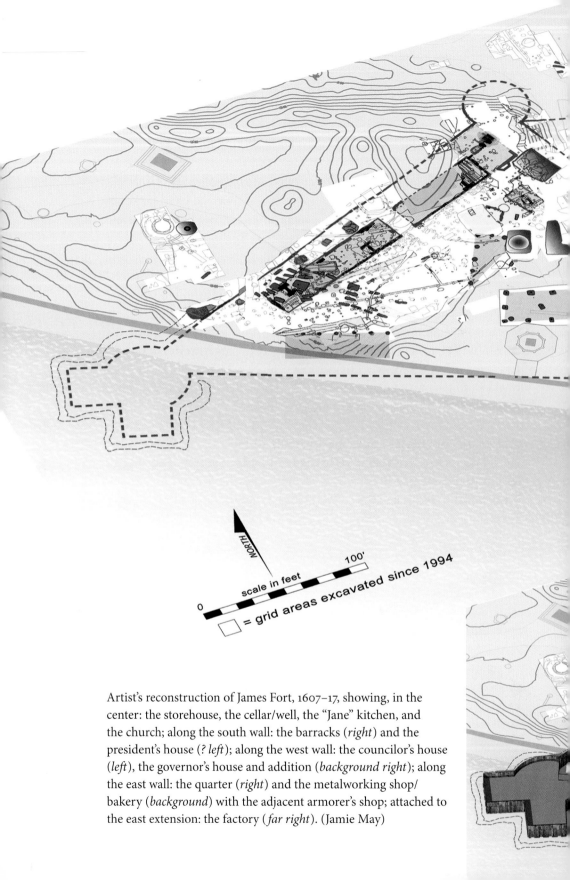

Artist's reconstruction of James Fort, 1607–17, showing, in the center: the storehouse, the cellar/well, the "Jane" kitchen, and the church; along the south wall: the barracks (*right*) and the president's house (*? left*); along the west wall: the councilor's house (*left*), the governor's house and addition (*background right*); along the east wall: the quarter (*right*) and the metalworking shop/bakery (*background*) with the adjacent armorer's shop; attached to the east extension: the factory (*far right*). (Jamie May)

NORTH

scale in feet

0   100'

□ = grid areas excavated since 1994

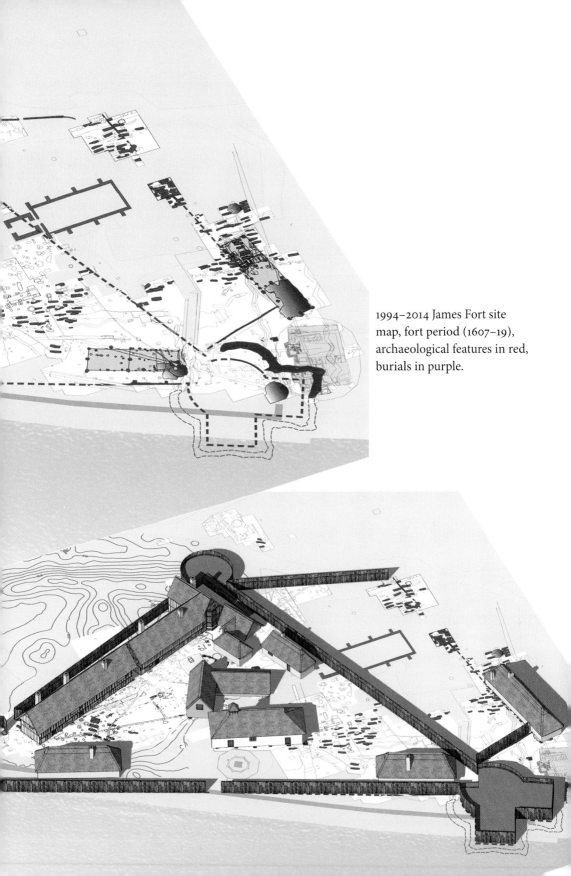

1994–2014 James Fort site map, fort period (1607–19), archaeological features in red, burials in purple.

INTRODUCTION

The American dream was born on the banks of the James River. Lured by the promise of a better life, in 1607 a band of adventurers established the first enduring English settlement in the New World: Jamestown. By 1620—the year the Pilgrims reached Plymouth—much of the James River basin, from the mouth of the Chesapeake Bay to within twenty miles of the site of modern Richmond, had been settled by the English under the sponsorship of the Virginia Company. The year before, a governmental body composed of men elected from the scattered settlements of Virginia had met for the first time on Jamestown Island. This assembly was the first expression of English representative government in North America.

Important as these accomplishments were, the written records pertaining to them are scarce, ambiguous, and sometimes conflicting: maps of questionable accuracy; a few letters and official reports; published accounts written by interested parties (most famous among them John Smith, his account including the dubious tale of his own dramatic rescue by the Indian maiden Pocahontas). Still, certain facts can be gleaned from these records. The colony's early history was evidently a troubled one, beginning with an alleged mutiny during the crossing from England (blamed on John Smith) and continuing through many struggles for power and incidents of civil unrest. The colony faced other trials and hardships as well, including a major battle with the local Indians within weeks of arrival, an unfamiliar semitropical climate, lack of freshwater, meager and spoiled food, drought, and accidents. The Virginia Company's goals—to find a route to the Orient, convert the New World natives to Christianity, find gold, and export raw and manufactured goods—were at best only slightly fulfilled. The hoped-for precious minerals and short, all-water route to the riches of the Orient were never found; the native population was far from willing to embrace the Church of England; and initial manufacturing projects did not prove lucrative.

These early years also witnessed periods of renovation, repopulation, and restructuring of the colony. The introduction of Caribbean tobacco by John Rolfe in 1613 did at last establish a cash crop that helped ensure the survival of the Virginia colony, although the success of hinterland plantations depleted the Jamestown population. A 1622 Indian revolt and the resulting death of nearly 350 colonists led to the end of the Virginia Company's rule, as Jamestown itself became a Royal Colony.

The documentary evidence of the precariousness of life in early James-town and of the gap between the founders' intentions and the colony's achievements led to a story of Jamestown that emphasized its shortcomings: "The adventurers who ventured capital lost it. Most of the settlers who ventured their lives lost them. And so did most of the Indians who came near them. Measured by any of the objectives announced for it, the colony failed."[1] In this interpretation, the colony's failure was ascribed to poor planning by the sponsoring Virginia Company, the incompetence or laziness of the colonists (qualities supposedly explained by the upper-class origin of half of the original settlers), and mistaken cultural assumptions about the Indians. This story, which continues to be told, has been held responsible for the diminished importance of Jamestown itself in American popular consciousness.[2] A comprehensive textbook survey concluded that "textbooks downplay Jamestown because it was a disaster."[3]

To call Jamestown a failure, let alone a disaster, is to oversimplify. Even the scanty documents, with their record of the colony's important firsts, its periods of thriving, and the energy and intelligence unceasingly invested in it, hint at a more complex story. The assertion of the textbook survey is correct to this extent, however: as the complex actuality of the early Jamestown experience faded with time, the importance of Jamestown to American history faded, too. Significant memories, significant truths were lost—seemingly forever.

My own engagement with Jamestown began more than four decades ago, far from Virginia. An undergraduate at Ohio's Baldwin-Wallace College, I decided to cheer myself up one gray March day by reading about Virginia,

In 1611 Ralph Hamor reported that "most" of the citizens of Jamestown were found at their usual pursuits of "bowling in the streets," much like the skittle players in this seventeenth-century Jan Steen painting. Such references led many historians to conclude that it was the "lazy" lifestyle of the gentlemen that turned the Jamestown settlement effort into a "fiasco." (*Skittle Players outside an Inn,* ca. 1660–63; © National Gallery, London/Art Resource, NY)

where I had heard that the sun usually shone and that American colonial history, second only to football as a passion in my life, was considered a serious subject. On a well-worn magazine cover, an aerial photo of Jamestown Island spread out before me. I was mesmerized. The color image showed a network of open archaeological trenches laying bare the foundations of the buried town. This gridwork was part of an effort in 1955 by the National Park Service to uncover remains of Jamestown for a 1957 exhibition celebrating the 350th anniversary of Jamestown's founding. Inspecting the strict order of archaeological trenches crisscrossing the park-like expanse of hallowed ground between unspoiled woodland and the spacious James River, I was amazed that archaeology could happen so close to my own time and place in history. At that time, all my knowledge of archaeology had come from *National Geographic* photo-essays on the pyramids.

Never much of a spectator, I could not help imagining digging with my own hands in that Jamestown soil. When I arrived at the College of William and Mary in Williamsburg, Virginia, as a graduate student interested in early American history, I naturally sought out the ruins at nearby Jamestown Island. I was especially curious about the 1607 fort that must surely have been uncovered in the 1955 excavations, the fort that first defined the limits of colonial Jamestown. At the excavation site, owned by the Association for the Preservation of Virginia Antiquities (APVA), I saw the moss-covered church reconstructed by the APVA, statues of Pocahontas and Captain John Smith, and, in the side of the nearby earthen Civil War fort, a curious windowed exhibit. The glass protected some exposed layers

An aerial view of excavations at Jamestown conducted by the National Park Service in the mid-1950s. This grid of search trenches located a number of seventeenth-century brick building sites, ditches, trash pits, and wells in preparation for the 350th anniversary of the founding of Jamestown in 1957. (National Park Service, Colonial National Historical Park)

of dirt in the fort bank, showing the actual soil surfaces that made up the bank: the Civil War zone, complete with lead bullets; beneath it the dark band of colonial trash; and the deepest deposit, a lighter soil containing arrow points and prehistoric Indian pottery. I was clearly seeing a layer cake of time, pre-Jamestown at the bottom, the colonial period in the middle, and the Civil War era on top. I took in the simple lessons. What is older is deeper; artifacts tell time; the earth can be an index of American history.

I asked a park ranger where the old fort site was. He pointed to a lone cypress tree growing way offshore and said, "Unfortunately, you're too late. It's out there—and lost for good."

I was disappointed to hear that this historic site had been swallowed by the waters that eroded the riverbank. I was confused, too. Looking back at the dirt under glass that said "colonial," I asked, "But what about here?"

He thought for a moment and replied with a shrug of his shoulders that I took as a "could be."

I did not forget James Fort in the ensuing years when I became an archaeologist specializing in the British Colonial America period, learning with my colleagues about that often-forgotten American century, the 1600s. Most of our work focused on rescuing farm sites along the James River, which were being rediscovered by real estate developers and resettled by retirees. The more we learned from the earth about the seventeenth century, the more we thought that the "colonial level" under the glass exhibit at the Civil War fort might be a sign that the 1607 James Fort was there. The likelihood seemed greater when Nicholas Luccketti, Bly Straube, and I restudied the field notes from the 1955 National Park Service excavations, the artifacts those excavations had uncovered, and some disturbances in the soil nearby.[4] Might those disturbances be vestiges of narrow slot trenches that had held seventeenth-century wooden palisade fort walls of the sort we had found elsewhere on the James? The bits of iron and pottery found with such trenches were old and military enough to have been part of James Fort.

A cross-sectional trench dug into the dirt bank of Jamestown's Civil War earthwork fort showing (A) Civil War period, (B) colonial period, (C) pre-1607 Virginia Indian period (*background*), and an L-shaped excavated ditch of unknown origin (*foreground right*). This excavated cross-section was left visible to Jamestown visitors as an archaeological exhibit for some years after the 1955 digging. (National Park Service, Colonial National Historical Park)

The first Jamestown Rediscovery excavation season (1994), in which visiting professional historical archaeologists and University of Virginia field school students aided, uncovered the first sign of James Fort, the dark soil trace of a wall line.

When the APVA decided to investigate its property on Jamestown Island archaeologically—this time in preparation for the 400th anniversary of Jamestown in 2007—I enthusiastically volunteered for the job. There was not much of a line ahead of me. Most archaeologists discounted any chance of finding traces of the early James Fort. At best there would only be signs that it had long since dissolved as the shoreline retreated before nearly four centuries of waves. So it happened that, thirty years to the day after I had first set foot on Jamestown Island, I found myself putting shovel to ground one hundred feet from the glassed-in cross-section that had originally inspired my curiosity. I did not have to miss out on digging at Jamestown after all.

An archaeologist must often practice more than one kind of patience. One September day in 1994, my digging was interrupted by a pair of tourists.

"What are you doing?"

I had been lost in the act of scraping loose dirt from a dark streak in the yellow clay. The accent of the speaker left no doubt that he was British.

"Archaeology," I answered, hoping to end the conversation so that I could get on with my digging. No luck.

"Have you found anything?"

He spoke so earnestly that I felt compelled to give a serious answer.

"Absolutely. See this black stain in the clay? Well, that's what's left of a 1607 fort wall . . . maybe from James Fort."

"Really?"

Silence for a moment. Then the man's companion said, "You mean that's it? That's all there is? America, the last of the world's superpowers, began as . . . just dirt?"

"I never thought about it quite like that," I said, "but yes, I guess it was just dirt."

"But," she continued, "shouldn't there have been a ruined castle or some marble columns or . . . something real?"

"No, there was just dirt," I answered. "But you know what else? I guess plenty of, well, just hope."

"Oh, brilliant!" they said in unison. "Brilliant indeed!"

The British visitors moved on, having grasped the concept that national stature was not necessarily synonymous with highly visible architectural ruins. The archaeologist exploring the beginnings of the United States discovers no medieval castles, classical temples, or Egyptian pyramids. "Just dirt" held out hope for the landless English immigrant, offering a way to break into an otherwise closed society based on the inheritance of family estates. "Just dirt" holds out hope to the archaeologist as well. Marks in the soil of Jamestown Island are the traces of a native people and English immigrants, evidence that has survived the ground-disturbing activities of succeeding generations and the eroding effects of the adjacent river. So we dig, in the faith that these traces bear America's richest heritage.

This hope and faith have now been

Discovery of aligned pockets of dark soil formed by rotting upright logs in narrow trenches revealed the architectural footprint of James Fort.

justified. The excavations at Jamestown have turned up more evidence than anyone had expected—most important, the site of James Fort, so long thought unrecoverable. Nor are these physical remains the only treasure to be discovered. The soil has yielded a new understanding of the early years of Jamestown; a new picture of its settlers, of their abilities, their lives, and their accomplishments; and a new story of the interdependence between the English settlers and the Virginia Indians.

This volume is divided into two parts covering my efforts over the space of twenty years (1994–2014) to unearth this once-lost treasure by the methods of historical archaeology. Part 1, chapters 1–4, which I call "Buried Truth," is an abridged version of my earlier book *Jamestown, the Buried Truth*. It covers the discovery of the location of James Fort and initial related archaeological discoveries made in 1994–2005 that revealed fresh perspective on the early years of life at Jamestown, some of its people, their circumstances, and their activities. In chapter 1, I review what can be learned about the nature and extent of the first Jamestown settlement and its settlers from documentary evidence alone. Chapter 2 recounts the exciting and painstaking discovery of James Fort and rereads the documents in the light of this archaeological discovery. In chapter 3, the recovery of early Jamestown burials becomes a means to understand more about the people of James Fort, the Jamestownians. Through an examination of the James Fort artifacts, chapter 4 addresses earlier and simpler notions of the nature and causes of what has been called Jamestown's failure, showing how the people of James Fort both acted out their preconceptions of Virginia and adapted to the realities of the New World. These uncovered artifacts illustrate the process by which Englishmen and -women began to be transformed into Americans.

Part 2, "More Buried Truth," reports the results of further excavation during the period 2000–2014 that led to a fuller view of the evolving design of the fort and a clearer understanding of Jamestown life. Chapter 5 recounts the discovery of Jamestown's first church (1608–16) and the chain of historical and forensic evidence leading to the identification of four Jamestown leaders buried in the early church chancel. Chapter 6 is an account of the excavation of a cellar bakery filled with debris from Jamestown's starving time, including the mutilated skull and severed leg bone of a cannibalized young teenage English girl. Chapter 7 discusses the excavation of five fort building sites: (1) the fort's storehouse complex, its deep storage cellar and well, from which was recovered cellar fill containing more than a half million objects discarded during the 1609–10 "starving time"; (2) an underground 1607 metalworking shop that was later turned into a substantial bakery; (3) a timber-lined replacement well filled with a rich collection of military and domestic garbage and trash that had accumulated in the well structure during a more prosperous post–"starving time" period, and a related armorer's shop or guardhouse; (4) traces of the first president's house, ca. 1609; and (5) an elaborate upscale reconfiguring of the governor's rowhouse during the term of Samuel Argall, 1617–18.

Throughout these chapters, readers will become acquainted with the tools of the archaeologist: the arts of computer manipulation, dendro-chronology, forensic sculpting, and X-ray, chemical, and DNA analysis; a knowledge of soil and water ecology and of the history of technology, architecture, and fashion; and, above all, the tireless practice of deductive reasoning. Put simply, my hope is that this book will give readers an op-portunity to glimpse, from an archaeological perspective, the genesis of the American dream.

Admittedly, the dream will, at times, be a nightmare even more vivid than the one earlier historians have portrayed. On the whole, however, the new archaeology offers a more balanced account of Jamestown's beginning. Jamestown's precarious attempt to plant English roots in the New World was a tale of trial and error. It was a story, too, of individual success and en-durance by our nation's founding grandfathers. Modern America took root for good at Jamestown. The pages that follow trace the story of the search and recovery of those telltale roots.

The buried truth lies ahead. Like any search for something buried, this search requires a map. So the quest begins not in the earth but in the library.

Part I
BURIED TRUTH

ONE

REIMAGINING JAMESTOWN

T	*he soil was good and fruitful, with excellent good timber. There are also
	great store of vines in bigness of a man's thigh, running up to the tops of
the trees, in great abundance . . . many squirrels, conies, blackbirds with crimson
wings and divers other fowls and birds of divers and sundry colors of crimson,
watchet, yellow, green, murrey and of divers other hues naturally without any
art using.*[1]

The exuberant eyewitness description given above of the Virginia wonderland came from the pen of George Percy, one of the first Jamestown settlers, who was to become governor of the colony almost by default when the dreamland turned into a nightmare two and one-half years later. Percy's account of the voyage to the New World is the most complete of the firsthand descriptions of the founding of Jamestown and the fate of the colonists during the first spring and summer in Virginia.

Eyewitness testimonies carry great weight in any search for the truth. A reading of the documents pertaining to early Jamestown is essential if we are to discover its buried secrets. But documents must be read carefully: the testimony even of eyewitnesses must be scrutinized, keeping in mind that the authors were not immune to dreams of gold and glory that might distort their accounts. It is important to ask, for instance, how much of the fruitful abundance Percy describes in his first sighting might have been merely an expression of the hopes of a new settler rather than reality.

An examination of the documents contemporary with Jamestown's founding offers hints of the precise location, configuration, and artifacts

Top: George Percy, highest-ranking original settler and lieutenant governor during the "starving time" winter of 1609–10. By Herbert Luther Smith. (Virginia Historical Society, Richmond) *Bottom:* Captain John Smith, by Simon de Passe. (Courtesy of the Library of Virginia)

of James Fort. In all, only a half dozen first-hand descriptions and three maps survive from the earliest years of the colony to guide an archaeologist's shovels and trowels. Here are the salient facts about the writers of these documents:

John Smith: Arrived in Jamestown 1607. Yeoman farmer's son, mariner, and soldier, often at odds with his less-experienced and higher-born colleagues. From 1608 to 1631 he published varying accounts of his twenty-nine months in Virginia, as well as heavily edited reports written by other settlers who stayed on. His sometimes-inconsistent accounts sought to justify his actions at Jamestown as well as promote colonization.

Gabriel Archer: Arrived in Jamestown 1607. Mariner and explorer, trained in the law. As recording secretary for the Virginia governing council, he described the earliest days of Jamestown in what appear to be official reports sent back to the Company in England. A devoted enemy of John Smith, he died during the "starving time" of 1609–10.

George Percy: Arrived in Jamestown 1607. Son of the Earl of Northumberland, Percy was one of the highest-ranked of the colonists on the social scale. He served as stand-in governor during the "starving time" and was reappointed in 1611. Percy wrote an account of the

1606–7 voyage from England and a refutation of Smith's 1624 *Generall Historie,* which had put much of the blame for the "starving time" on Percy's shoulders.

Ralph Hamor: Arrived in Jamestown 1610. A stockholder in the Virginia Company and, later, in the 1620s, a member of the governor's council, he published an apparent promotional report in 1615 that described a flourishing Jamestown in 1611–14 and urged further investment and emigration.

William Strachey: Arrived in Jamestown 1610. Secretary of the colony. His letter of 1610 includes an account of the colony as he saw it in May–July 1610 and a summary of earlier events, which Percy apparently dictated to him. The most polished of the early reporters, he wrote the most exact description of James Fort, but his reliance on Percy casts some doubt on the accuracy of his account of Jamestown's first three years.

"The Ancient Planters of Virginia": Writing in the spring of 1623, these surviving original settlers thought the Crown should know about the mishandling of the colony under the leadership of the Virginia Company treasurer, Sir Thomas Smythe. Although cast to shed ill light on Smythe, the account by the "Ancient Planters" includes details about Jamestown houses and hardships during the early years.

Don Pedro de Zúñiga: The Zúñiga map of Virginia was delivered to King Philip III of Spain in 1608 by his ambassador to England, Don Pedro de Zúñiga. This is believed by some to be a tracing of an early map by John Smith. The map includes a minuscule sketch of James Fort. Zúñiga repeatedly urged King Philip to wipe out the colony.

Johannes Vingboons: The Vingboons chart is a Dutch navigational chart showing structures on Jamestown Island as well as downriver forts, all in an area labeled "New Nederland."

THE FORT

In May 1607, Virginia looked like the Garden of Eden to Percy and probably to the 104 English "gentlemen, artisans, laborers and servant boys" seeking a place to settle in the name of King James I, and, more important, a place to reap profit for their investors, the Virginia Company of London. At this point, Virginia appeared to be what they expected: the ideal place to plant a permanent colony of English people, to find gold and a route to the rich Orient, and to convert the natives to Christianity. The Virginia Company officials had instructed the adventurers to settle at least one

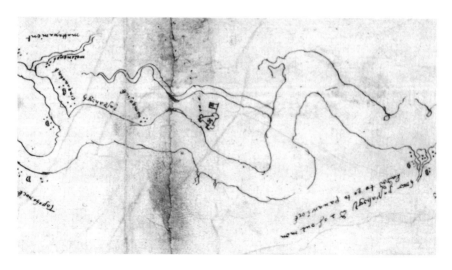

Known as the Zúñiga map (1608), this is one of three known seventeenth-century renderings of James Fort. (Ministerio de Educación y Cultura de España, Archivo General de Simancas, MPD,19,163)

hundred miles from the ocean, in a place where a major river narrowed, offering defensive positions on either side of any attacking ship—which would surely be Spanish, avenging past English privateering raids. As an alternative, the colonists were advised to settle "some Island that is strong by nature."[2] Led by Christopher Newport and Edward Maria Wingfield, and following their instructions, the three ships entered the largest river of the Chesapeake, which they named after their king. The party then sailed as far as sixty-five miles northwest looking for that defensible narrow stretch of river. Reaching the Appomattox River without having found an uninhabited place with the right requirements, the colonists turned back toward the bay. On May 13, the group decided to settle a point of land that was actually an island at very high tide. Why there? Percy explained that here the channel was so close to the shore that ships could be tied to the trees.[3] Other considerations made Jamestown Island the settlement site of choice. Again the Virginia Company's instructions came into play: the colonists were not to upset the Virginia Indians, especially by settling on land the natives already occupied. Jamestown Island was vacant. Although the island was a mere thirty-five miles from the open ocean, from which the Spanish could launch an attack, it still qualified as a naturally defensible place, with its narrow neck of land to guard against assault from the mainland Indians

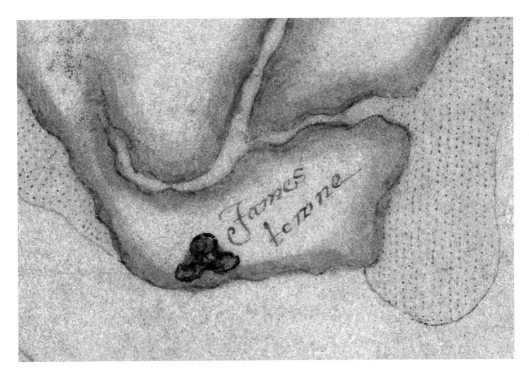

Tindall map of Virginia, 1608, showing original map of James Fort ("James towne"). (© The British Library Board)

and its naturally hidden location in a sharp bend in the river. The several ridges at Jamestown Island provided ideal sites for a fort, particularly the third ridge from the west, the highest point of land on the north shore of the river bend. It is also possible that, although the Indians did not then occupy the land, they had been there in the not-too-distant past. By 1607 their cleared land might have evolved into a fair-sized grove of straight, tall, second-growth hardwood trees, ideal for building timber palisades and blockhouses.[4] Captain John Smith deemed Jamestown Island "a very fit place for the erecting of a great cittie."[5]

The next day the colonists—all men—filed ashore, onto what the English adventurers decided to call Jamestown Island on the north shore of the James River.[6] That first landing day, Smith reports,

> now falleth every man to work . . . cut down trees . . . pitch tents . . . some provide clapboard to relade the ships . . . some make gardens, some nets . . .

Jamestown Island from the west.

The island was a busy place, with the men doing exactly what they needed to do for survival: clearing the land, establishing shelter, preparing to live off their own gardens and the native fish, and fortifying themselves despite Company instructions not to upset the Indians by doing so. Like Smith, chronicler George Percy tells of throwing up a brush fort. Percy also writes of establishing a military guard "to watch and ward."[8] This exercise was wisely done. The settlers soon were challenged by the Paspahegh Indians from the nearest village.

Arriving with a hundred men in arms—a message that the English soldiers were essentially outnumbered and surrounded—the Indian leader "made signs that he would give us as much land as we would desire."[9] Of course, the settlers already believed they had ownership by the English king's patent of the whole of continental North America. In any case, they must have rapidly accepted the offer, surely one that meant no more than the 1,600-acre Jamestown Island. But the deal seemed to go sour when one of the Indians grabbed a soldier's hatchet, prompting a scuffle in which a native was struck on the arm. The chief and his warriors left in anger.

The Indians seemed to be a forgiving lot, for two days later forty appeared at the Jamestown "quarter" with a deer. In addition, they offered to stay in the "fort" all night. Sensing ambush, the English denied the overnight and proceeded to flaunt their own military prowess. "One of our gentlemen" put on a demonstration to prove English weapons superior to the Indian arrows. He first set up a leather "target" (hand shield) for Indian target practice. An arrow penetrated a foot into the leather. Next a "steel target went up which shattered his arrow all to pieces."[10] This set the stage for open warfare one week later.

On May 27 Captain Gabriel Archer described the first battle, "a very furious assault to our fort" by some

This seventeenth-century Dutch image of soldiers and their tents on a river in the Low Countries is reminiscent of John Smith's 1607 description of the colonists' first day at Jamestown Island. (*River Landscape with a Tent*, Philips Wouverman, copy credited to Verlag Hanfstaengl, Munich, in Walter Bernt collection, Fine Arts Library, Harvard University)

two hundred warriors who "came up allmost into the fort, shott through the tentes." The battle "endured hott about an hower," hurting "11 men [Smith reported 17 casualties] (whereof one dyed) and killed a Boy. . . . We killed divers of them . . . how many hurt we know not. . . . Foure of the Counsell that stood in front were hurt in mayntayning the Forte, and our President, Master Wynckfield (who shewed himself a valiant Gentleman) had one shott clean through his beard."[11] Wingfield seems to have escaped harm literally by a whisker, but the other four councilors in town, John Martin, John Ratcliffe, George Kendall, and Bartholomew Gosnold, were apparently not so lucky. However, the seriousness of their wounds drew no further comment from Archer. Wingfield, who presumably now knew the men would need more than their beards, brush, and canvas to stay alive, ordered that the settlement be immediately and this time seriously fortified. The camp was to be enclosed with palisades (logs set side by side in the ground)—the men "labored pallozadoing our fort"—and the cannons were mounted.[12] These activities marked the beginning of James Fort. In only nineteen days, the enclosure stood complete. According to Percy, on June 15 "we had built and finished our fort, which was triangle-wise, having three bulwarks at every corner like a half-moon, and four or five pieces of artillery mounted in them."[13]

Building the fort was no easy task for such small numbers in so short a time. As if cutting and hauling logs, probably weighing eight hundred pounds apiece, and digging at least one thousand feet of trenches to seat them were not enough of a challenge, almost daily the workmen had to dodge Indian arrows shot from the surrounding woods and marsh grasses.[14] The constant threat of incoming arrows, the heat of a developing Tidewater Virginia summer, and the stress of the fear-driven building schedule would eventually take its toll on the men:

> [W]ithin ten days [June 25, 1607] scarce ten amongst us could either go or well stand, such extreme weakness and sickness oppressed us. . . . When they [the ships] departed, there remained but the common kettle [which amounted to] . . . half a pint of wheat, and as much barley . . . for a man a day, . . . and this contained as many worms as grains . . . our drink was [river?] water our lodgings castles in the air. . . . our extreme toil in bearing and planting palisadoes so strained and bruised us . . . in the extremity of the heat . . . made us . . . miserable.[15]

In the days that followed, Percy chronicled the deaths of twenty-four colonists, including the councilor Bartholomew Gosnold: "Our men were destroyed with cruel diseases as swellings, fluxes, burning fevers, and by wars, and some departed suddenly, but for the most part they died of mere famine."[16] Later Smith claims sixty-seven were dead by September, but finally "most of the soldiers recovered with the skillful diligence of master Thomas Wotton, our chirurgeon [surgeon] General."[17] Given all this stress, it is unlikely that any further work was done on the fort for some weeks after the June 15 "completion" date. When the popular Captain John Smith took over as the colony's manager in September—President Wingfield having been impeached for allegedly hoarding food—Smith oversaw the building of some thatched houses. In the fall of 1607, a number of emissaries from James River Indian tribes expressed intentions of peace, and every four or five days Pocahontas (the great chief Powhatan's daughter, who had befriended Smith) and her attendants brought the men provisions.[18] Despite these friendly actions, concern for security probably caused the new houses to be built inside the fort.

The exact form, size, and degree of sophistication of the council's fort cannot be determined from these early records, but it seems that much of the fort in its original configuration did not last long. In January 1608, after a supply ship and a hundred fresh men arrived from England, fire either seriously damaged or completely destroyed the fort. The new supply itself was to blame. Apparently something flammable in it, presumably gunpowder, set fire to "their quarters . . . the town . . . palisadoes . . . arms, bedding, apparel . . . much private provision . . . and [the reverend] Hunt lost all his library." On top of that disaster, the winter of 1608 was one of "extreme frost," and copper, one of the colonists' main means of exchange for food, had been rendered almost worthless by the ships' crewmembers' illegal Indian trade. That winter saw a rash of deaths in which, Smith reports, "more than half of us died." Despite these hardships, Smith reports a "rebuilding [of] James Towne," which included repairing the partially burned palisades, building the first substantial church, building a "Stove" (kitchen), and reroofing the storehouse—a first reference to the existence of the latter. By summer Smith carried on with his voyages of discovery on Virginia's waterways away from Jamestown, with the presumption that the fort had been brought back in order.[19]

Yet whenever Smith returned to Jamestown from his explorations, once in July and again in September 1608, he wrote that he found the town in decay and the people "all sick, the rest some lame, some bruised—all unable to do anything but complain . . . many dead, the harvest rotting and nothing done." In September the council and company elected Smith president. Under his new leadership further construction and an apparent redesign of the fort were carried out. The fort was "invironed with a palizado of fourteene or fifteene foot, and each as much as three or foure men could carrie . . . we had three Bulwarks, foure and twentie peece of ordnance . . . upon convenient plat-formes . . . [the overall plan] reduced to the form of this ( ) [figure omitted but later called "five-square"]."[20]

Smith also restored discipline in the disorganized and disheartened militia: "the whole company every Saturday exercised in the plain by the west bulwark prepared for that purpose, we called Smithfield where sometimes more than an hundred savages would stand in amazement to behold how a file would batter a tree."[21]

Likely among the audience watching the troops perform were the first two immigrant women, Mistress Forest and her maid, Anne Burras, and eight Germans and a Pole who had arrived with the second supply, the latter brought to make pitch, tar, glass, mills, and soap ashes. Nothing more is known about Mistress Forest, but Anne Burras soon met John Laydon, one of the few hearty survivors of the original 104 settlers. They married, presumably in Smith's recently built church. The mission of the Germans also was successful, for when Newport sailed back to England in late 1608, he carried, among a cargo of clapboard and wainscot, Jamestown-made "trials of pitch, tar, glass . . . [and] soap-ashes."[22]

In 1608–9 the "five-square, James towne" seemed to prosper under Captain John Smith's strict leadership. That spring, although Smith apparently found enough unspoiled food in the store to make it to the fall harvest, he wrote that he instituted a "must work or no food" policy to make sure, among other things, that there would be a harvest. His work-for-food policy paid great dividends at the fort, where the men "quietly followed . . . [their] business that in three months produced . . . tar, pitch, and soap-ashes, . . . a trial of glass, made a well in the fort of excellent sweet water which was wanting, built twenty houses, recovered the church, provided nets and weirs for fishing and built a blockhouse in the neck of our isle."[23]

But again, by the summer of 1609, the corn in the store rotted while the men "digged and planted" thirty or forty acres under the direction of two fettered Paspahegh prisoners, Kemps and Tassore, who were so "well used they did not desire to go from us." And the settlers caught more of the giant and nutritious sturgeon fish "than could be devoured by dog and man," which they transformed into bread. With that staple as well as various wild roots and fruits, according to Smith, "[w]e lived very well." But not for long. The same summer seven of a nine-ship supply flotilla made it in from England intending to revitalize the colony. Those ships also brought certain gentlemen who set out to murder Smith and "to supplant us rather than supply us." More than two hundred men took the new supplies away from Jamestown, going to live at the Falls of the James or downstream at the Nansemond River. When Smith sailed to the Falls in search of supplies in the autumn, he returned with a life-threatening wound to his thigh caused by, as he put it, someone "accidentally" firing his powder bag. He soon decided to return to England, "seeing there was neither chirurgian nor chirurgery in the fort to cure his hurt." George Percy was named president.[24]

In reporting the condition of the colony at the time of his departure, Smith's *Generall Historie* offers one of the most complete state-of-the-fort descriptions—one that of course made his tenure as president look positive:

> Leaving us with . . . ten weeks' provision in the store, . . . twenty-four pieces of ordinance, three hundred muskets, snaphaunces and firelocks, shot, powder, and match sufficient, curats [cuirasses], pikes, swords, and morio[n]s [helmets] more than men, an hundred well-trained and expert soldiers, nets for fishing, tools of all sorts to work, apparel to supply our wants, six mares and a horse, five or six hundred swine, some goats, some sheep. . . . Jamestown was strongly palisadoed, containing more than fifty or sixty houses.[25]

But Smith also made clear his opinion that he was forced to leave behind the seeds of destruction, namely, "poor gentlemen, tradesmen, serving men, libertines [who were] ten times more fit to spoil a commonwealth than either to begin one or but help to maintain one."[26] The 1609–10 winter that followed became known as the "starving time." A flotilla of supply ships under the newly appointed lieutenant governor Sir Thomas Gates was shipwrecked in Bermuda. Indians besieged the fort.[27] The colonists' livestock was quickly eaten, including the horses, and some of their weapons were traded away for Indian corn. Some of the "poorer sorte" even resorted to survival cannibalism. Only 60 of the 215 left at Jamestown survived.[28]

By spring, the *Deliverance* and the *Patience,* replacements for the governor's wrecked flagship, the *Sea Venture,* arrived from Bermuda to find "the palisades torn down, the ports open, the gates from off the[i]r hinges . . . and empty houses [some] rent up and burnt [for firewood]. . . . [T]he Indians killed . . . our men [if they] stirred beyond the bounds of their blockhouse." Lieutenant Governor Gates was accompanied by William Strachey, who began his relatively precise record of Jamestown's events and appearance in 1610. The supplies brought in from Bermuda soon disappeared, and the expectation of resupply from the Indians proved to be wishful thinking. The situation declined so badly that Gates ordered an evacuation of the town. On June 7, 1610, "we . . . buried our ordinances before the front gate which looked into the river."[29] With thirty days' supply, the survivors sailed downriver. According to one account, Gates planned to "stay some ten days at Cape Comfort . . . to wait the arrival of a supply ship."[30] More official accounts say that the party was in a headlong nonstop retreat back to England. In any event, Gates did not have to go that far or wait that long.

Not far downriver the evacuees met an advance party from the incoming supply fleet of the new governor, Thomas West, Lord De La Warre. After only thirty hours' respite from Jamestown, the demoralized group had to backtrack and prepare for the new governor's arrival. Thereafter, the new leadership and especially the new supplies quickly seemed to rejuvenate the town.

Strachey's next description of the fort is considerably more positive than his first and remains the most exact we have. Only three days after his return to the abandoned town, Strachey observed:

> [T]he fort growing since to more perfection, is now at this present in this manner: . . . about half an acre . . . is cast almost into the form of a triangle and so palisaded. The south side next the river (howbeit extended in a line or curtain sixscore foot more in length than the other two, by reason the advantage of the ground doth require) contains 140 yards, the west and east sides a hundred only. At every angle or corner, where the lines meet, a bulwark or watchtower is raised and in each bulwark a piece or two well mounted. . . . And thus enclosed, as I said, round with a palisade of planks and strong posts, four feet deep in the ground, of young oaks, walnuts, etc. . . . the fort is called, in honor of His Majesty's name, Jamestown.[31]

Percy's and Strachey's descriptions agree that James Fort was triangular with watchtowers and/or bulwarks at each of the three angles, where ordnance was mounted. That design seems to be consistent with the two early maps, the Robert Tindall map and the Don Pedro de Zúñiga map. The former shows the lower Chesapeake Bay, the James and York Rivers, and the land between them from the bay to seventy miles inland. The caption reads: "Draught of Virginia by Robarte Tindal Anno 1608." Jamestown Island is drawn and labeled "Jamestown," and near the western end of the island there are three circles attached by straight lines forming a triangle. This appears to be the James Fort plan described by Percy and Strachey. The Zúñiga map shows a larger area including part of the eastern coast of modern North Carolina and much of Tidewater Virginia. It depicts "Jamestown" also basically in the form of a triangle, but the bulwarks at the angles are more complicated: two partial circles and an attached square form on the two river sides and only a relatively large circle to the north. The scale of both maps seems to defy any attempt at learning how far the fort was from the western end of the island.

In 1611, after De La Warre's illness forced him to leave Jamestown, there

Above: Thomas West, Third Lord De La Warre, first resident governor of Virginia, 1610–11. (From Alexander Brown's *Genesis of the United States* [Boston, 1890]) *Right:* Sir Thomas Gates, lieutenant governor of Virginia, 1610 and 1611–14. (From the original portrait by C. Jansen, in the possession of Sir Leonard Brassey, from Alexander Weddell's *A Memorial Volume of Virginia Historical Portraiture, 1585–1830,* 1930)

arrived yet another Company-appointed governor, Sir Thomas Dale. That year the optimistic settler Ralph Hamor described what seems to be a rather different Jamestown:

> The Towne . . . is reduced into a handsome forme, and hath in it two faire rowes of houses, all of framed Timber, two stories, and an upper Garret, or Corne loft high, besides the three large, and substantial Storehouses, joyned together in a length some hundred and twenty foot, and in breadth forty, and this town hath been lately newly, and strongly impaled, and a faire platforme for Ordnance in the west Bulwark raised.[32]

His glowing account of the "handsome forme" of the town and the "faire rowes of houses" paints a picture of a renovated and expanded fortified area. Hamor never really says the town plan expanded outside the limits of the original fort in any particular direction, but he does mention houses scattered beyond the town. This handsome town, whatever its form, did apparently include a governor's residence, built by and for Lieutenant Governor Gates presumably when he took office in the summer of 1611. This building was expanded by other governors as they saw fit: "The Governor's house in James Town first built by Sir Thomas Gates Knight at the charges and by the servants of the Company, and since enlarged by others by the same means [is to] continue forever as the governor's house." The establishment of an official residence was a reflection of the 1609 Company charter, which vested both the commercial and the governmental affairs of the colony in the hands of the Company. Before then, the governing council, directed ultimately by the king himself, carried on the affairs of the colony. Now that the resident governor had the power to govern, he presumably needed some building much more substantial than an "air castle" at Jamestown to reflect his authority.[33]

There are no more detailed descriptions of James Fort/town, but there are hints that its development was an on-again, off-again process through the decade. Governors Gates and Dale, even though they kept their main residence at Jamestown (1611–16), apparently let the fort slowly decay. Dale neglected Jamestown in favor of another fortified town he was building upriver at a place he called Henricus. Even before Dale's neglect, another document, if it states the truth, paints a Jamestown again in shambles by 1613. A Spanish prisoner held at Jamestown, Don Diego de Molina, smuggled a letter to the Spanish ambassador in London, urging a Spanish invasion of Virginia and a quick surrender of the disgruntled "slaves" at Jamestown, who were protected only by "fortifications . . . so fragile that a kick would destroy them . . . a fortification without skill and made by people who do not understand them."[34] Molina also said that the palisade walls were so full of gaps that the enemy outside was safer than the defenders inside.

Things were no better in 1617, when yet another new lieutenant governor arrived at Jamestown, Captain Samuel Argall. Planter John Rolfe's disparaging description of the town is almost an echo of Gates's discovery of Jamestown just after the "starving time":

In James Towne he [Argall] found but five or six houses, the Church downe, the Palizado's broken, the Bridge [a wharf to the channel?] in pieces, the well of fresh water spoiled; the Store-house they used for the church, the market-place, and streets, and all other spare places planted with Tobacco, the Salvages [Indians] as frequent in their houses as themselves, . . . the Palizado's not sufficient to keepe out Hogs.[35]

Rolfe failed to mention that his own actions might have been in part responsible for Jamestown's decay. His development of a profitable tobacco strain that would thrive in Virginia soil had begun to drain the Jamestown population to hinterland tobacco plantations and diminished the settlers' interest in keeping up the fort—that is, except as they could grow tobacco in any vacant space there. Nevertheless, Argall set out to make things right by repairing the defective town. During his administration (1617–19) a 20' × 50' church was built.[36]

Also during Argall's tenure as governor, the Dutch were busy mapping Virginia, claiming it lay in "New Nederland." The area was so labeled on a circa-1617 detailed chart of the James River from its confluence with the Appomattox to the Chesapeake Bay. This chart, drawn from a ship as it sailed along, is one of 156 maps included in a worldwide *Atlas of the Dutch West India Company*. Known as the Vingboons chart for its maker, Johannes Vingboons, the map shows Jamestown Island, individual houses around modern Hopewell, and two other early Virginia forts: Fort Algernon at Point Comfort and Charles Fort at nearby Strawberry Bank. The downriver forts appear as attached gable-end buildings, three at Algernon and two at Charles Fort.[37] Jamestown is depicted in an identical way—attached buildings—and located about one-third of the way from the western end of the island. The Dutch charts, intended as navigational guides, usually show buildings as they would appear from a distant ship, not as mere symbolic structures. So either each of these forts had prominent multisection storehouses—"three large storehouses joined together in length"[38]—or the chart symbols depict blockhouses or watchtowers, the most visible features of forts from a distance. If they are defenses, then Jamestown and Fort Algernon appear almost identical—three blockhouses each—while Charles Fort had only two and perhaps a palisaded "yard." In fact, the Jamestown Island buildings are labeled "Blockhouse Jamestown." If the triple houses mark the exact location of the town, as they almost certainly do, then the map locates the fort some distance from the now-eroded western end of the island. Allowing for distortion in scale, the storehouse or blockhouse symbol appears to be located precisely where the later church tower stands today.

Other documentary descriptions of James Fort's private and public buildings are vague but suggest that for months the town looked like a temporary army camp. First came the tents and the "castles in the air." As late as September 10, 1607, there were "no houses to cover us, our Tents were rotten and our [thatched roof] Cabbins worse than nought."[39] Three years

later, however, things seemed to have improved some. Strachey described the houses in the fortified town:

> [T]o every side, a proportioned distance from the palisade, is a settled street of houses that runs along so as each line of the angle hath his street. . . . The houses were all burnt by a casualty of fire the beginning of the second year . . . which since we have better rebuilded though as yet no great uniformity, either for fashion or beauty of the street. . . . The houses have wide and large country chimneys [wood, clay covered?] . . . [they] cover their houses now (as the Indians) with the barks of trees, as durable and good proof against storms and winter weather as the best tile . . . which before in sultry weather would be like stoves, whilst they were, as at first, pargeted and plastered with bitumen or tough clay.[40]

Detail of ca.-1617 Dutch (Vingboons) chart of the James River showing Jamestown Island and vicinity. (National Archives, The Hague, The Netherlands)

Regardless of how improved these shelters became, it is clear that they were never intended to last long. According to Strachey:

> We dwell not here to build us bowers.
> And Halls for pleasure and good cheer:
> But halls we build for us and ours,
> To dwell in them whilst we live here.[41]

There was a constant repair and replacement program: "we were constrained every yeere to build and repaire our old cottages, which were always decaying in all places in the Countrie." These so-called "cottages" may have been prone to decay, but they were not scarce. By summer 1608, "we had about fortie or fiftie severall houses warm and dry." The town houses increased to "some fiftie or sixtie" a year later. If the figure is not exaggerated, some of these houses had to stand outside the rather constrained space in the fort Strachey described.[42]

There is very little record of James Fort after the Dutch navigators produced the 1617 chart. A last-minute warning saved the fort from damage during the disastrous Indian uprising of 1622. A year and a half later, James Fort, other forts, and a number of the houses in Virginia were all very much at risk. By August or September 1623,

> James Citie . . . [and other parts of the colony] have been suffered by the Colony of late to grow to such decay that they are become of no strength or use . . . there are no places fortified for defense & safetie . . . the plantations are farr asunder & their houses stand scattered one from another, and are onlie made of wood few or none of them beeing framed houses but punches sett into the Ground And covered with Boarde so as a firebrand is sufficient to consume them all. . . . The fortifications antientlie used were by Trench and Pallizado and (which now are all gone to ruyne . . . [lined out]) and diverse blockhouses made of timber . . . [lined out] great Tymber built uppon passages and for scouring the Pallizadoes: all which now are gone to ruyne.[43]

The documentary evidence of the nature and extent of James Fort and the early town is often ambiguous. We know that much of this evidence could have been distorted for self-serving reasons. The 1623 document written by the "Ancient Planters" is significantly at odds with the earlier accounts. According to these surviving original settlers, in January 1608 the town had only forty occupants, most "at the point of death—all utterly destitute of houses, not one as yet built, so that they lodged in cabins and holes in the ground [and soon thereafter] . . . there were [only] some poor houses built."[44] They do, however, mention the houses Gates constructed, presumably in 1611, that constant repair left still standing when the "Ancient Planters" wrote in 1623.

Overall, a fairly consistent image emerges from these accounts. James Fort was some sort of triangular enclosure, between one and two acres in size, built on ground located on the James River shore near the southwestern end of Jamestown Island. James Fort became Jamestown soon in the literature; it included houses of varied quality, a church, a storehouse, and other buildings, and it grew in size. Many people died there from a number of causes, primarily disease, starvation, and battle with the Virginia Indians. The town had a number of episodes of neglect and decline, but each new governor's term brought the town back to serviceable condition or renovated and expanded it. The early fort fell into final decay and disappeared by 1624, when James I dissolved the Virginia Company and took over the colony for the Crown.

THE PEOPLE

The eyewitness accounts of Jamestown's first seventeen struggling years paint a picture not only of James Fort but also of the people involved in its founding—including the eyewitnesses themselves. Other available documentary evidence can tell us more of the events and people that affected the fabric of the developing Jamestown Island settlement. Demographic and biographical information can be gleaned from records of individual Englishmen who first landed there as well as of the people who came soon thereafter: the "diverse other" men and women. Their age, social standing, colonial and military experience, and place of origin in England all influenced how they reacted to the alien Virginia environment. Documents also tell of another people whose presence had a tremendous impact, both positively and negatively, on the siting and survival of Jamestown: the Virginia Indians. To a certain extent, they can be known individually, too. Finally, we can even come to know some of the story of the Spanish, whose constant threat of invasion influenced Jamestown's first development and whose failure to invade early on inadvertently let English roots take hold.

First, let us consider the Englishmen and their last hours ashore in England. It is technically false to state, as most history books do, that the first three ships disembarked for Virginia from London. Rather, the settlers last trod English soil at a place called Blackwall, slightly downriver from London, adjacent to the foreboding-sounding Isle of Dogs.[45] Blackwall in the early seventeenth century amounted to alehouses and churches supporting the docks of the emerging English maritime trade. Today, at the end of a street named Blackwall Way, is a place known traditionally as Blackwall Stairs, where the remnants of very old wooden stairs are visible at low tide. Local lore has it that the Virginia-bound legion of men and boys boarded the ships there in December 1606. Until at least 1897, a Tudor half-timber structure stood nearby, called the Sir Walter Raleigh House by local historians—an inn where travelers, presumably once Sir Walter himself, awaited transport out of the Thames.[46] Conceivably this inn would have been the freshest memory of an English house that most of the future Jamestown settlers would carry with them during the tedious crossing to the New World. There must have been great longing to return to that rugged inn and the alehouses of Blackwall when the three outbound ships lay becalmed in bone-chilling weather near the mouth of the Thames for over a month—almost half of the anticipated length of the voyage.[47] Who were

Map of London area, dated 1610, showing Blackwall, the point of embarkation for the original Jamestown settlers. (© The British Library Board)

these shivering would-be colonists waiting for the winds and their fortunes to change?

Certain biographical facts are commonly known about some of the Jamestown leaders. We know, for example, something of the members of the first council selected by the Virginia Company before the voyage, their identities revealed at the opening of a sealed box containing a list of people preselected by the Company to rule the colony at the voyage's end: Edward Maria Wingfield, John Martin, Captain George Kendall, John Ratcliffe, Bartholomew Gosnold, and Captain John Smith.[48] They all had military/combat experience acquired either in fighting the eighty-year wars in the Netherlands, in privateering, or in establishing the English plantations in Ireland. Captain John Smith had fought not only in the Netherlands but also in France and Transylvania. Gosnold led the capture of a Spanish galleon and took a colonizing party to settle briefly off Cape Cod in 1602. Except for Smith, they all were gentry, some urban and some rural.

What is not so well known are their ages, which ranged from twenty-seven (Smith) to fifty-seven (Wingfield). The rest of the council were in their forties, except Gosnold, who was thirty-six, and Kendall, thirty-seven.

The so-called Sir Walter Raleigh House (now demolished) at Blackwall, near London, traditionally known for housing hopeful settlers waiting to board ships to America. (Tower Hamlets Local History Library and Archives, London)

At a time when fifty-six was the average life expectancy, these men were primarily "seniors."[49] (Thus, in his youth as well as in his lower social status, Smith did not fit the norm of the leaders.) The rest of the party for whom biographical data has been determined so far ranged in age from the forty-six-year-old Christopher Newport of Harwich to nine-year-old James Brumfield of Lincolnshire. The average age of the noncouncil men was about twenty-five.[50]

The settlers' home parishes and probably their family seats were either the Greater London area (including the Kent/Sussex counties to the southeast and Essex), Suffolk, the Greater Peterborough area, and John Smith's Lincolnshire. Of the original colonists whose place of origin can be determined, twelve came from the City of London, and an equal number came from the Greater London area and East Anglia. Those from East Anglia—the river port town areas of Suffolk, Norfolk, Lincolnshire, and Cambridgeshire—were younger than those from the Greater London area. A small percentage came from other towns or counties but not from any other single region in England. Fourteen came with relatives: cousins, fathers, sons, and brothers. Six had some kinship with Gosnold.[51]

From these statistics, drawn from research still in progress, one might begin to speculate how and why these men and boys wound up filing down those Blackwall stairs to begin their Virginia adventure. Finding gold was considered to be a realistic expectation, as was the assignment of land in Virginia to planters or adventurers.[52] It is logical to assume that many of the immigrants were the younger sons of gentry, with little prospect of inheriting the family lands in England. Insofar as we can now determine, at least six of the gentlemen were younger sons; the gentleman Bartholomew Gosnold, for example, had an older brother. Prospects for acquiring land in Virginia must have been appealing to these younger gentlemen, as to other immigrants well into the seventeenth century.[53] But land could not

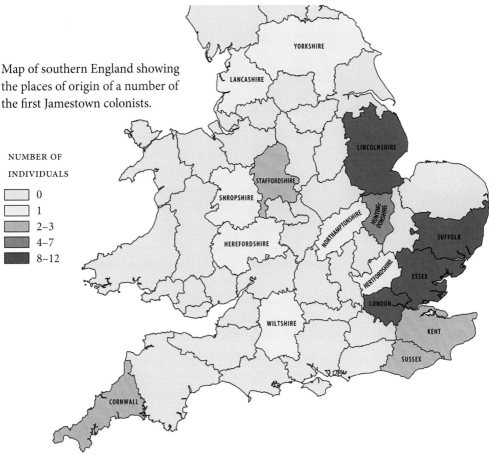

Map of southern England showing the places of origin of a number of the first Jamestown colonists.

NUMBER OF INDIVIDUALS

- 0
- 1
- 2–3
- 4–7
- 8–12

CORNWALL
Robert Beheathland
George Kendall
Richard Simmons

ESSEX
Henry Adling
Gabriel Archer
Edward Browne
Robert Ford
Matthew Fitch
George Martin
John Martin
Eustace Clovill
Edward Morris
Christopher Newport
Kenelme Throckmorton

HEREFORDSHIRE
Richard Crofts

HERTFORDSHIRE
Roger Cooke

HUNTINGDONSHIRE
Edward Harrington
Nicholas Scot
John Stevenson
William Love
Edward M. Wingfield

KENT
Edward Pising
Thomas Wotton

LANCASHIRE
Robert Pennington

LINCOLNSHIRE
John Smith
John Herd
William Laxton
Robert Fenton
James Brumfield
Richard Dixon
John Dods
Nathaniel Pecock

LONDON
John Capper
Thomas Emery
Richard Frith
James Read
Thomas Gore (Gower)
William Garrett
George Cassen
Thomas Cassen
William Cassen
Richard Mutton
William Roods
Thomas Sands

NORTHAMPTONSHIRE
Jereme Alicock

SHROPSHIRE
Ellis Kinistone
(Kingston)

STAFFORDSHIRE
Edward Brinto
William Smethes
George Walker

SUFFOLK
William Brewster
Anthony Gosnold
(brother)
Anthony Gosnold
(cousin)
Bartholomew Gosnold
George Goulding
Thomas Webb
Thomas Cowper
Edward Brookes
Anas Todkill
William Unger

SUSSEX
George Percy
Drew Pickayes

WILTSHIRE
John Martin Jr.

YORKSHIRE
Lancelot Booker

have been the primary consideration for many others. At least three other gentlemen, including Wingfield and Martin, were the eldest sons in their families.[54] Clearly, they were gentlemen with other motives, perhaps just the adventure of it all.

How did word of the voyage get out in an age when only one in ten could read and where the roads were hardly passable? The distribution patterns of geographic origins suggest that the principal leaders may have been the principal sources of information as well.[55] It is logical to assume that the settlers from London learned of the venture through the promotional program of the Virginia Company based there. Thomas Smythe, the London merchant, "whose wealth and influence played so large a part in the formation of the first Virginia Company," and who may have had a personal hand in collecting the London recruits himself, was Bartholomew Gosnold's cousin-in-law.[56]

Born in 1571 near Ipswich, Suffolk, Gosnold, with his brother, Anthony, and sisters Elizabeth and Margaret, attended school at his uncle John's moated manor, Otley Hall. Through his uncle, secretary to the Earl of Essex, Gosnold became a daring mariner, venturing to the Azores in 1597 and accumulating booty by privateering against the Spanish. Essex intended to fund a New World voyage to include Gosnold, but Essex's implication in the 1601 Essex Rebellion and his ultimate execution left Gosnold no support for the trip. The following year the Earl of Southampton—cousin of Edward Wingfield—stepped forward to fund the Cuttyhunk colony near Cape Cod, of which Gosnold was appointed admiral. Although the colony lasted only a month, Gosnold became known as an outstanding mariner and immediately began planning to sail to the southern coast of America.

Gosnold gathered the leaders and many of the other first settlers from among his East Anglian friends, neighbors, and relatives. He must have been a particularly effective promoter, since, like few others, he could describe firsthand the Atlantic voyage and at least part of the area then known as "Virginia." Gosnold would have been able to assure his listeners that the new Virginia adventure would be different. He had learned from the Norumbrian (New England) shortcomings and successes. He could well have said with conviction that the south of Virginia was a paradise in comparison to the northern latitudes.[57] John Smith credited Gosnold with being the principal promoter of the Virginia venture.[58]

By 1605 the plans for a southern colony led by Gosnold were much advanced, and by then included Wingfield, Gosnold's cousin Thomas Smythe,

Left: Otley Hall, Suffolk, England, the moated manor house of Bartholomew Gosnold's uncle, and possibly the meeting place where Gosnold, Edward Maria Wingfield, Christopher Newport, John Smith, and Richard Hakluyt planned the Jamestown voyage and settlement. *Right:* Otley High House, Suffolk, the manor of Bartholomew Gosnold's father, Anthony.

and Gosnold's friend, the soldier and traveler John Smith. In on the planning as well was Richard Hakluyt, the vicar of nearby All Saints Church, Weatheringsett, and the king's official geographer. It was Hakluyt who put into print the most vivid accounts of the English explorations in the New World and the most forceful and convincing arguments for founding English colonies. Otley Hall may have been used as the forum for the planning meetings of these promoter/friends and as a base for recruiting men from the vicinity. Judging from the way the East Anglian hometowns cluster on the map of southeastern England, it is logical to assume that Gosnold was an accomplished recruiter for the Virginia venture from the environs of Otley.

When the fleet sailed, however, Christopher Newport became the commanding admiral, and Wingfield, a chief stockholder in the Virginia Company, an aspiring president. As second-in-command despite his experience as a mariner, Gosnold must have watched helplessly as the fleet floundered near the mouth of the Thames for the first month of the voyage. Gosnold must also have been frustrated enduring Newport's long southern route to Virginia via the Canary and West Indian Islands when he already knew the benefit of the faster northern route. It was, in fact, at their first stop in the Canary Islands that Gosnold's friends, John Smith and Stephen Calthrope, along with John Robinson, were implicated in a mutiny. Smith was "restrained," probably in chains. By the time the fleet got to Nevis in the Virgin Islands, Newport ordered gallows to be constructed to hang him. The hanging never happened, possibly because Gosnold intervened.

We pick up the Jamestown story again in Virginia. After an unspecified illness of three weeks, the talented Gosnold died on August 22, 1607, and was buried in or near James Fort with full military honors. By the fall of 1607, according to Smith, sixty-seven of the original 104 settlers had died, and George Percy recorded the deaths of twenty-four colonists during the months of August and September 1607.[59] The greatest number of the gentlemen, eleven of those reported by Percy as having died, came from London.[60] Others who died during the rest of the summer came from just about every other region in England. It is perhaps significant, however, that the men Captain John Smith took with him during his two voyages of "discovery" that summer, one to the Falls of the James and the other into the Chesapeake, included the men and boys from his home area of Lincolnshire and Norfolk. They were among those who apparently survived the summer death toll (or at least were not included in George Percy's list of the dead). Of course they were away from Jamestown Island during the real heat of the summer, sailing on the open water, which gives more credence to the assumption that Jamestown Island with its marshes and lack of fresh spring water may have been responsible for the quick demise of so many. On the other hand, perhaps Smith chose the strongest and healthiest of the group to go with him, thus culling out the people who might have survived had they stayed at the fort.

The story of Jamestown traditionally focuses on Smith and other leaders, so much so that a number of people whose actions immeasurably affected the settlement become invisible. John Smith listed 213 settlers' names among those who made the first few Jamestown voyages, dismissing the rest as mere "diverse others."[61] These anonymous "diverse others" should not be so quickly dismissed. Contributing just as significantly to the Jamestown story were hundreds of other unnamed colonists, both men and women, the Virginia Indians, and even the Spanish.

The Virginia Indians' first significant impact was on the siting of Jamestown itself. Historians have long maligned the choice of the Jamestown site, owing to the unhealthy nature of the low-lying marshy island and the danger posed by the island's location deep within Powhatan's territory. The island is so low-lying today that 80 percent is below the water level of storm flooding.[62] The lack of springs meant that only brackish river water or shallow wells could serve the colony, a fact often listed as contributing to Jamestown's high death rates. So why choose this place? Percy explained the choice by the proximity of the channel, but it is clear that the experienced military leaders saw the highest ground and the surrounding water as a natural defense against the expected enemies: the Virginia Indians and the Spanish.

To the natives themselves, "Virginia Indians" were neither "Virginian" nor "Indians." Those were their English names. In 1612 William Strachey, author of that precise James Fort description, wrote, "The severall territoryes and provinces which are in chief commaunded by their great king Powhatan, are comprehended under the denomynation of Tsenacommacoh, of which we may the more by experyence speak being the place wherein our abode and habitation hath now well neere six years consisted."[63] Tsenacomacah was the native name of the territory under the control of their leader, Powhatan, or at least that part of the territory explored and first settled by the English. It follows that the native people could be called Tsenacomacans. But to the English, the people they met along the banks of the rivers were variously called savages, salvages, naturals, natives, barbarians, heathens, or Indians. (Today most people, including modern descendants, refer to the Virginia Indians of Powhatan's chiefdom in Tidewater Virginia simply as Powhatans.) In the same way, the Powhatan River became the James River, named for King James I.[64] In the eyes of many of the English, the land was vacant, the "savages" only another form of wildlife on the "untamed" landscape. In fact, the replacement of Tsenacomacan terms by English names was a first phase of the establishment of an English population to rule or replace the Tsenacomacans themselves. The king had claimed all of Tsenacomacah and beyond to the western sea and north to modern New Jersey, as long as no other "Christian" nations had any settlements there. To rename places with English names meant conquest.

The Tsenacomacans had their own names for themselves, their villages, their rivers, and even the new English arrivals, Tassantassas (King James and his people).[65] We can know this, ironically, only from English accounts, biased as these observations of a foreign culture are. Nonetheless, these depictions of Tsenacomacans provide a profile of a significant group of players in the Jamestown story, telling of a nation with a sophisticated language, customs, government, and economy.

The southernmost river in Tsenacomacah was the Powhatan (the modern

John Smith's map of Virginia, which essentially delineates the boundaries of Powhatan's geographic influence, an area the Indians called Tsenacomacah. (First published in 1612; courtesy of the Library of Virginia)

James River), named for the longtime native leader of the united chiefdom that greeted the English colonists in 1607. Who was he? Some speculate he was the cousin of Don Luis, who met the Jesuit settlers of the Chesapeake in 1570.[66] It was Don Luis who went to Spain with the Jesuits and upon returning led a massacre of the missionaries. Whether or not the speculation is correct, Powhatan is almost invariably characterized by the English as the single most powerful chief among the Virginia Indians: "He is of parsonage a tall well proportioned man, with a sower looke, his head somewhat gray, his beard so thinne that it seemeth none at al, his age near 60; of a very able and hardy body to endure any labour."[67]

Powhatan, also known as Wahunsonacock, was the head of a huge family whose genealogy we can know in some measure. A variety of records,

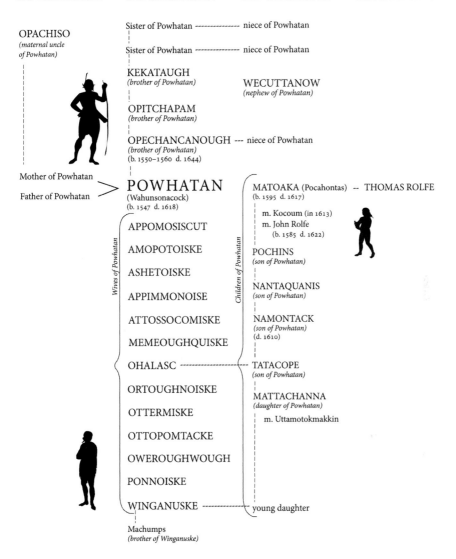

| 1ST GENERATION | 2ND GENERATION | 3RD GENERATION | 4TH GENERATION |

Sister of Powhatan ---------------- niece of Powhatan

Sister of Powhatan ---------------- niece of Powhatan

OPACHISO
(maternal uncle of Powhatan)

KEKATAUGH
(brother of Powhatan)

WECUTTANOW
(nephew of Powhatan)

OPITCHAPAM
(brother of Powhatan)

OPECHANCANOUGH --- niece of Powhatan
(brother of Powhatan)
(b. 1550–1560 d. 1644)

Mother of Powhatan

Father of Powhatan

POWHATAN
(Wahunsonacock)
(b. 1547 d. 1618)

Wives of Powhatan

APPOMOSISCUT

AMOPOTOISKE

ASHETOISKE

APPIMMONOISE

ATTOSSOCOMISKE

MEMEOUGHQUISKE

OHALASC ------------------

ORTOUGHNOISKE

OTTERMISKE

OTTOPOMTACKE

OWEROUGHWOUGH

PONNOISKE

WINGANUSKE ------------

Machumps
(brother of Winganuske)

Children of Powhatan

MATOAKA (Pocahontas) -- THOMAS ROLFE
(b. 1595 d. 1617)
m. Kocoum (in 1613)
m. John Rolfe
(b. 1585 d. 1622)

POCHINS
(son of Powhatan)

NANTAQUANIS
(son of Powhatan)

NAMONTACK
(son of Powhatan)
(d. 1610)

---- **TATACOPE**
(son of Powhatan)

MATTACHANNA
(daughter of Powhatan)
m. Uttamotokmakkin

---- young daughter

A hypothetical Powhatan family genealogical chart, based on English sources.

mainly Smith's *Generall Historie* and Strachey's *Historie of Travell into Virginia Britania,* list the names of thirty of Powhatan's relatives and in-laws.[68] Of his three named brothers, the most can be known of Opechancanough, werowance (chief) of the principal village on what the Tsenacomacans called the Pamunky River (modern York River). Upon Powhatan's death in 1618, Opechancanough became ruler either after or along with another brother, Opitchapam. Opechancanough led two devastating assaults against the English in 1622 and 1644. When he was more than ninety years old, he was shot and killed at Jamestown, where he had been imprisoned after the 1644 attacks on the English settlements.[69]

One source claims Powhatan had "many more than one hundred" wives. The names of at least a dozen of them are recorded.[70] One wife, Oholasc, served as queen of Quiyoughcohannock. The names of seven children of Powhatan's, five sons and two daughters, are also on record. Three sons were werowances, and Captain John Smith described the fourth, Nantaquawis, as the "manliest, comliest and the boldest spirit I ever saw in a salvage." Matachanna, one of Powhatan's two daughters, married Uttamatomakkin (Tomocomo), a priest who traveled with her more famous sister, Pocahontas, and her English husband, John Rolfe, to England in 1616–17.[71] Tomocomo was not impressed with the land of the strange Tassantassas— but apparently Pocahontas was.

Pocahontas, the favored daughter of Powhatan who befriended John Smith, was kidnapped and proselytized by the English. She married John Rolfe in 1614, ushering in a period of peace between the settlers and the Indians. She also went to England, was received by the king, and shortly thereafter started for home. Lord Carew, in a letter to Sir Thomas Roe in 1616/1617, wrote that she waited "reluctantly" for favorable winds for her return voyage, sorely against her will. In the end, she died before sailing to Virginia.[72] She is presumably buried in the chancel of St. George's Church, Gravesend, rebuilt after it burned in the early eighteenth century. Because of that fire and the rebuilding, Pocahontas's exact burial spot remains a challenging puzzle for archaeologists and interested direct descendants of the Jamestown colony.[73]

Besides Uttamatomakkin and Pocahontas, a number of individual Tsenacomacans are recorded to have spent time with the English. Kemps, an Indian prisoner in the fort, taught the colonists to raise corn, and while he was a slave of George Percy, he guided the English during raids on the "Pasbeheans and the Chiconamians."[74] Pepasschicher also guided the English. Nantaquawis, also called Mantiuas, a son of Powhatan, traveled with them, and Machumps was "sometyme in England." Powhatan had Amarice killed for staying in the fort without his permission.[75]

It is a fact that Pocahontas married John Rolfe in 1614. Her first husband was an Indian named Kocoum. In asking permission from Sir Thomas Dale to marry Pocahontas, Rolfe seemed to be saying indirectly that such an intercultural marriage would be frowned upon by the English or at least be unusual. Other evidence suggests that intermarriage was officially scorned. Unofficially, however, there are strong reasons to suspect considerable mixing of the two cultures: the all-male population of the settlement during the first sixteen months would have spurred such mixing; and in 1612 the Spanish reported that as many as "40 or 50 of the men had married with the salvages."[76]

Despite the suggestion that Tsenacomacans had considerable access to the English and to Jamestown itself, serious animosity between the Indians and the English almost wiped the colony out during the "starving time" of 1609–10. Some Virginia Indians besieged the fort that winter, and the siege was so effective that "it is true, the Indians killed as fast without, if our men stirred but beyond their bounds of their blockhouse, as famine and pestilence did within."[77] The Indians withheld even their occasional food deliveries. One explanation for the trouble may be the arrival at Jamestown of twenty women and children on the *Blessing* in the fall of 1609; perhaps

Painting from an engraving from life of Pocahontas, the favored daughter of Powhatan, made shortly before she died in England. She was buried at Gravesend, east of London, in 1617. (Oil on tapestry, by Mary Ellen Howe, from an engraving by Simon de Passe; on loan to the Virginia Historical Society, Richmond)

the siege was a result of these newcomers' presence. It certainly must have sent a strong signal across Tsenacomacah that what might have been perceived as a small, perhaps temporary all-male trading post was growing into something quite different: a permanent settlement of families.[78] Extermination of the invaders may have appeared to be the only course of action.

Whatever the effect of the immigration of women and children on Tsenacomacan foreign policy, these newcomers certainly constitute another group of anonymous "diverse others" who influenced the developing "new

England." We already know that the first English women, Mistress Forest and Anne Burras, came to the colony in the fall of 1608. They were not the only English women in town for long, however. According to the Spanish ambassador to England (and spy) Don Pedro de Zúñiga, one hundred women joined the four or five hundred men in the Gates 1609 flotilla to the colony.[79] The *Blessing* women accounted for twenty of these. Perhaps half the remaining eighty arrived as the remains of the fleet limped into the Jamestown port during the summer of 1609, and with the Bermuda ships *Deliverance* and *Patience* that arrived at Jamestown in May 1610.[80] The names of the women who arrived on the *Blessing* are not known, but Temperance Flowerdew, wife of the future governor, Sir George Yeardley, came in 1609, as did Thomasine Cawsey, Elizabeth Joones, and Amtyte Waine, in time for them, along with the women from the *Blessing,* to experience the "starving" winter of 1609–10. The list of named women grows to thirty-five by 1618, if the dates and the census of 1624–25 are reliable.[81] When Sir Thomas Gates returned to Virginia in 1611, he brought along his daughters, Margaret and Elizabeth.[82] There must have been hundreds of anonymous "diverse other" women who braved the crossing and the "seasoning time" of a Virginia summer as well. The three female burials uncovered by archaeologists beneath the third and fourth Statehouse foundations on the western edge of the town site may be evidence that few women survived at Jamestown for long. All three were dead before the age of thirty-four.[83]

The siege of James Fort almost ended the colony. The two Bermuda-built ships that arrived in 1610 came not only with women but also with far too few provisions for a starving colony and the new arrivals. By June 1610 Gates decided to move the survivors out of Jamestown and set sail for England. Thanks to what has been characterized as last-second divine intervention, an advance vessel, followed by the arrival of Governor De La Warre and abundant fresh supplies, turned the deserters back to Jamestown in what seemed to be the nick of time. A more careful reading of one account of that so-called chance meeting, however, reveals that Gates knew that De La Warre was on his way and was going to wait for him for "ten days at Cape [Point] Comfort" at the mouth of the James. After that time he was "otherwise so to go for England" with whatever he had left on board of his thirty-day rations.[84] This waiting period made good sense. Upon his arrival in the James from Bermuda two months earlier, Gates had found thirty people with Percy at Point Comfort, literally healthy as clams, living off the seafood there. They had thrived while their fellow colonists held the

Left: King James I of England, artist unknown. (Colonial Williamsburg Foundation) *Right:* King Philip III of Spain, by Diego Velázquez, ca. 1634/35. (Museo Nacional del Prado, Madrid)

fort and died like "dogges." The wait for De La Warre was not a desperate measure, then, but a chance to be revived by the Point Comfort seafood before risking a voyage home with meager supplies, in the event that De La Warre's flotilla did not arrive. The notion that chance alone saved a failed Jamestown might well be an exaggeration.

Just as the Virginia Indians and the population of English women presented challenges as well as benefits to Jamestown, so did another group: the Spanish. The Jamestown colonists always had to prepare to defend against invasion by the ships and the troops of the Catholic Spanish. The threat was not entirely external: the first president, Edward Maria Wingfield, and perhaps other Englishmen had strong Catholic backgrounds, and the arrest and execution of Captain George Kendall seems to have been carried out because he was a suspected agent of the Spanish. The Spanish king, Philip III, received a steady stream of secret information directly from a "confidential person on His Majestie's [English] Council" concerning Jamestown events and details.[85]

The settlement was in a precarious place indeed, according to the Spanish. A letter from the Spanish ambassador in London, Don Pedro de Zúñiga, reporting to Philip details of Zúñiga's conference with James I, claimed that King James himself had said that if the Spanish wanted to "punish" (remove) the Jamestown colonists, "neither he nor they could complain." In fact, according to Zúñiga, King James called the Jamestown colonists "terrible people." Zúñiga was almost certainly exaggerating, trying to maneuver Philip to send troops to wipe out the colony, for in all his surviving letters he consistently urges Philip to do this. Regardless of what James I might have said or thought of Jamestown, clearly the Spanish desired to erase it from their "Indies." On January 17, 1608, Philip endorsed a plan proposed by his Council of War whereby he "command[ed] that there should be prepared whatever was necessary to drive out the people who are in Virginia . . . [and] not to let anyone hear what is being done."[86] Presumably the plan was to send a fleet then lying in preparation at the Windward Islands to annihilate Jamestown. But there also seems to have been another proposal to the king for the colony's destruction, involving a double agent at Jamestown.

In a March 1609 letter to King Philip, Zúñiga refers to his dealings with Baron Arundell, a disgruntled English Catholic who proposed to aid the Spanish by sailing on the pretext of a voyage of discovery, choosing a man in Puerto Rico to be planted as a spy at Jamestown. The man would be taken to Jamestown and instructed about the geography of the James River region and the nature of the English forts there so that he could relate to King Philip "by what means those people can be driven out without violence in arms."[87] What "means" the baron had in mind to erase Jamestown without firing a shot is a mystery. One theory is that a Spanish agent might have been sent to secretly lace the common kettle with arsenic. Such a poisoning might explain the periodic mass deaths at Jamestown, although it cannot account for deaths that occurred before March 1609 (sixty-six in the summer of 1607, and at least thirteen in 1608).[88] Alternatively, it is more likely that Arundell knew that the population of the colony had had enough of Virginia, and any offer to be ferried back to England might look far better than an impending winter without Smith's negotiating talents with the Indians.[89] Or maybe he thought it possible to gain enough of Powhatan's trust to persuade him to stage a more concerted siege of the fort. Then Jamestown would indeed be wiped out without resorting to Spanish arms.

In any case, Arundell's plan most likely would not have been executed. Once approved by the king—in itself a two-month process with the passage

The Somerset House Conference, 1604, artist unknown. This historic meeting between Spanish and English diplomats ended twenty years of fighting among the English, the Spanish, and the Dutch. The resulting peace treaty removed some of the threat of Spanish sea power and must have played a major role in Spain's later reluctance to destroy Jamestown. (National Portrait Gallery, London)

of letters to and from Spain—the series of voyages, the training period for the chosen spy, and the devising and execution of the plan would have required many more months. Apart from the question of time, after reading of the proposed Arundell scheme, Philip III did not approve of dealing with Arundell. He urged Zúñiga to act with "great caution with the Baron of Arundell." Over the next two years, the king merely kept asking for inside information about the colony without giving the green light to crush it.[90]

The fact that the Windward Islands fleet never sailed to Virginia and that the Spanish let Jamestown take root by neglect, chance, or design has turned out to be one of the greatest diplomatic success stories in the history of the English nation. Thanks to what these "diverse other" Spanish did not do, Jamestown survived.

TWO

REDISCOVERING JAMESTOWN

James Fort: The Documentary Evidence

Imagining what James Fort really looked like from documents alone can be frustrating. For example, according to Percy, the overall configuration of James Fort was "triangle-wise." What does that mean? Was it or was it not a triangle? Or was it "triangle-wise" because it was not an equilateral triangle? Or was it "sort of" a triangle, meaning Percy saw more than three sides, perhaps a short fourth wall? If the fort had three joining walls, then it was not "like" a triangle but in fact *was* a triangle. Percy also reported that the fort had "three bulwarks at every corner like a half moon." So were there as many as three protruding bulwarks at every corner, making a total of nine, or only three bulwarks total, one bulwark where each of three walls connected? Can a triangle even have corners? They actually have angles. Does the word *corner* suggest a fourth side? Is each of the three bulwarks a half moon, or demi-lune—a military architectural term for a corner defense shaped like a wedge with an inner curved wall—or do the three points at each corner together form a half moon? When Percy refers to "four or five pieces of artillery in them" (the bulwarks or the half moons), does he mean four to five guns total or four or five in each of three bulwarks, totaling twelve to fifteen mounted guns?

The Zúñiga map, likely a 1608 tracing of a draft version of Smith's Map of Virginia, and the Tindall map seem to settle the question about the number of walls in the fort—three—but the shapes of the corner bulwarks, if they are architecturally correct, do not look anything like traditional half moons (see illustrations on pp. 16 and 47). Are these supposed to be circular bulwarks and rectangular gates on the river side, with a larger single circular bulwark on the land side? Is what looks like a flag on a flagpole really a flag at all, or is it a plan of a palisade connecting to a rectangular outer enclosure? Is the slightly off-center X a designation for the church? And what about scale? As drawn, the fort encompasses at least fifty acres and winds up near but not directly on the western end of the island. Surely the size does not reflect reality, although the relative location might. Almost certainly the asymmetrical shape of the triangle suggests that this symbol is no mere generic fort icon, intended only to locate the building in relation to the ocean and rivers for the guidance of future invading Spanish ships. Yet the church does not deserve even a sketch-plan view. Can the map details, or some of them, be taken literally? If only some qualify as truth, then which ones?

The other map of Jamestown Island made during the Virginia Company period, the Vingboons chart of the Powhatan (James) River, likely dating to 1617–20, shows only a triple-gabled building to designate "Blockhouse Jamestown." Is this chart intended to show everything a ship's captain might

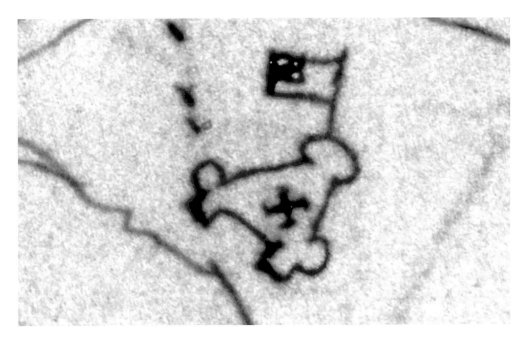

Detail of 1608 Zúñiga map showing corner bulwarks and a cross possibly marking the church. (Ministerio de Educación y Cultura de España, Archivo General de Simancas, MPD,19,163)

recognize as he finds his way upriver? If so, had the fort walls already disappeared by the time the chart was drawn, leaving only the fort's most prominent building? Or was the chart maker selective, leaving out the palisades in favor of the clearest landmark for navigators?

Eyewitness documents provide no clearer guide to the location and appearance of James Fort. In July 1610, William Strachey described a very precise one-half-acre triangle and stated the dimensions of the three curtains (technically, walls between bulwarks): river side, 140 yards; land sides, 100 yards each. But his dimensions describe a fort interior at least twice the size of his one-half-acre estimate (1.1–1.75 acres). So can his measurements of the walls be trusted?

Even more puzzlingly, in a description of the fort in 1608, almost two years before Strachey wrote, Captain John Smith reported that the fort was "reduced" to a five-sided form. Does "reduced" in this sense mean "made smaller," or does it mean "changed" or even "enlarged," as it might have meant in seventeenth-century usage? Philip Barbour, modern editor of Smith's complete works, admits that only in the 1624 version does Smith state the pentagonal shape, while in two earlier versions of the same document the exact form was not specified. So was the fort really five-sided, or did Smith's memory dim during his fifteen-year absence? Our understanding of the fort's design is further confused by colonist Ralph Hamor's description of a "town" again "reduced," this time into a "handsome forme" with two "faire" rows of timber-framed two-and-a-half-story houses. What is a "handsome forme"? Does this phrase describe a linear form outside of the original triangle, as most scholars have decided, or does it imply that the timber houses paralleled the palisades in the original triangular fort? Did the 1617 Dutch chart maker perhaps record one of these rowhouses in sketching the triple-gable icon? Do these seemingly conflicting details reflect architectural change as Jamestown-the-fort evolved into Jamestown-the-town?

For all their numbers and other seemingly objective facts, these documents raise as many questions as they answer. Add to these records the obviously subjective testimonial descriptions of Jamestown penned in 1623–24 by eyewitness settlers criticizing or defending Thomas Smythe's twelve-year reign as treasurer, and envisioning Jamestown during the Company period becomes even more impossible.[1] Any attempt to make a composite from these various sources would likely leave us with the proverbial camel designed by committee. More documents might help, but after a century of historical research, the odds of finding new evidence of Jamestown's fort in the library or the attic are small. The archaeologist's recourse is to seek out more substantial evidence in the form of physical remains. In the case of Jamestown, however, few scholars held out hope for this form of research. Philip Barbour said it best. After reading the negative report of National Park Service archaeology, he concluded, "[A]rchaeological evidence can prove nothing [about the fort design], for the undoubted site has been washed away into the James River."[2] The planners of the 350th anniversary of Jamestown's founding must have shared this belief: in 1957 they supported a document-based reconstruction of the fort in a historical theme park completely off the island.

FINDING JAMES FORT: THE CHALLENGES

By 1994, most people agreed with Barbour that the site was "washed away into the James." There was little reason to think otherwise. As early as 1837, when William Randolph visited the Jamestown site, his eyewitness account of the fort's erosion lent credence to the belief that the site was now submerged with the island's western end, marked by a lone cypress tree some one hundred yards offshore.[3] Since that eroded section was the only part of the island once close to the deepwater channel—the mooring spot that Percy described in 1607—belief in the demise of all traces of the fort made perfect sense. That is, if the fort and the landing point were on the same site. But what if they were not?

The Association for the Preservation of Virginia Antiquities (APVA) decided to ask that question. Beginning in 1994, the APVA sponsored archaeology "to locate and then uncover any remains of that first Jamestown settlement, especially traces of the Fort as it was originally constructed, and determine how it evolved to accommodate a growing population during the Virginia Company years, 1607–1624."[4] The effort might have seemed predestined to failure. Not only did the weight of evidence, both historical and archaeological, suggest that the fort had melted before centuries of wave action, but there were twenty-two and a half acres of relatively unknown ground to search.

Other built-in challenges presented themselves as well. Given the long and widely shared assumption that the first colonists located the fort on the doomed west end of the island, proof to the contrary would have to be extraordinarily conclusive. Any evidence found of a fort design would have to correspond to the seventeenth-century eyewitness descriptions, at least demonstrating some sort of triangular shape. In particular, in order to be sure that the site of the first fort had been located, any artifacts unearthed had to be found in undisturbed deposits that were old enough and military enough to relate directly to that early fort era, 1607–10. The discovery of wall fragments here and there, scattered building remains, and a few objects of a military nature dating to the 1607 period would not be enough to prove anything. After all, those remains could be evidence of an outer fortified area, such as Smith's five-sided town, that grew up somewhat later than the original 1607 palisaded structure.

What happened on the Jamestown site in the centuries after 1699, when the capital moved to Williamsburg and most occupants abandoned the town, promised both to help and to hinder the archaeological process of excavation. During those years the land slowly reverted to agricultural fields. On the one hand, that was good news for future archaeology. With the exception of the construction of a Confederate earthen fort in 1861, no extensive ground-disturbing construction took place to destroy the buried evidence of occupation. No modern town grew into and over the original town site to obliterate and conceal seventeenth-century remains, such as had happened at Plymouth, Massachusetts, for example. On the other hand, the eventual plowing of the western end of the Jamestown site between circa 1750, when the church was dismantled, and 1893, when the APVA acquired the land, was bad news for archaeologists. Plowing the land for farming would have blended the upper foot or so of the heretofore-intact layers of seventeenth-century town remains. Objects left on the site through the seventeenth century would have been mixed together in the plowzone as one layer, making precise dating difficult. In addition, plowing would have destroyed some evidence of soil levels deposited one on top of the other. As a consequence, surviving bits of James Fort and other seventeenth-century features would be exposed all at once, regardless of the sequence in which they had been created. A hole dug in 1607 that held a wall post and a filled-in drainage ditch that once marked a 1680 property line could appear archaeologically to be from the same moment in time.

Not all was lost, however. The plow would only have gone so deep, usually a foot or so. This level could be shoveled off and screened for artifacts relatively quickly. Once a large area could be exposed in this manner, then relationships among any traces of the fort, such as the alignment

View of Jamestown Island showing extent of agricultural fields, ca. 1930. (National Park Service, Colonial National Historical Park)

After the Virginia government center moved to Williamsburg, much of the Jamestown site reverted to agricultural fields. Constant cultivation churned through the shallowest remains of the town, leaving undisturbed deeper seventeenth-century building postholes *(left),* ditches *(right),* cellars, pits, graves, and wells.

or lack of alignment of a wall line and a building foundation, could help determine which things had existed at the same time. Three or more post-holes forming a straight line would likely be the anchor points of a standing structure, probably a long-vanished timber fence line. A set of these holes in a rectangular pattern would quite likely form the footprint of a building once supported by posts anchored in the ground. Any other building foundation found to be aligned with a series of these post lines or post-line rectangles could confidently be assumed to have been built or planned at the same time.

Obviously, determining these significant relationships in space and time would require uncovering large continuous parcels of ground. Unfortunately, extremely large parcels could not be uncovered all at once, nor were there any clues as to which parcel might hold the evidence of such aligned structures. So the best possible excavation process at Jamestown was the "quilt" method. Once the digging lifted the plowzone, the excavation would progress by adding one completed ten-foot square at a time to an over-all plan, revealing the pattern of the original town design, the direction of walls, plan of buildings, direction of ditches, and location of pits and graves. This quilting process would follow a trail of the Jamestown remains. If the excavated angles of walls and buildings datable to the first quarter of the seventeenth century took on a triangular form, a "triangular-wise" palisaded fort with half-moon bastions could be identified. In other words, archaeological proof of the fort could only be mustered by a deliberate, ever-expanding excavation strategy, moving from one excavated area to an adjoining area, wherever the apparent pattern of fort-period fragments led. Bit by bit, James Fort could emerge from its earthen shroud.

But twenty-two and a half acres—the size of the APVA property on Jamestown Island—was no small shroud. Excavated by the quilt method, that area would amount to 9,900 ten-foot squares. Before we began digging, therefore, it was critically important to narrow the boundaries of the site. Three factors helped us make the best educated guess where the center of the fort might lie.

The first factor was our knowledge of the site of seventeenth-century Jamestown's church. The foundations of the church had been uncovered in 1893–1903 by Mary Jeffery Galt, who excavated a number of burials and two superimposed church foundations next to the brick church tower—the only remnant of the original town still standing above ground. According to William Strachey, the church was in "the middest" of the triangle.[5] So if local lore was correct, and the fort site was "undoubtedly" submerged offshore to the west, then the church in the fort also had to be gone. In that case, the present foundations and tower were evidence of a seventeenth-century relocation campaign in which the church was rebuilt a quarter mile to the east of its original site. Although it was known that the first substantial church, originally erected in 1608, was rebuilt in 1617 and again in 1639–46, there was no record that the church was relocated. In fact, churches were rarely moved from their original locations, sanctified by prayer and the human burials in and around them. Why should the church at James Fort be any exception? It followed that the early fort likely surrounded the enduring church foundations and tower. If so, initial digging between the shore of the river and the church tower would intersect the fort's south wall line.

The brick church tower is the only aboveground remnant of seventeenth-century Jamestown.

Second, it made sense that archaeological ground should be broken at a place where military and industrial objects datable to the first quarter of the seventeenth century had already turned up. In fact, such artifacts had been found in and about the church remains at various times during the first sixty years of APVA ownership, beginning with the excavation efforts of APVA founder Mary Jeffery Galt. The two superimposed church foundations she uncovered established what she thought was the footing of the 1608 church building. Also, during the installation of an underground utility line in 1939, workmen unearthed a stray "pot." Fortunately, the location of the find was recorded, and the relic itself was saved in a collection of other objects serendipitously discovered on the APVA property over the years. Researchers studying the collection recognized the vessel as an intact crucible with a fragment of a second

Crucibles (one fragmented and capping the other) likely used for glassmaking in 1608, found during the installation of utility lines "near the Pocahontas statue," 1939.

crucible, originally used in its intact form as a lid for the first vessel, fused to it by molten glass.[6] Smith's records of a successful trial run of glassmaking in 1608 suggest that these objects might have been left in James Fort during that first glassmaking operation.[7]

In the 1950s, in an endeavor titled Project 100, National Park Service (NPS) test excavations found a number of apparently random old ditches and trenches in and around the Civil War earthwork. An early seventeenth-century deposit of artifacts associated with a blacksmithing/gun-repairing operation was also uncovered, hinting at some sort of fort connection. Nevertheless, the archaeologists heading this research effort concluded that "in all probability it [the fort] stood on ground that has been washed into the James River."[8]

The third factor in our decision was speculation that the fort site might be recoverable. In the early 1960s, British archaeologist Ivor Noël Hume conducted a survey of the reports, history, and collections of a number of past excavations of colonial sites in Virginia. Noting the church burials found by the APVA under Galt and the possible "starving time" burial ground found by the NPS in the 1950s, Noël Hume concluded: "[T]ogether the two graveyards provide brackets between which the fort site probably existed." The site he indicated was located in the vicinity of the Confederate earthwork, which seemed to be a logical assumption. But by the early 1980s he had completely changed his mind. He came to believe that the fort had indeed eroded away, not on the western but rather on the extreme eastern end of Jamestown Island. Virginia Harrington, an NPS Jamestown historian, took strong exception to this eastern-end erosion theory and called for excavations in the area of the church and the Confederate fort, if only to prove the area barren.[9]

Twenty-five years after the NPS archaeologists decided that the site of James Fort did not survive, the Project 100 records and artifacts were re-

South churchyard, ca. 1940, with original location of Pocahontas statue and hence the place where workmen found the 1608 crucibles. For that and other reasons, this appeared to be the most likely place to start the search for James Fort in 1994.

viewed by a new generation of archaeologists building on the excavations and theories of the recent past and armed with decades of firsthand experience in excavation of outlying seventeenth-century fortified settlements in the Chesapeake region. Study of the random field tests that had uncovered apparently disconnected fragments of ditches and a trash pit could not confirm or deny that these were parts of James Fort. But an evaluation of the artifacts from primarily undisturbed or underrecorded deposits proved more promising. Lessons learned from fieldwork on other James River early plantation sites and new interpretation of the early seventeenth-century artifacts by museum scholars made possible more precise identification of these objects. It was now clear that the arms and armor in the Project 100 collection dated to the first quarter of the seventeenth century, thus testifying strongly to the existence of an underlying James Fort in the vicinity of the Confederate earthwork. Some of the ceramics found were types that might date to the James Fort period as well. Consequently, the study led to the "strong recommendation that an area excavation be conducted . . . on the interior, surroundings of, and, wherever possible beneath the Confederate earthwork."[10] At the least, these excavations might detect some architectural pattern in the assorted ditches and trenches exposed by Project 100, connecting the random-appearing dots; at best, the excavations might find James Fort.

Once the most promising area to search for the fort was determined, a final pre-digging exercise focused the search even more. The Zúñiga map of 1608, as out of scale as it is, provided enough data to create a hypothetical fort plan. This model could be transposed onto the modern churchyard landscape, thus giving some guidance for the initial digging. The measurements recorded by William Strachey set the scale for the model. Strachey's measurements were taken to be the length of the fort's curtain, not including the corner bulwarks.[11] The bulwarks were assumed to be at least large enough to accommodate cannons the size of demi-culverins (or at least fifty feet in diameter). Given these assumptions, the hypothetical fort became 1.75 acres in size. The central church tower served to anchor the model of the fort to the modern landscape. If fragments of the actual fort appeared as the dig was carried out, the fort model could migrate and perhaps change scale based on the reality of the discoveries. In other words, ongoing archaeological discoveries would correct and recorrect the hypothetical fort model until it fit precisely onto the modern landscape.

That was the plan as I, a crew of one, put the first shovel into the ground on April 4, 1994, at a spot predetermined by blending fact, artifact, theory, and hope—at a place surrounded by all the promising signposts: the church, the Confederate earthwork, and the James River shoreline. The decision where exactly to shovel first came down to a discussion I had with Ivor Noël Hume, the project's first advisor. Since the 1980s, when Noël Hume had offered his theory that the fort had washed away to the east, his discovery of the glassmaking crucibles in the APVA collections had brought him to the yard between the church and the river. As we stood there, however, we were still uncertain where to start. Finally, we both eyed a slight depression in the lawn next to an active gravel service road, a clear sign that that place must have been disturbed sometime in the past. Since it did not seem like a good idea politically to dig into and therefore to cut off a major useful Park Service road with the very first trench—at least until we could prove there was something under it—the roadside depression seemed as good a starting place as any. With much finger-crossing, the first real digging into the depression began the next day. There is no way to describe the elation I felt when that digging almost immediately produced fragments of early seventeenth-century ceramics. The incredible chain of discoveries that fol-

Jamestown Rediscovery excavations begin, April 4, 1994.

lowed, literally connecting the dots, unfolded like a mystery novel over the course of the first eleven electrifying years (1994 to 2005) of the Jamestown Rediscovery Project.

JAMES FORT: CONNECTING THE DOTS

South Palisade

As spring turned to the summer of 1994, the crew of one had the great fortune to be augmented by a number of professional archaeologists experienced in seventeenth-century British colonial sites. Consequently, a number of ten-foot squares could be opened up at the same time. Some of them revealed a distinct black streak angling through the undisturbed yellow clay. Parallel to that streak, a number of individual dark stains appeared at regular intervals. Careful scraping of the surface within the boundaries of the discolored streak showed patterns of soil color, a line of circular dark areas of loam within the light-yellow clay. There was little doubt that such soil stains were archaeological evidence of a palisade wall: marks of decayed circular or split timbers once standing side by side and held upright by solid packed clay in a narrow, straight-sided, flat-bottomed trench. Transformed by time into rich loam, the dark stains retained the exact shape of the vanished logs they had replaced. Carefully excavated, they left an exact mold of the timber, five inches to one foot in diameter. The precisely dug, straight-sided, and flat-bottomed trench, probably two and one-half feet deep originally, would have met the requirement for firmly supporting

Excavations during the first season discovered a palisade line and the source of the utility-line crucibles: a number of pits containing thousands of other discarded early seventeenth-century artifacts.

palisades. The line ran 17 degrees south of a compass east–west alignment for more than fifty feet from a point where it had been destroyed by a later seventeenth-century drainage ditch on the east and the construction trench of a seawall on the west. Establishing this line as the south wall of James Fort would provide a key interpretive tool for the future, presenting the possibility that other structural evidence that might align with it in some meaningful and mathematical way could identify other pieces of the James Fort puzzle.

The form of the wall trench and the soil stains left by decayed posts therein clearly marked a palisade. Whether or not this could be identified as the wall of James Fort depended on establishing its date of construction and how long it had stood. Finding datable artifacts in fill deposited during construction and destruction was the key to uncovering the age. There could be no doubt of a 1607–24 chronology. Excavation of the post molds' backfill, made up of the decayed post and the clay deposited as the posts were raised, did strongly suggest, however, a connection to the fort period (that is, prior to 1623–24, by which time, according to eyewitness documents, James Fort was a ruin). A tobacco pipe crudely made of local clay and a ceramic crucible base found in the fill of one of the related wall-support posts were so similar to those found at a 1585 minerals lab workshop site at Fort Raleigh, North Carolina, that they likely dated to the early James Fort years.[12] A fifteenth- to early seventeenth-century Venetian glass Nueva Cadiz trade bead, a late sixteenth-century Scottish snaphaunce pistol lock, and a Hans Krauwinckel (1586–1635) casting counter (German calculating token) were found where some of the palisade timbers once stood as well. So all of these late fifteenth-century to early seventeenth-century objects fit quite nicely into the fort era—good news for the fort-seeking hopeful. The palisade we had discovered was definitely old enough to be part of James Fort.

And, the palisade trench and the related postholes seemed to be strong evidence that we had found one wall of the fort. Could there be other footprints?

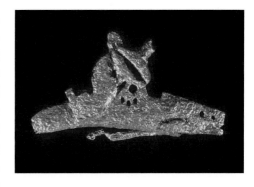

Late sixteenth-century Scottish snaphaunce pistol lock found in the fill of the south palisade line.

A fifteenth-century German coin-like jetton (originally made for calculating) and a sixteenth- to seventeenth-century glass trade bead found in the south palisade line.

South Bulwark

Expansion by more ten-foot squares moving east from the riverside fort wall eventually uncovered another possible palisade trench, but one with a distinctively different plan. Instead of striking off in a linear pattern, this wall line formed an arc about twenty-five feet long. Starting at the base of an APVA granite monument, the trench extended toward the riverbank, gradually becoming shallower until it disappeared. A larger and deeper ditch mirrored the curve of the smaller trench, nine feet to the north and east. The parallel trenches—presumably contemporaneous—immediately brought to mind the circular bulwark of

Discovery of the south palisade wall trench (1), curved bulwark palisade, and accompanying ditch (2) together suggested that James Fort had been found.

the 1608 Zúñiga map. The trench ranged from five inches deep, where it was cut by the foundation of the monument base, to one-half inch deep, where grading—possibly during the Civil War—had wiped it away. The palisade trench itself held only Indian pottery, further evidence that this trench was dug in historically virgin ground, establishing a construction date of circa 1607. By 1996, the discovery of the south palisade trench, the curved bulwark trench with its accompanying ditch, and the early dates and military nature of the associated artifacts became early compelling signs that we were indeed finding the "lost" remains of James Fort.

The form of the wider and deeper ditch, or dry moat, and the artifacts associated with it strongly suggested that the ditch was part of James Fort. The moat was deepest near the monument and contained various layers of dirt that told the story of its life. At the bottom, rain-washed clay and decayed plant material had slumped in from the rampart side as top layers of clay on the bank washed back in. Then organic topsoil-like fill, alternating with mixed soil containing small lumps of subsoil clay, filled the top of the bulwark ditch, the mixture of dirt resulting from the partial leveling of the rampart when the fort was abandoned. (Natural washed clay would not produce lumps, but shoveled soil would.) As the natural erosion levels built up, glassmakers evidently poured a layer of hot slag (waste produced during glass production) at the northwest end of the bulwark ditch. The glass waste spilled into the ditch from the north, presumably coming from a manufacturing site inside the fort, carted through a nearby gate and then tipped into the partially open ditch. We know that glassmakers arrived in 1608 and sent a "trial of glass" back to England before the end of the year. So the presence of the slag deposit shows that the entrenchment had been open long enough to receive the glass waste and accumulate some eroded silt between May 1607 and 1608.[13] The excavation of the fill along the bulwark ditch exposed two occurrences of digging and backfilling: a right-angle trench to the east and a later extension of the bulwark ditch to the south. But the fill sequence could still indicate that both of the earlier ditches could well have stood open and then been abandoned and back-filled at about the same time.

The moat location and the apparent extra-thick plowzone and survival of

Artifacts associated with signs in the ground of the fort configuration proved old and military enough to establish construction as early as 1607: a late sixteenth- to seventeenth-century English Borderware jug and an iron breastplate from a suit of armor.

old topsoil next to it provide more information about the bulwark design. They suggest that an earth wall or rampart once stood over and along the curved palisade. The builders would have used the dirt removed from the entrenchment to build this wall. This dirt would also have created the two and one-half feet or so depth of soil necessary to support the palisade logs. Digging an entrenchment and piling up a rampart were standard procedure in fort construction, requiring an attacking enemy to struggle through the entrenchment and then scale the rampart before getting to the palisade. The right-angled ditch extension east of the curved palisade trench and the bulwark ditch suggest a more complicated bulwark design than a simple circle. The ditch strays from the circular pattern to become simply a straight line for thirty feet, where it makes about a 90-degree turn toward the river. Following this early seventeenth-century fort footprint was challenging. Most of the ditch existed beneath the remains of a burned building post-dating the existence of the fort by at least two decades. That building's construction made a significant impact on the fort remains, complicating our efforts. The 46' × 30' structure, which once stood on a deep foundation of stone, had a basement and included two massive exterior brick chimneys, one each in the two twenty-three-foot-wide basement rooms. Original construction of the basement and one of the chimneys cut into the bulwark ditch extension, which had already been backfilled. Fortunately, the ditch had been dug two feet deeper than the cellar floor of the building, so it survived that later construction. Since the building was an integral part of the seventeenth-century Jamestown story, however, everything that was removed from it in order to record the earlier fort footprint had to itself be recorded and interpreted. What turned out to be the ruins of the 1640s house/warehouse of merchant/politician John White required months of excavation.[14]

Eventual digging beneath the basement floor of the White building determined that the bulwark ditch was originally at least four feet below the estimated original fort-period ground surface and perhaps six feet wide. But because the ditch extended to the eroded shoreline and was therefore lost at that point, its precise design must remain somewhat conjectural. In light of the shape of the south and west James Fort bulwarks as shown on the Zúñiga map, it would make sense to speculate that the advance earthwork and palisades mounted on it formed three sides of a square bulwark (perhaps one of two such bulwarks) for cannon. This rectangular shape does not sound like the bulwarks Percy saw as "like a half-moon."[15] But the

Overhead view from under a protective tent of the bulwark ditch found beneath the John White building foundation, view facing south.

extended bulwark is probably an addition to the curved ditch and so not part of the original construction that Percy described as standing in June 1607. These rectangular bulwarks may well have reworked a simple earlier circular-walled bulwark.

More soil layers and another feature found inside the confines of the bulwark also suggested that the design of the bulwark changed over time. The White building debris and shoreline deposits—sand and domestic trash deposited in an apparent attempt to extend the shoreline in 1901—extended southwest until they rested upon a circular pit, filled with washed-in clay and dark organic soil holding scores of artifacts dating circa 1610. This collection included a number of gun parts, 1602 Irish halfpennies, an ornate horse bit, and a medical instrument known as a spatula mundani, which was used to treat constipation. The medical implement turned out to be quite precisely datable to 1609, as there was record of it being sent to the colony with a chest of other medical instruments in that year.

The pit itself may have originally functioned as a relatively safe place

Circular pit inside southeast bulwark; possibly a place to store powder near the bulwark gun platform.

to store gunpowder for the bulwark cannons. How it fit into the overall scheme of the curvilinear bulwark is problematic. It is located in a position that would have been in the path of the circular palisade if it had originally completed the circular form suggested by the surviving palisade trench. Consequently, both the magazine and the later rectangular bulwarks could not have been original to the first fort design but rather were part of changes made later. Could these changes all be examples of "[the fort] growing . . . to more perfection," as Strachey reported in 1610? The dates of the reworked bulwark ditch and the magazine could certainly fit that explanation, but the Zúñiga map, on which these shapes seem to appear, was made two years earlier. Here it seems no explanation fits all.

This evidence of construction and remodeling, however difficult to understand completely, does bear witness to the military prowess of the Jamestown leaders. Wingfield, Gosnold, and the other captains "contrived" (designed) the fort in May/June 1607. Since the colonists were constantly under fire from the Virginia Indians during construction, a secured fortified area had to be constructed as quickly as possible. A triangle requiring only three walls could be built in the shortest period of time. Circular bulwark walls, strengthened by advance moats and mounds, reflect the battle experience these leaders brought with them from their service in the Netherlands and Ireland. Such English designs, while archaic in comparison to what the Spanish were building in Europe, were good enough to repel the Virginia Indians, an enemy without muskets and cannons. The designers admitted, "We have made ourselves sufficiently strong for [attacks from] these savages."

This construction may not have been considered "sufficient," however, to repel cannon-wielding Spanish ships at undermanned Jamestown. The rectangular-shaped advance batteries would be a necessary addition as time and arrow-free days would allow. Given the months of off-and-on

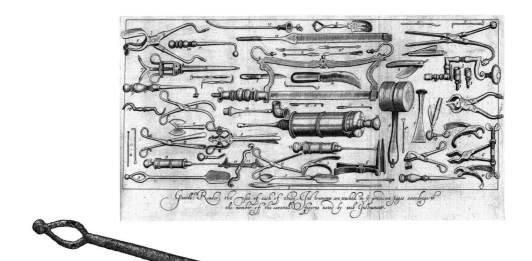

Early seventeenth-century surgical tool (spatula mundani) devised by the English surgeon John Woodall, and his illustration of it along with the other tools of his trade. (Illustration from John Woodall's *The Surgeon's Mate*, 1617, courtesy of the University of Bristol Medical School Library)

siege and starvation at the fort for the next three years, it is likely that any improvements more in keeping with European standards had to wait for Lord De La Warre's rescue mission in the summer of 1610 and his "perfection" of the fort.[16]

East Wall

Once the southeastern bulwark and south wall lines appeared to be established archaeologically, finding any surviving evidence of an east wall became the focus. As the bulwark began to take shape, a relatively faint linear soil stain angling off to the north, which had been found during the very first season of excavation, acquired added significance. It was already known that the stain was old enough to be from the fort period, because it had been severed by the digging of a circa-1620s drainage ditch. As there were no signs of the telltale rotted palisade posts, however, the feature had been written off as a small drainage ditch. Tracing the stain back toward the bulwark area for some fifteen feet established that it was straight as an arrow, it had the required straight sides and flat bottom of a palisade trench, and it terminated directly opposite the path of the curved bulwark palisade five feet from the monument base, which stood between the two paths. The bulwark line did not emerge from the statue base and thus connect directly with the east line, but this gap probably indicated that there had been a gateway between the two.

Once it was clear that the trench was part of the fort design and likely the east wall of the triangle, four spaced trenches were dug at intervals along the projected line. These trenches all uncovered more of the east line, defining it for one hundred feet. No upright timber post molds were found, though. While the 45- to 46-degree angle between the east and south wall trenches would fit a triangle of Strachey's overall dimensions, this lack of evidence that timbers stood in the trench would make it hard to prove that this line was part of the fort at all. At the same time, however, Virginia Indian artifacts, found in testing the trench, along with the absence of any European artifacts, once again suggested that this indeed was an original and early part of the fortification.

Trenches near the church determined that, unlike all of the other areas excavated in the James Fort vicinity, this area had never been plowed. Certainly, plowing near the church tower, the only remnant of Jamestown still above ground, or in the adjacent graveyard would have been considered off-limits. While plowed soil can indeed have its advantages archaeologically, the discovery of uncultivated ground was promising in its own way. Unplowed land preserves soil layers in their original context from the time of their deposition up to the present. In theory, then, the entire depth of the original palisade trench might have been left undisturbed along some of the east line, offering the possibility of viewing a complete palisade cross-section.

The excavation process to that point had approached the palisade lines literally from top to bottom. On the south, that method was logical, allowing each stain left by the timbers to be removed individually. On the east line, however, no post molds were visible at the surface to dig out. So an attempt was made to examine the east line by digging, not from top to bottom, but from the side of the trench, which had a good chance of revealing any deeper evidence of posts. This process proved only partially successful. Primarily, the side view revealed backfilled gouges, which turned out to be signs of holes dug to remove the posts. The removal of the posts accounted for their invisibility at the top of the trench. In other words, most of the original upright timbers did not rot in place but were dug out and removed, leaving no rotted timber molds. One mold *was* found, however, at the end of the section that had been dug out and removed, proving that there actually were posts in the line at one time.

The question then became, What time? The fill was devoid of any artifacts capable of establishing the date of the palisade construction or removal. All that was found were some fragments of animal bone, shell, and stone worked by natives years or even centuries before the construction of the fort. This slight evidence could argue for a palisade built and then removed in or soon after 1607, when no historical artifacts would be lying around to become mixed in the wall destruction holes. It was tempting to suggest that the wall came down soon after some of the palisades burned in January 1608.[17] That explanation had several problems, however. There was no obvious sign of fire in the palisade fill, nor was there evidence that the wall was rebuilt before Strachey would have written about it in 1610. A test trench on the side of the Confederate earthwork along the projected line of the east palisade suggested the same palisade-removal scenario. Nothing more than a ditch filled with mixed soil, in alignment with the other sections of the east line, was found—still no post stains. Nonetheless, except where a large shallow 1680s-era pit (dated by wine-bottle fragments found there) and nineteenth-century road grading wiped it out, the line could now be clearly identified for at least 240 feet from the riverside bulwark to the Civil War earthwork. It was also clear from the nature of the soil layers above the backfilled palisade trench that the Civil War earthwork was constructed from dirt redeposited as soldiers or slaves dug through the 1607 fort soil to create a moat next to it. Excavations beyond the earthwork to the north, along the projected line and distance suggested by Strachey, found that the east line disappeared somewhere in between. Although the east line might have been discovered, there was no sign of a north bulwark.

North Bulwark

Until the summer of 2003, our excavations to the north, based on our model and Strachey's measurements that produced a 1.75-acre fort, were leading nowhere. So far, digging precisely in the places suggested by those dimensions had uncovered only a single but straight palisade trench. But this trench made no sense as part of the missing bulwark: it ran straight north for at least 130 feet, then entered a surviving branch of a swamp known as the "pitch and tar" swamp. A bulwark wall would not take that course:

by definition it had to form a securely closed-in space with a wide range for cannons. Once again, however, the Zúñiga map offered a possible explanation. One curious aspect of the map was a rectangular shape connected to one of the bulwarks of the triangular fort by a short line—a shape that looked like a flag set on a flagpole. Could what had been taken for a flagpole actually be a wall connecting the circular fort bulwark to a flag-shaped enclosure, possibly an enclosed garden? In that case, the straight palisade trench running to the north might be that wall (see illustration on p. 47). As for the north bulwark itself, that corner of the triangle seemed lost.

But there was another possibility: finding an end to the east palisade should reveal the starting point of the adjoining bulwark. That end of the line had to lie in the last place left to look, under the corner of the Civil War fort. Why? Simply a process of elimination. Previous skipping ahead beyond the earthwork corner, digging directly along the projected line, had come up empty, and trenches on the other side of the earthwork corner along the line exposed a continuing wall line. Perhaps the elusive end of the line was in between, under the earthwork corner. So it was—and more. The "end" actually joined two other palisade trenches, one a section of the curved bulwark wall and the other an additional line, in all likelihood part of an eastern expansion of the palisaded area. At long last the triangle was two-dimensional.

A measurement of the full length of the east wall, from the riverward to the landward end, produced the true curtain-wall dimension, 266 feet. This figure did not jibe with the one-hundred-yard curtain reported by Strachey. Had he miscalculated? At that point a miscalculation by Strachey seemed to be the most plausible explanation of the discrepancy.

At least we now knew that our fort model, based on a curtain of one hundred yards, was clearly too big. On and off for years, that model had led the search for the north bulwark astray, literally on the wrong side of the road. And while finding the junction of the three palisades—east wall, bulwark, and later extension—had revealed more of the fort plan, the road grading and the earth scouring conducted during construction of the Civil War earthwork left the size of the actual bulwark for conjecture. The few feet of the bulwark palisade that survived this destruction appeared to curve enough for us to project a regular wall with a sixty-foot diameter. Such a wall would be slightly larger than the projected circular form to the south. This shape certainly tended to corroborate the Zúñiga map, which shows a

Excavation below the Jamestown Civil War earthen fortification (*background*) revealed the junction of the James Fort east palisade wall trench with the north bulwark and another slightly later palisade protecting the "town" to the east.

larger bulwark to the north, a smaller one to the south and west. The map also shows that the north bulwark was more oval than the other two. In addition, the map's flagpole image—what we had tentatively identified with the single north-running palisade—connects directly to the bulwark wall at about 45 degrees west of a center line through the triangle. Allowing for the sketchy nature of the Zúñiga map, however, both the compass direction of the map and the reality of the palisade on the ground extending west of center suffice to justify the conclusion that the "flagpole" was a palisade— and that the Zúñiga map reliably depicted the design of James Fort.

What does not appear on the map but did materialize on the ground was a third palisade found attached to both the dug-out east wall and the north bulwark trenches. That extra palisade trench was deeper than the other two and had visible post molds. This palisade was clearly a later addition to the fort triangle, serving to expand the area enclosed by the fort. As a later construction, it would logically not have appeared on the 1608 map. An expansion of the fort area could also explain removal of the east wall. If the expanded area to the east was completely enclosed by additional palisades, then the east wall would have become obsolete, an unnecessary barrier inside the fortified area. Discovery of yet another related palisade trench going east and a closer look at seventeenth-century eyewitness descriptions of the town's defenses together proved that James Fort changed its shape through the years, and that these additions would continue to complicate our search for the original triangle. Nevertheless, the search for that original third side—the west wall—continued.

West Wall

Although the length of the east wall had begun to cast some doubt on the dimensions of Strachey's fort model, it still seemed a good plan to excavate inside the Civil War earthwork, where our model indicated the missing west wall line should be. A digging season there proved discouraging. There was no topsoil, plowzone, or palisade line. It seemed that all evidence of the wall, if it had ever been there, had been destroyed in the construction of the 1861 fort. By early 2003, not finding traces of the elusive west wall began to cast some doubt on the relationship of the palisade trenches and apparent bulwarks on the south and east. A fort at least had to be a triangle.

However, the digging in the Civil War fort was far from wasted. The scouring in 1861 could not destroy ground features that were deep enough—a well, for example, which would be far deeper than a palisade trench. Sure enough, a few feet outside of the missing hypothetical west wall, a well datable to the fort period appeared inches below the surface. This discovery proved to be a time capsule full of James Fort artifacts. *Where* the well turned up was puzzling, however. It did not seem to make sense that a water source for the fort would lie beyond the safety of its palisade; a fort under siege with no water could not hold out for long. Could this fort-period well have once actually stood inside the fort, perhaps conveniently near its center, and not outside? Could the palisade wall we sought be missing not because it had been graded away but because we were looking for it in the wrong place? If the fort was much larger than we had projected it, the palisade might actually be far to the west of the well. In other words, the model that had guided the digging might be too small. If the well indeed marked the middle of the fort, then the fort would have been at least twice as large as predicted.

Had Strachey miscalculated more seriously than we had suspected when the one-hundred-yard curtain wall he specified seemed to be only 266 feet long as found? That was a possibility. Perhaps, instead, Strachey's dimensions were accurate after all, and this well was only one of many later water sources. In that case, at least one of those wells remained to be found within the border of the fort's palisades. The west wall, too, remained unfound.

Knowing just how deep the Civil War scouring had gone in 1861 might show whether or not it could have wiped away the palisade. The key to determining this depth would be establishing the pre-1861 grade close enough to the well to gauge accurately how much dirt was missing. If the pre-1861 soil level was more than two feet higher than the present surface inside the earthwork, then any evidence there of the west wall would certainly be gone. The only place to find this all-telling soil would be under the Civil War earthwork itself. We had always considered disturbing the Civil War landscape to be a last resort. That landscape was itself a visible piece of Jamestown Island history. The ques-

A brick-lined well in the original parade ground, Smithfield, known to be just west of James Fort (*left*), beside a brick-lined Civil War powder magazine (*right*).

tion of the relative significance of these two historical records had been put to Civil War preservationists at the beginning of the Jamestown Rediscovery project. They concluded that this earthwork, because it had never seen battle, could be sacrificed to some degree for the James Fort search, providing that the excavation only disturb as much as necessary and record the earthwork in sufficient detail to make possible an accurate reconstruction. Fair enough. However, the thought of having to dig through four to twelve feet of soil deposited from 1861 to the present was daunting. A search trench designed to prove why the hypothetical wall was missing to the west did exactly that, and in a surprising way. The wall was not found near the well, because it had never been there in the first place. The true wall location—the last, vital side of the triangle—turned up, quite by chance, in the search trench instead. The fateful test trench, about forty feet west of the well, exposed a five-foot-long dark palisade stain right at the base of Civil War fill. Post molds survived, and the profile fit the regular palisade form. James Fort was found!

From that point, multiple excavation trenches were dug along the extended line, tracing it to the bank of the river, where the seawall construction had ended the shoreline erosion in 1901. At that place, the eroded Civil War earthwork on top of the early seventeenth-century fort left a cliff of sorts. The palisade trench appeared in the face of the cliff in a natural cross-section next to an associated pit or ditch filled in with an artifact-rich dark loam. Digging continued intermittently away from the river on each side of a Civil War mound, exposing sections of the palisade trench for a total of two hundred feet. Once this last essential piece of the three-sided fort revealed its alignment on the ground, the entire triangle came into clear focus. Projection of each line came to an intersection with each of the two others, revealing at long last the true dimensions of the fort: 304± feet on each land side (100 yards) and 425± feet (140 yards) along the river, forming a 1.1-acre enclosure. The continued presence of James Fort on Jamestown Island was a fact.

Strachey had told us that his measurements of 100 yards, 100 yards, and 140 yards were of the curtain walls. Again, in standard military terms, a fort curtain is the length of the wall between bulwarks. Our model, with its hypothetical circular bulwarks, had been based on the belief that Strachey meant a traditional curtain. What we found on the ground yielded the Strachey measurements—but only if the measurements were made from points where the walls intersected. These intersections actually occurred inside the bulwarks that we had found archaeologically. Strachey had given accurate measurements, but from different reference points: he was technically not measuring a curtain wall. Rather, he had described the distance between the points where the lines of the walls intersected. Few if any reading his account had ever understood it that way, despite the qualification offered in his next sentence, locating the bulwarks and a watchtower "where the lines meet." This episode is a rare instance of signs in the earth enabling us to verify and even correct a written account. The power of this physical evidence to help us decipher a firsthand account should also be a sobering reminder of how easily seemingly straightforward eyewitness accounts can be misunderstood. Strachey's measurements of James Fort were accurate—he just had his own definition of "curtain."

View of west palisade wall trench and apparent west bulwark trench at the point where the river erosion was cut off by a concrete wall in 1901.

In misreading Strachey, we had also developed a hypothetical model of James Fort that was more than a half acre larger than the actual fort. Does it matter that the fort was actually about a third smaller than its traditionally understood size? Undoubtedly, what counts most is what we can learn from the initial enduring English presence in America. Yet to recapture the landscape of colonization accurately is to understand colonization in context. The bigger picture depends upon that context.

So the site of James Fort, once considered completely lost on eroded land, exists almost intact on uneroded land. Shoreline erosion dissolved only the west bulwark, probably half of the south bulwark, and about three-quarters of the south wall, leaving about 90 percent of the overall fort intact on land. This discovery was a real gift for Jamestown as it approached its 400th anniversary. But there were to be other birthday presents. Our excavations also revealed the expansion of the original fort design and began to define the evolving plan of the early town.

FIVE-SQUARE FORM

James Fort became known as Jamestown rather quickly in eyewitness accounts. This change in terms suggested that the form and substance of the settlement was evolving from strictly a fortification to a town-like setting. Documentary accounts have given us some idea of the changing town design and the types of houses and public buildings within and about the fort. Archaeological remains bring the design and structures of Jamestown into clearer focus.

Signs of the developing Jamestown had appeared early on in the excavations. Removal of plowed soil beyond the south bulwark uncovered an add-on palisade trench. This trench forged a right angle with the east wall line but left a gate-width gap between them. The palisade had run for sixty feet until it ended next to what soil stains hinted were the remains of a backfilled cellar under a post-supported building. Excavation a few inches below the plowzone along the length of the palisade revealed the clearest stains of decayed upright timbers yet found. While the extended plan was clear, the chronology—when this line became an addition to the triangle— could not be precisely established. Once again, only prehistoric Indian artifacts appeared in the fill.

But the writings of Smith, Strachey, and Ralph Hamor seem to leave little doubt that the triangular James Fort did not encompass all of Jamestown

Skillful removal of clay originally tamped around the town palisade posts to hold them upright leaves a perfect soil cast of each wall timber along the extended fort wall line.

for long.[18] Their descriptions, read in light of the extended palisade, may also explain both the removal of the east wall of the original triangular fort and the eventual location of the Jamestown church where its tower and reconstruction stand today, directly on and outside the east wall. After Smith was appointed president (September 10, 1608), he wrote that "James towne being burnt, we rebuilt it [the overall plan] reduced to the form of this ( ) [figure omitted but later called "five-square"]." The word "reduced" is the key to understanding what Smith describes. To repeat, today the word clearly means "made smaller," but in seventeenth-century usage the word might have meant "changed," "restored back," or maybe even "made larger." To Smith, "reduced" could well have meant "changed" and "enlarged," because he reports that by the summer of 1608, Jamestown consisted of forty or fifty houses. If this is no exaggeration, there were far too many structures here to fit into the now established and relatively small 1.1-acre triangle.[19] Another palisaded enclosure, probably rectangular in shape, might well have been attached to the original triangle, resulting perhaps in Smith's pentagon. The curious third palisade discovered at the north bulwark might have extended out to a connecting wall to form this "five-square" as well. The dimensions of this presumed eastern enclosure would add only about one-half acre to the triangle, still probably too small for all these new houses. Perhaps the palisade at right angles to the east wall, possibly more substantial than the earlier palisades, was one of the walls Strachey described as either added or reconstructed/repaired by Sir Thomas Gates and his men after Lord De La Warre arrived in 1610.[20]

These extra palisades would have secured the land east of the original triangle, the Smith five-sided housing development, and possibly even the 1611 town of Hamor's description, "reduced into a handsome forme [with] two faire rowes of houses . . . newly, and strongly impaled."[21] These archaeological signs of a changing palisade configuration may at least suggest why the east wall of the triangular fort was eventually dismantled: the wall wound up inside the expanded palisaded area and therefore no longer served as a barrier to attacks from outside the compound. It too had become obsolete. Again, the dates of these events remain uncertain: we know only that the triangular configuration must have existed until July 1610, when Strachey so accurately measured it. The additions and renewals so far discussed must have occurred, then, after that date—possibly soon after, as part of De La Warre's renovations.

The enlargement of the fortified town also explains why the church tower would have come to straddle the site of the fort's original east wall. The discovery of the outlines of James Fort had revealed to us that Jamestown's church must have been moved after all, despite the aforementioned rarity of such a move and the absence of records attesting to the relocation. As time passed and James Fort grew, the church must have needed to be recentered as the hub of the larger community. According to Strachey in 1610, the original church of 1608, central within the triangular fort, was in shambles. Strachey also wrote, however, that De La Warre ordered it repaired, meaning that it was upgraded in place. So the resiting of the church, from the center of the triangular fort/town to the center of the expanded town, apparently occurred in 1617, when Samuel Argall ordered construction of a new and smaller church, 50' × 20' compared to the 1608 size of 60' × 24'. During the Galt-Tyler church excavations of 1901, a cobble foundation of the dimensions of Argall's church was found on a site that would lie beyond what we now know to have been James Fort's original east wall.[22] This location suggests that the construction of the church under Argall in 1617 was indeed an occasion for the church's recentering. The new town walls must have gone up before that, but exactly when is in some doubt. There were no artifacts in the various expansion palisades to date construction. Still, it stands to reason that by De La Warre's time the new five-square fortified area beyond the triangle continued to grow. So it makes sense to date the dismantling of the east wall and the redesign and expansion of the fort to sometime between late 1610, after Strachey saw the complete triangle, and 1617, when Argall built his church. If that church provides evidence for identifying the new center of town, we can perhaps make a good estimate of the town's size in 1617. Supposing the expansion to be rectangular, the new town would have been three times the size of the original triangle, a total of three to four acres. Archaeological remains of what could be the new east wall—a relatively vague palisade trench aligned with the post building and traceable, except where later graves cut through it, for more than one hundred feet north—suggest that this estimate of acreage might be generous. In order to delimit a significantly larger fort, capable of enclosing more houses, the line found would have to make a turn to the east, then continue to encompass more space in that direction. A trench of this sort remains undiscovered.

JAMES FORT'S BUILDINGS

The size of the area required to contain the buildings of John Smith's or Ralph Hamor's descriptions depends upon just what actually did constitute James Fort houses: Holes in the ground? Castles in the air? Cabins? Two-story timber buildings? A study of the buildings of James Fort can address not only these questions but others as well: How were English ideas of building adapted to the Virginia environment? What evidence can be found for a town plan? What can we know about the use of individual buildings? And what can the buildings tell us of the historic events we know to have transpired in Jamestown?

At least two of these questions are related: if what people lived in at James Fort were whimsical "air castles" or nothing more than flimsy tents, then the archaeological search for a town plan could have been doomed. Such structures probably left few archaeological signs in the earth. (It is possible, however, that four pits found paralleling the west wall of the fort, all dating to the first three years of settlement, are signs of crude quarters supported by lean-to roofs attached directly to the palisade.) Most other types of more permanent construction, however, could leave solid archaeological traces, such as cellars, postholes, and masonry foundations. Fortunately, all these building signs were present. Excavations by 2005 located

Crude pit-like cellars and small, almost random postholes found at Jamestown along the west palisade wall trench suggest that lean-to structures, like those shown here on the set of the Jamestown movie *The New World,* once stood along the west and likely the east James Fort palisade walls. (*The New World,* © MMVI, New Line Productions, Inc. All rights reserved. Photo courtesy of New Line Productions, Inc.)

clear evidence of five James Fort–period buildings: four inside the fort (hereafter, for reference purposes only, called the barracks, the quarter, and the rowhouses or rows) and a fifth in the east extension (the factory, a building outside the fort for storage and trade with the Virginia Indians). The barracks, quarter, and rows each aligned with the three walls of the triangle, and the factory basically paralleled the east fort wall in the fort extension. This arrangement certainly suggests the plan described by Strachey: rows of settled houses along each palisade wall. Three structures—barracks,

This silver English halfpenny bearing the Tudor rose and thistle of James I, king of England and Scotland, and minted from 1606 to 1608, was found in one of the pit cellars, indicating a likely 1607–8 date for these makeshift quarters.

quarter, and factory—are of strikingly similar design, while the rows are something quite different (as will be discussed below). The almost identical archaeological remnants of the first three are a cellar and a number of slightly irregularly aligned postholes. It is possible that each of the buildings began as a cellar hole with a crude roof covering it. Over time the larger post-supported buildings were added, incorporating the original cellar. (The four possible lean-to cellar buildings along the west wall, on the other hand, never evolved to the post-building stage.) The spacing of the postholes, in which vertical support timbers would once have been seated, reveals rectangular floor plans. All three similar buildings are one room wide and multiple rooms in length, and all retained their cellars at one end.

What people in these buildings lost or threw away is as important to the Jamestown story as the remains of the buildings themselves. Such objects become accidental and impartial records of life that went on in each structure. Recovery and interpretation of what seems to be lowly trash gives unusually clear insight into the past. The cellars of the barracks, quarter, and factory generally contained the same sequence of artifact-rich fill layers. An initial accumulation of tracked-in or washed-in fill built up on each of the dirt cellar floors, containing objects that were left there while the cellar was in use. Above these time-capsule-like occupation zones, a distinctly similar deposit of dark humus mixed with lumps of clay subsoil and nails appeared. This rather strange mixed-soil layer filled all the cellars to a depth that would have rendered them unusable. Thus it became reasonable to conclude that the fill was a result of the collapse of the building above—the falling of earthen walls. Above these layers were garbage and trash-laden deposits, filling the cellar holes up to what later became a plow-zone. All this material can now reveal what went on (and when) inside and outside of the cellars; it can provide insight as well into the superstructure and purpose of each building; and it can tell us something, too, of the life span, destruction, and afterlife of the buildings and their sites.

The Barracks

Archaeological remains of the barracks floor plan consisted of twenty-six imprecisely aligned, irregularly spaced postholes of random depth, forming a 55′ × 18′ rectangle divided into at least two rooms with a cellar and a fireplace. Relatively small post molds survived in most of the postholes, indicating a light timber framing. The rather random and insubstantial nature of these remains, especially in light of the fallen earth-wall layer in the cellar, provides clues to how it was built.

Buildings with cellars like this found beneath the factory all contained (*from bottom to top*) occupation zone, collapsed mud walls, and garbage and trash deposits.

The small circular posts, one as under-sized as three inches in diameter, and the varying depth of their seating postholes suggest that the building frame was supported by what John Smith called "cratchets," basically nothing more than forked sticks. Smith wrote that the 1608 church was "a homely thing like a barn, set upon cratchets covered with rafts, sedge, and earth; so also was the walls." He added that "the best of our houses [are] of the like curiosity but the most part much worse workmanship."[23] Cratchets work almost like crutches: the wall plate timber rests in the V-shaped fork exactly as an arm rests on top of a crutch. No intricate carpentry is needed to hold the plate timber in place. Such a structure also would not require holes dug to any uniform depth; the depths might vary according to the random natural length of the cratchets themselves. The misalignment of the cratchet poles from side to side means the building probably had no crossing ceiling beams, with the exception of the west-end room, where the posts do line up crosswise. Without ceiling beams to tie them together, the walls of such a house would seem hardly capable of supporting a roof.

Pattern of support postholes (*right*) and the cellar and pit complex remains of the barracks.

However, if the walls were made of thick earth, as Smith's reference to hard mixed clay and the presence of a mixed loam and clay deposit in the building cellars suggest, the wall would indeed be strong enough to support the roof even without ceiling cross ties.

These building details of the Jamestown barracks point to a particular English building tradition known as "mud and stud," a style common in the postmedieval East Midlands region of England—especially the eastern half of the county of Lincolnshire, where more than three hundred buildings in this style still stand today. Construction of such buildings begins with a framework of slight timbers either seated in the ground or based on stone pads. Between the uprights, crosspieces are added to the upright frames, and vertical slats or studs are nailed to the crosspieces. The resulting interior skeleton-like frame gives support to the wet mud walls until they can dry enough to stand on their own. Some walls are as thick as a foot or more. On the outside of the mud wall, fabric presents a smooth, uninterrupted clay surface that requires frequent recoating, often with a thin covering of lime plaster. Roofs of these buildings are traditionally of a light framework, with natural pole rafters lashed together to form a hip or half-hipped roof. Lincolnshire mud-and-stud wall lines tend to zigzag to conform to the natural curves of pole roof framing.[24] Should one of these Lincolnshire buildings with an earthfast frame collapse and become an archaeological site, the remains in many respects would match the James Fort barracks. The major difference, of course, would be that the uprights in Lincolnshire are heavier and therefore, unlike cratchets, need to be held together by joinery.

Not surprisingly, the chief designers/builders of the early houses at Jamestown were most likely from Lincolnshire. Captain John Smith of Alford, Lincolnshire, reported that he directed the building of houses. William Laxton, a Lincolnshire carpenter who was among the original settlers, must have been familiar with the mud-and-stud tradition.[25] In light of the abundant wooded land of Jamestown Island and the perfectly adhesive nature of the underlying clay, this building style, so familiar to Smith and Laxton, should have instantly dictated the housing process. Strachey attests to a rebuilding after the 1608 fire, although his was not an eyewitness account as

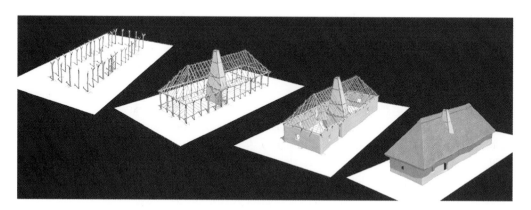

Stages in the construction of the mud-and-stud barracks, based on the pattern of its support postholes, the fill in the cellar, and what is known of the English architectural tradition. (Architect, Earl Mark; Virginia Polytechnic Institute and State University)

he did not arrive in the colony until 1610. His description of the Jamestown of 1610, however, is consistent with the alignment between the fort walls and the buildings we had found: "To every side [of the fort,] a proportioned distance from the palisade, is a settled street of houses that runs along, so as each line of the angle hath his street."[26] Only the lean-to cellar buildings along the west fort wall are too near the palisade for a "street" of any kind to have existed there. So the lean-tos must have been abandoned and filled in to create the street "to every side" of the triangle by the time Strachey penned his description.

Whitt Cottage, Thimbleby, Lincolnshire, England, a classic example of a surviving postmedieval mud-and-stud building, which exhibits a traditional building technique likely transported to early Jamestown.

The cellar/pit in the end of the barracks included an original clearly cut cellar hole that experienced a number of earth-removing and filling episodes. Any pit or irregular hole in the ground presents interpretation problems for the archaeologist. Why did people dig these holes in the ground near their houses? To get dirt to fill something else in? To quarry clay for other uses, such as brickmaking or preparing daub? To create the hole itself—perhaps to serve as a mix basin for brick or daub clay, or perhaps to serve no higher calling than becoming a lowly trash dump? The purposes of the barracks cellar/pit seem to be almost all of the above. While the purpose of the cellar/pit was unclear, it did help us to date the barracks itself. It was eventually filled with refuse, but on the floor someone left an artifact that establishes an early seventeenth-century date for the building's use. A single tiny clay tobacco pipe bowl with a teardrop-shaped heel design lay on the earthen floor surface. Fortunately, the sizes and shapes of colonial-period pipe bowls can indicate when the pipe was made and when it was in general use. The earliest pipe bowls had a very small capacity, probably owing to the scarcity and price of tobacco when Europeans began using it. We know this from viewing datable seventeenth-century Dutch paintings depicting pipe smokers and from the shapes of pipes found on other dated archaeological sites. Bowls began small, growing in size and evolving in shape as time passed. The pipe bowl in the pit appears to match the bowls shown in the earliest such paintings, suggesting

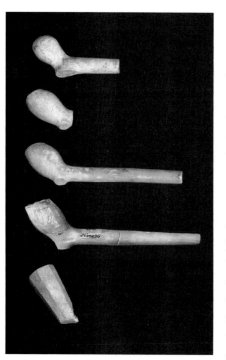

The shapes and sizes of tobacco pipe bowls from early Jamestown have proven to be consistent evidence in determining the date ranges of a number of key components of the Jamestown archaeological record. *From the top:* 1580–1610 (from the barracks cellar/pit); 1610–30 (a rowhouse builder's trench); 1610–30 (a Statehouse burial); 1630–40 (Berkeley Row); and a faceted stone pipe bowl of ca. 1620 (from the Smithfield well).

a manufacture/use date of 1580–1610. This same pipe bowl shape appears at Jamestown with regularity in other deposits where late sixteenth- to early seventeenth-century coins and other precisely datable objects have been found. Pipes from other New World sites set the date of their use more precisely. Bowls with the same shape and teardrop heel have been discovered at the site of Fort Saint George in Maine, which only existed for one year in 1607–8, and at the wreck site of the *Sea Venture,* the Jamestown supply ship that sank in 1609.[27] In the barracks, a sizable section of a broken Virginia Indian–made earthen bowl decorated with impression marks of wrapped cord—a type known to be in use when the colonists first arrived—rested in the cellar fill with the circa–1607–10 pipe bowl. This suggests a very early seventeenth-century date for use of the cellar, and probably for the construction and occupation of the barracks itself. It also reflects English reliance on Indian corn, perhaps delivered in these earthen bowls, further evidence, like the shift away from clay to bark as a building material, of the impact of Indian neighbors upon the colonists.

The consistently early dates and the military nature of the vast quantity of the more than 44,000 artifacts found within the remaining series of related pits reveal that the barracks was indeed part of the James Fort enterprise. Precisely datable artifacts included three coins ranging in date from 1590 to 1602, casting counters or jettons (small copper coin-like discs used in mathematical calculations) dating as early as 1580, Elizabethan lead tokens from the 1570s, and a lead cloth seal that dates no later than 1603.[28] Thousands of European pottery fragments were also found—English,

Dutch, French, German, and even Spanish types—all of manufacturing dates within the period. Triangular stone-hard vessels known as crucibles were among the ceramics from the barracks cellar/pit as well. One fragment from the pit proved to fit onto the broken, glass-coated pair of crucibles from the aforementioned 1930s utility trench. The crucibles, along with thousands of fragments of broken English window glass (cullet) found in the pit trash layers and similar debris related to glass-melting from nearby deposits, suggest the fallout from glassmaking, undoubtedly debris from the "trials of glass" to which Smith referred in 1608. Military arms and armor of the late sixteenth to early seventeenth century also found their way into the pits, including an intact cabasset-type helmet, sections of body armor, gorgets (neck guards), a couter (elbow protector), and tassetts (leg armor). The armor, firing mechanisms from muskets (matchlocks), and lead shot are un-

A German stoneware bottle known as a Bartmann (bearded man) with decorative coat of arms (Italian), made ca. 1610, from the barracks cellar/pit.

deniable evidence of a military post. All this support for a date of 1607–10 tells us that the barracks is the remains of one of the earliest Anglo-American buildings yet found in North America.

A vast quantity of discarded food remains and animal bones was found in the cellar/pit as well, giving vivid testimony to the struggle for survival at Jamestown during those first precarious years, 1607–circa 1610.[29] This approximate date for the bones is suggested by the objects found with them, but an even more precise date is established by interpreting the bones in the context of the documentary record. According to Strachey's report, when he and the shipwrecked Bermuda contingent of Governor Gates's original flotilla arrived at Jamestown in May 1610, they brought with them some food gathered during their nine-month shipbuilding stay in Bermuda. Among the easiest to gather was the cahow, a Bermudan bird that failed to understand the importance of flying away from hunters. The shipwrecked colonists quickly recognized this free lunch and almost certainly kept the cahow in some preserved state as naval provisions. Among the bones found in

Late sixteenth- to seventeenth-century iron helmet (cabasset) found in the barracks cellar/pit and the conserved breastplate from the bulwark ditch.

the barracks cellar/pit were those of the cahow. The cellar also held Bermudan conch shells, a number of tropical fish common only to Bermuda, and some pieces of Bermudan limestone. There is no record of supplies coming from Bermuda to early Jamestown at any time other than May 1610. These uniquely Bermudan foods and other supplies must have been brought to Jamestown by the ex–*Sea Venture* passengers, eventually to be cooked and eaten by them and the surviving settlers of the "starving time" at Jamestown. The bones wound up in the barracks cellar/pit sometime afterward.

These relics of transported Bermuda supplies tell us something more. The number of these bones and shells is small in comparison to the remnants of what must have been the colonists' provisions from the Virginia woods and rivers. To understand the full meaning of the meager Bermudan supply, it is necessary to revisit estimates of Jamestown's population after the "starving time."

Smith's publication, *The Generall Historie*, reports that only 60 of the 500 people at Jamestown survived the "starving time."[30] A combination of numbers from several eyewitness accounts, however, suggests that while the death rate at Jamestown was appalling, it has been exaggerated. By adding and subtracting population estimates, using accounts of individual and group deaths and reports of numbers arriving on various ships, one can estimate that by the fall of 1609—the beginning of the "starving time"—215 people were living at Jamestown and 30 more in its environs.[31] At the time the group arrived from Bermuda, according to Strachey's figures, 90 were left alive in the colony, with 60 of these living in the town. So the number of deaths during that time was less than half the total reported by Strachey (155 compared to 440). However, with the influx of the estimated 135 *Sea Venture* survivors, the total population at Jamestown would have jumped to 195.

In this context, the few remains of Bermudan foods fill out the harrowing story told in documents. The Bermudan contingent would not have carried many extra supplies on their trip to Jamestown, as they had no way of knowing that they would find a starving colony; nor would they know that their own arrival would amount to a dangerous explosion in Jamestown's already stressed population. The ensuing events, however, showed that the Bermuda contingent, instead of saving the colony, imposed a new burden on Jamestown.

Taking over leadership of the colony from George Percy, Sir Thomas Gates immediately saw the need to assess the ratio of population to provisions. Gates at first concluded that the Bermudan food supplies should be kept in reserve for a possible retreat voyage back to England. In the meantime, he would send parties out to forage among the Powhatan, hoping to gather enough food to get the colony back on its feet. Having no luck with that plan, Gates figured that enough food was left to supply the colonists at Jamestown for sixteen days if he rationed two cakes (possibly a type of dried fish cake) per person per day.[32] If no supplies could be found during that period, the colony would be abandoned.

We have already heard the rest of this story: after sixteen days, no food materialized. The colonists would have to leave. They buried the ordnance and whatever else might be reclaimable if they ever came back, gathered up everything else of saleable value, then headed downriver toward the open ocean. Their interim destination was the Grand Fishing Banks off Newfoundland. It should be stressed again that Gates and the retreating

Collection of discarded food bones and shells from the barracks cellar/pit. Some, like the butchered bones of horses, rats, and poisonous snakes, are grim reminders of "starving time" diets, 1609–10.

Jamestown settlers could have planned to stop at the Charles and Algernon fort area and wait at least ten days for possible English supplies to arrive.[33] There, the settlers knew, they could live off shellfish for the short term, as Percy's party had done while awaiting Gates's arrival from Bermuda two months earlier. Just over a day after the settlers had left Jamestown under Gates's direction, an advance boat arrived from Lord De La Warre's ship, announcing the imminent arrival of the latest new governor. Luckily, De La Warre brought with him enough supplies to save the colony. With the addition of the De La Warre entourage, the Jamestown population could well have been 345. If De La Warre actually brought provisions to support the total population for a year, as reported, his ships must have been heavily laden indeed.

While the bones from Bermuda in the barracks cellar/pit reveal the pressure put upon the weakened colony by the arrival of Gates's contingent, the other discarded food remains found there graphically depict the sufferings of those who had tried to hold the fort during the "starving time," the winter and spring of 1609–10. The presence in the pit of poisonous snake vertebrae and musk turtle gives some indication that life at Jamestown had reached crisis proportions. Butchered horse bones and the bones of black rats, dogs, and cats also powerfully demonstrate how desperate conditions must have become. Fifteen bones or bone fragments of a large dog or dogs were recovered from the fill in the nearby dry moat. These did not show signs of butchering, but their proximity to other bones that did may indicate that, while these animals were brought to Virginia as hunters or weapons of war, they might eventually have become a food source.

X-rays of skull fragments show that dogs at Jamestown lived hard lives even before they may have ended up on the dinner table. One radiograph shows a small piece of lead shot embedded in a dog's skull. This injury was not the cause of death: the X-ray also shows that the bone had healed around the shot. The injury may have resulted from combat after the Indians acquired muskets (as early as 1608, according to John Smith).[34] Documentary sources indicate that the Indians realized the strategic importance of the colonists' dogs. Gabriel Archer reports that a Virginia Indian attack on the Jamestown settlers in May 1607 resulted in the killing of "our dogs." Of course, the Indians may have had nothing to do with the wounding of the dog, which could also have resulted from a stray hunting shot. There is some evidence that the injured dog did belong to the colonists rather than the Indians: a rendering of one local Indian dog suggests that such dogs were relatively small with very distinctive skull shapes. (Some believe that relatives of these Indian dogs, the American dingo, still roam free in the backwoods of coastal North Carolina.)[35] While the exact breed of the dog with the head wound is not known, it has characteristics of a mastiff.[36] There is no question that this dog was relatively large, perhaps in the forty-five- to fifty-five-pound range. According to records, greyhounds and mastiffs were at Jamestown.

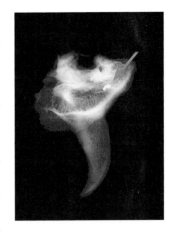

X-ray of dog (possibly a mastiff) jawbone showing lead shot in a healed wound.

Resorting to killing and eating one of their key means to hunt and so to live off the wild surely demonstrates the extremity of the hunger of the Jamestown colonists in the "starving time." But once the settlers were confined to their "blockhouse," as Strachey reports, domesticated animals, such as dogs and cats, and even indoor animals like rats would have become the only source of food for the besieged colonists. Percy apparently was not exaggerating when he wrote, during the "starving time," "Then having fed upon horses and other beasts as long as they lasted, we were glad to make shift with vermin, as dogs, cats, rats and mice."[37] As we will see, later excavations revealed that a few of the colonists even resorted to survival cannibalism.

The Quarter

Building remains of the quarter closely resemble those of the barracks: the cellars of the two buildings were similar in size and in location (at one end of the building), and they contained similar fill. The width of each building was seventeen feet, and the framing holes were spaced with similar randomness. It can be concluded that the quarter had been another mud-and-stud building. In the period postdating the fort, however, the quarter site had suffered considerable damage, probably starting with the growth of a nearby oak tree. Grading during the creation of the adjacent Civil War earthwork in 1861 took a sizable bite out of the site. Finally, the building remains were unmercifully shaved and punctured by the grading of a road in the late nineteenth century and the installation of a commemorative fence around the church, which was reconstructed in 1907. It is amazing

Excavated site of the quarter building showing wall posts and cellar of another example of likely mud-and-stud construction.

that any trace of the quarter survived all these earth-shattering impacts. Excavation of what trace remained was limited by the church tower, which had been constructed on the quarter's southern end, preventing a determination of the building's length.

Even the deepest disturbance, however—the nineteenth-century road—left a few inches of the northwest corner posthole intact. The rest of the building footprint fared still better. Building remains nearer the seventeenth-century church tower were within the aforementioned no-plowzone, where soil was left untilled, presumably out of respect for the church graveyard. The unplowed building surface stood four feet above the cellar floor. This establishes its undisturbed original depth. As much as two feet of the original seventeenth-century surface in and around the west side of the barracks were missing. But by the same token, at least that much earth is probably missing all across the fort site except in the immediate vicinity of the church tower.

The cellar's occupation zone—a six-inch-deep deposit accumulated during the time the cellar was in use, now covered by the fallen mud-wall level—lay on top of a group of artifacts whose position suggested that they had all been abandoned there at the same moment, creating an accidental time capsule. In one corner, charred wood and clay marked where a cooking fire once burned, and beside it, a Virginia Indian pot was found, still containing traces of turtle bone. A butchered hip-bone of a pig and a butchered turtle shell lay nearby, suggesting that pork, or a combination of pork and turtle, comprised the menu. Near the pot lay a large Venetian trade bead. So was the cook a Virginia Indian—perhaps a woman? Might she have been one of the forty or fifty Indian wives of English settlers, according to the Spanish claim?[38]

From foreground to background: Butchered turtle, crushed Virginia Indian pot containing remains of cooked turtle, large trade bead, butchered pig bone, sheathed dagger, and charred wood on scorched clay cellar floor—a moment in time at the quarter.

The Indian (?) cook had been surrounded by weapons. A sheathed dagger was found within arm's reach of the cooking fire, and behind it lay a musketeer's bag of gunflints, lead balls, and powder. Iron shovel blades were on the floor as well. The shovels and weapons in a cellar were no real surprise: cellars would be likely places to store such objects. The fire, however, is hard to explain. How and why would someone burn a fire on the floor of a mud-and-stud building's cellar, when the ceiling—the floor above—would presumably have been made of wood? A possible answer is offered by evidence that the cellar had originally had a lightly constructed, wooden dividing wall. This wall might speak to an earlier tent-pit structure, perhaps one of the mere hole-in-the-ground shelters settlers first lived in, according to that negative report of the "Ancient Planters" in 1623.[39] In this earlier structure, a fire might have blazed away on the pit floor without danger. The artifacts and documents together could suggest, then, that the mud-

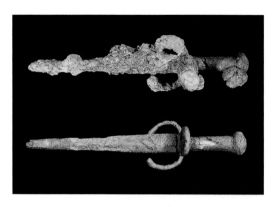

Late sixteenth-century dagger, from the quarter cellar, before and after conservation.

Musketeer's "kit" on the quarter cellar floor, includes musket balls, a gunflint, a single-charge powder bandolier, and the copper pouch base.

and-stud superstructure was an evolution from an earlier crude cellar/house. In any case, the dagger, Virginia Indian pottery, a large Venetian glass trade bead, and copper objects date the cellar to the first few years of settlement. The building's association with the east wall of the triangular James Fort, superseded by later renovations, further suggests this dating. The quarter, too, then, is an example of the very beginnings of house construction in Anglo-America.

The Factory

The most complex floor plan of the mud-and-stud buildings appeared in the factory, whose architectural details and artifacts could reveal something of its use during the first three years of the settlement, 1607–10. The factory was eventually found to be the largest of the mud buildings, seventy-two feet long, and there was clear evidence that it was divided into at least three and perhaps four rooms. The southernmost room was built over a comparatively enormous, partially wood-lined cellar, constructed in two phases under a superstructure that was supported by the now-familiar irregularly spaced upright posts. The fort's palisade wall was connected to the building at what appeared to have been its original southwest corner post. At some point the cellar was expanded into an L shape by digging beneath the building's superstructure.

A series of entrance steps descended from the west at the head of the cellar, fanning toward the south as they entered the subterranean room. Although the cellars of the barracks and the quarter had been unlined, this cellar showed clear signs of decayed timbers on the east and north walls. Cavities in these walls left molds of these timber supports. The east wall of

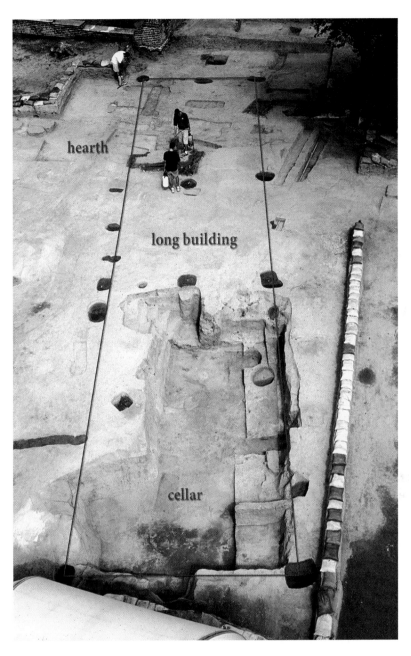

Archaeological remains of the factory attached to James Fort by palisade, showing wall postholes and three rooms: cellar with stairs and drainage barrels (*foreground*), central room, and "workshop" (*background*) with three brick hearths.

the factory held back a mixed-clay liner, presumably packed behind the timber to waterproof this wall, which was closest to the edge of the building above. The west wall did not have such a lining, presumably because it was well away from the outside wall line of the building. The original south wall would also not have required waterproofing clay, as it too was well underneath the superstructure.

Natural subsoil clay in the L addition made up the cellar floor, but a mixture of sandy clay leveled the floor in the north half of the room. In that section, the floor held two barrels buried upright, which apparently served as sumps whenever the cellar took on water. Judging from the lower few inches of washed sand on the floor and in the barrel, flooding was not uncommon. A fire had burned in this cellar along the west wall. Charcoal on the floor and clay heated enough to turn red pinpointed a fire "place." There was no evidence along the clay cellar wall above the fire area that there had ever been a flue. Here again was a puzzle: How could a fire exist in a basement below what had to be a wooden floor without setting it on fire? Had the factory, like the quarter, possibly been a pit house before it was transformed into a mud-and-stud building? Documents suggest a more intriguing explanation.

In addition to the stairs, walls, and floor, excavations uncovered a line of small postholes cutting into the subsoil below the dirt floor just south of the stairs. These holes suggested the presence of some sort of partition there before the floor level was raised. A wall in that location would not make much sense unless there was need, as in a prison, to secure the cellar space at times from access via the stairs. Perhaps both that barrier and the fire are explained by one of John Smith's tales. Smith wrote about putting one of two Powhatan brothers in a "dungeon" until the other brother returned a stolen pistol by sunup.[40] Failure to comply would result in the execution of the prisoner. That night, taking pity on his prisoner, Smith allowed him to burn a charcoal fire. The fire, apparently flueless, naturally would have produced poisonous carbon monoxide. No wonder the prisoner was unconscious by the time the brother returned the pistol. Thinking him dead, the brother loudly and justifiably cried foul, at which time Smith told him that if he promised to end the thievery of arms forever, Smith would bring his brother back to life. The brother agreed. A stiff shot of "aqua vitae" (strong alcohol) did the trick, and, according to Smith, he thereafter had little trouble getting his way with the Indians. He had the power to raise the dead, or so they thought.

So a flueless charcoal fire, which perhaps burned only once, and an inner security wall at the base of the cellar steps might identify the site as Smith's dungeon. Jail or not, it is clear that the cellar did serve as part of the Jamestown defense system. Shelves cut into the north and south walls could have been built there to serve musketeers. These shelves would have given an elevated firing position through a ground-level opening. Like the other two fort-period cellars, the factory cellar held several distinct types of fill, laid in this sequence: washed sandy clay at the bottom; above that, the aforementioned fill that washed in along the floor from the south and into the barrel sump; on top of that, a deposit of what has to be the collapsing of mud-and-stud walls; then a rich vein of trash and garbage spilling in from the south and east. Finally, brown loam filled the resulting depression, presumably to enable easy plowing of the cellar-building site. Three of these layers represent the end of the life of the cellar: the wall collapse, the trash and garbage, and the leveling loam. The same sequence is

"J. Smith taketh the King of Pamaunkee prisoner, 1608." (Plate 45, *The American Drawings of John White*, vol. 2; Folk Art Collection, Special Collections Research Center, Swem Library, College of William and Mary)

observable in all three mud-and-stud buildings, with the exception of the trash layer, which is missing in the quarter. Such a deposit may have been wiped away in the quarter with all the nineteenth-century earthmoving.

What these layers tell is the same story of construction, use, and demise that can be discerned in the barracks and the quarter. First, the builders dug a cellar, presumably stockpiling the mixed topsoil and clay and maybe even living in the cellar for a time. Then the light cratchets went up as a frame above the cellar and beyond. As a network of lighter studs lined the walls between the major upright poles, the stockpile fill was spread (pargeted) onto the frames. A light sapling roof frame was built separately and then raised up as forked-pole wall posts went into place. The light roof was hipped for strength. When the mud walls were dry and stable enough, thatch was added to complete the roof. The cellar then was used for a concentrated period of time, likely during the stressful first three years, 1607–10. Sometime after that, the mud walls collapsed into the cellar as the building disappeared. Last of all, a rich layer of trash went into most of the remaining cellar space.

That topmost layer of trash is rich not only in its abundance and variety but in its capacity to illuminate the early history of Jamestown's fortifications. This capacity derives, first of all, from one distinctive characteristic of the trash deposits in the cellars of the barracks, quarter, and factory, and, for that matter, all of the rest of the early fort trash deposits (the fort moat and the circular magazine at the south bastion, and the west bulwark ditch): all these deposits were apparently created at one and the same time.

How do we know this? All of the deposits contained pieces of some of the same ceramic vessels: that is, in archaeological terms, there could be some cross-mending. If broken pots found at different deposits across a site mend together—that is, if the pieces of the same pot found in different deposits fit together—then it is possible that the deposits came from the same source. And, ceramic cross-mending among the cellars and other features theoretically suggests a massive deposition all across the site at about the same time. Not only did such cross-mending characterize these trash deposits, but all held almost identical artifacts: scrap copper, jettons, armor, weapon parts, the same types of broken pottery (especially Delft drug jars), and food remains. Another similarity in the trash layers is that the most recent artifacts in all of them date to no later than 1610; therefore, all four cellars seemed to have a similar backfilling date.

Why so much was thrown away at the same time after 1610 remains an important question. One possible answer might be called "the De La Warre cleanup." In June 1610, when Lord De La Warre with his fresh troops, supplies, and settlers arrived to save the day after the "starving time" of 1609–10, the trusted William Strachey wrote that the new governor "brought the fort to more perfection" and, among other things, "cleansed the town."[41] What exactly was perfected, what was cleansed, is not very clear. Cleansing likely meant clearing the grounds of accumulated litter, repairing or removing shabby buildings, and repairing and/or perhaps redesigning palisade lines. These activities might possibly account for the great number of contemporaneous 1607–10 trash deposits. But if De La Warre filled all the cellars, moat, and bulwark trenches in 1610, what was left of the original

James Fort thereafter? The fort cannot have disappeared, since Strachey described its form as triangular, just as Percy and Smith had described it earlier, with two 300-foot sides on the east and west and a 420-foot side on the south made of "planks and strong posts."[42] And these are exactly the dimensions of the one and only fort found archaeologically.

Another explanation for the trash layer may lie in Strachey's earlier description of the town, written about what he saw on May 20, 1610, the day he arrived with the previously shipwrecked party from Bermuda. Strachey made a strong point that the town was in shambles, with the main gate off its hinges and the houses and palisade torn down and cut into firewood. Although we have explained the dismantling of the fort's east wall as part of an intentional expansion, some of the removal could have resulted from a desperate gathering of firewood. If this east palisade had not yet become an interior wall, its removal would have explained why, as Strachey remarked, the Indians could kill anyone who ventured from the "blockhouse" (to which the survivors may have been confined because it was the only place secure enough to provide protection).[43] Razing a palisade, even in part, would have left the whole settlement wide open to attacks from the Powhatan.

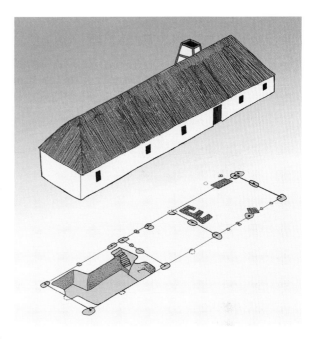

Archaeological plan (*below*) and mud-and-stud conjectural reconstruction of the factory.

The "blockhouse" could mean, of course, the blockhouse built near the isthmus at the extreme western end of the island, or the blockhouse on Back River. But it is also possible that some settlers were seeking safety in the factory or other fort buildings, all of which would have become, in a sense, blockhouses as soon as some palisades were gone. Strachey also noted that the surviving settlers were suffering from pestilence within the blockhouse. If they were in fact trapped inside the buildings for their own safety, then it is not beyond the realm of possibility that their garbage and trash could wind up in the cellars below them. Under siege by the Indians, who would risk an appearance beyond the protection of the blockhouse walls just to get rid of rubbish?

Some of the trash found in the cellars, however, does not fit this explanation. The debris included industrial waste from glassmaking, pipe making, metallurgy, and the reworking of armor. Starving and trapped settlers would hardly bide their time busily manufacturing things and dropping the waste in the cellar below. The siege explanation also does not account for what appears to be the collapsed walls found below this industrial waste in the factory. This redeposited clay layer can only be the consequence of wall destruction. So a blockhouse confinement, brought on by an Indian siege, cannot convincingly explain the cellar garbage.

Since the artifact and food remains from the backfilling of the factory cellar could have been hauled in from anywhere on the fort site during the 1610 cleanup operation, they might have little to say about what human action took place in the immediate vicinity of the extension building. But some objects were found embedded in the factory cellar subfloor and in its relatively thin occupation layer, obviously dropped and lost right there as people used the space. For example, a Nuremberg 1580 jetton, a fragment of a French Martincamp ceramic flask, and a 1573 silver English sixpence all date to the late sixteenth century. These artifacts tell us that the cellar was being used as a cellar during the very early fort period—more evidence that the triangular fort expanded sooner than later in its early years, certainly by the time De La Warre completed his many "perfections." Together with the building floor plan, the artifacts also offer clues to the use of the building. In the northernmost rooms of the complex, more than one hundred jettons were found in the plowzone as well as scattered across the top of or embedded in a thick clay floor. Again, being *in* the floor means they were dropped when the room was occupied. Perhaps most telling of all, a fragment of a glass alembic (a domed vessel used in distilling) was found in the floor, almost certainly broken off of the alembic recovered from the trash levels in the cellar under the southernmost room. There, a ceramic boiling vessel known as a cucurbit rested in the fill with the alembic. The alembic and the cucurbit are the two main components of a distilling operation. These objects and other specialized ceramic vessels found with them—including crucibles, a distilling dish, and a dipper—are all implements required for the detection and refinement of precious metals. These artifacts may also

Ceramic boiler, known as a cucurbit, found in the factory cellar. This vessel is part of a still, indicating that scientists with the early settlers had the equipment to test for gold and other precious metals that ultimately eluded them.

be the only clue to the purpose of the three brick fireplace hearths found in the north room, as no other evidence of industrial waste appeared in any of the fill from the occupation period.

The fire in the largest hearth—which showed evidence of two periods of construction—had been hot enough to partially melt the brick surfaces. Since distilling requires only enough heat to boil liquid, either something else was being heated there, or the continuous fires took their toll on the surface of the brick. Distilling is still one of the most likely uses of the rooms. The process also requires a collection vessel at the end of the line, and French Martincamp flasks could have been used for that purpose.

Jettons would not have been used in distilling, so their presence in the northern room in such great numbers is rather puzzling. Their presence might suggest that the northern room was some type of accounting office or perhaps occupied by the cape merchant, the man appointed by the Company to keep track of the supplies and any material that could be shipped home to turn a profit. If the space was an accounting office, then the James Fort cape merchants who were responsible for the Virginia Company "store" were based there in 1607–10.[44] It is also possible, and probably more likely, that jettons were used, not for their original purpose of calculation, but for a currency. Official coinage might not have been readily available that far away from England.[45] If that is the case, then what were the settlers buying there? And if the jettons had intrinsic value, why had they been lost and scattered on the floor in such great numbers? Perhaps the jettons were used to buy food from the Virginia Indians. It would make sense that such transactions should occur in a building that was somewhat secure, yet outside the actual triangular fort (see illustration on p. 97 and related text).

But plowing disturbances had made understanding the northern room(s) difficult. An even greater source of difficulty was the churchyard burial ground that extended across the building site. More than a dozen burial shafts pierced the earth floor, especially in the northern room, so that only segments of the original floor between the burial shafts remained intact. Fortunately, most of the hearths survived the burials. Also, the earthen floor that escaped the burial disruptions held not only the jettons but also two curious artifact caches in small, shallow holes. One such hole contained an English-made (Borderware) candlestick datable post-1580, two Hans Krauwinckel jettons also post-1580, and a very unusual 1577 Livonian silver coin. Stranger yet, next to the main hearth, someone had buried dozens of quartz pebbles, apparently in an early seventeenth-century case bottle sealed with a pewter stopper, but with the bottom of the bottle broken away. The artifacts were located between the eastern wall line of the factory and the chimney, suggesting they were buried in what must have been a lobby entrance, a small room between the front door and the chimneystack. Lobby entrances were common in lowland English houses of the postmedieval period; the room acted as a holding space for strangers, a place to decide whether or not they were eligible to venture into the more private main rooms. Small collections of objects placed in voids along chimneystacks and under floors have turned up in postmedieval houses in Suffolk as well. Some argue convincingly that these English caches were placed there by superstitious country people, believing that articles as personal as shoes would keep evil spirits, such as witches, from entering the house through the one opening that could not be closed, the chimney flue.[46] The caches in the factory's lobby floor could well be a sign that Suffolk superstition was alive and well at Jamestown.

A metallurgy shop? A store? A prison? A factory? These are questions and possible answers as to the use of the building. We can only speculate, also, about whether this extension building was set apart from but attached to the triangular walls of James Fort for any special reason. What is less speculative is that the factory, in common with the other mud-and-stud buildings, reflects a local vernacular tradition. What may be most intriguing are the hints that these remains, like the remains of the barracks and the quarter, offer of the colonists' complex interactions with the Virginia Indians: learning from their building techniques, relying on their food supply, entering into human relationships more complex than those of enemies or neighbors keeping at a well-regulated, cautious distance. Whatever we can or cannot know of the form and life span of the factory, we can be sure that negotiating these relationships formed one of the major challenges of these struggling years of the colony.

Governor's Row

Remains of the third and fourth buildings inside the James Fort triangle, the rowhouses (hereafter rows) tell a different story architecturally. This story, in turn, offers new insight into the Virginia Company's steadfast commitment to making a success of their Virginia enterprise despite the obvious challenges to survival presented by nature and the Virginia Indians during the first two years. Excavations on the west side of the fort triangle beneath the Civil War earthwork and its underlying plowzone revealed remnants of cobblestone foundations, defining the limits of two enormous buildings paralleling the west wall line for more than 170 feet.

Grading for the Civil War earthwork and plowing by farmers had again seriously disturbed portions of the buildings' remains, but enough escaped these disturbances to define the basic plans. The southernmost structure measured 90' × 18' and had three chimneys with back-to-back fireplaces in them. The double hearths make it probable that this structure had at least six rooms, one fireplace in each. There were no cellars. The solid cobble footings indicate the buildings were of box-frame construction, with sills protected from contact with the decaying effect of the wet clay beneath. These footings were built for permanence beyond that of their mud-and-stud predecessors. Inside the foundation, however, were signs that timber floor joists had been laid directly on the ground.

The foundation to the north measured 66' × 18' with one back-to-back brick chimney toward the northern end. There the Civil War grading was

Overview of the two building sites found in the fort with cobblestone foundations and back-to-back brick-chimney foundations (probable governor's residence [*foreground*] and the rowhouse [*background*]). Note also the west fort palisade trench (*upper right*), cellars/pits, and postholes from lean-tos along the wall, and postholes from what appear to be, at this writing, pre–governor's residence/rowhouse post-in-the-ground structures (1607–10?) to the left of the cobble line.

lighter than elsewhere, allowing more of the floor joists to survive. This row appears to have been divided by the chimney into a seventeen-foot-long room to the east and probably one heated and one unheated room to the south. Grading to the south, however, may have erased one or more chimneys. Although grading for the Civil War earthwork erased most of the west wall line, both of its corners were spared. The northern row has a brick addition of yet undiscovered design or dimensions. Discovering signs of such permanent buildings raised a number of significant questions: Were they old enough to be a part of the town plan of the fort era, or did they belong to the post-fort town? What did they look like? What were they used for?

One fact proves that the rows date to the fort era: the distance that separates their foundation from the west wall of the fort is generally the same as that separating the barracks and quarter from their parallel palisades. Like these other buildings, then,

Discovery of a clay tobacco pipe bowl of a 1610–30 style in the builder's trench of the rowhouse corroborates the documentary construction date of 1611.

the rows were part of the early, fortified Jamestown, standing on the opposite side of the "street" from the fort wall. Unlike these mud-and-stud buildings, however, the rows do not appear to have been part of the original 1607–9 house construction. A Bermuda limestone was used in the southernmost chimney foundation, the type of stone used as ballast in the Bermuda-built ships that arrived with Gates in 1610.[47] For that reason, the rows must date after June 1610. Archaeological test excavation of the trench dug and then filled around the cobblestones by the builders at the time of construction produced fragments of pottery and tobacco pipe bowls lost by the workers. One bowl shape dates it to after 1610, which corroborates the evidence of the limestone (see illustration on p. 84).

Finally, it is significant that twenty-one single and three multiple burials lay about and beneath a chimney and the wall of the southern row, all par-

A late sixteenth-century London series of attached dwellings, likely a prototype of the James Fort rowhouse complex. (From John Thomas Smith's *Antiquities of London* [London, 1791]; Victoria and Albert Museum, London)

allel or perpendicular to the west fort wall. Burying people inside the fort would have been out of the view of the native Indians, thus following the instructions of the Virginia Company: "Above all things do not advertise the killing of any of your men, that the country people [Virginia Indians] may know it, if they perceive that they are but common men . . . you should do well also not to let them see or know of your sick men."[48]

Excavation of the two double burials established that these were likely the graves of four of the twenty-five gentlemen Percy listed as dying in the first disastrous summer of 1607 or soon thereafter. Like the use of Bermuda stone, the 1607 date of the graves underlying the row is more evidence that the rows were not part of the very first years. What is more, the graves lay in aligned cemetery fashion in an area with no other indication of contemporary use of that space, while the lean-tos along the palisade—the earliest shelters—were built beyond the burial space limits. In other words, those who lived in the fort before the construction of the rows knew the graves were there and avoided building on or among them—while in later years, when this row was likely constructed, the probably unmarked graves were perhaps lost from memory.

Could this substantially built rowhouse be one of the "faire . . . houses" Ralph Hamor crows about in his *True Discourse*? Could it even be the governor's residence built by Sir Thomas Gates in 1611?[49] The Hamor document is usually dismissed as propaganda, falsely hyping the colony as a great success in order to offset the gruesome stories of immigrant deaths that

Three oversized postholes in the center of the triangular James Fort mark the likely location of the Virginia Company storehouse. Later post-fort disturbances such as the construction of a brick-lined cellar in a mid-seventeenth-century house (*foreground*) may have erased more evidence of the earlier building.

had been circulating in England. His description of "two faire rowes of houses, all of framed Timber, two stories, and an upper Garret, or Corne Loft" seems too good to be true of the heretofore-struggling Jamestown. In fact, Hamor's later indictment of the mismanaged town in a written attack on the Virginia Company treasurer, Thomas Smythe, gives an opposite account, depicting the houses as "mean and poor."[50] Hamor's extreme shift gives more reason not to trust his facts. Nevertheless, with their masonry footings and multiple chimneys, the rows could well be the buildings Hamor describes.

These footings could support a two-and-one-half-story timber-framed building, perhaps of the scale of a London rowhouse of that time.[51] While practically all such buildings went up in flames during the Great Fire of London in 1666, an engraving of a rowhouse built in 1577 for the support of poor widows seems to fit the Jamestown buildings' multichimney plan and Hamor's "faire" houses.[52] The division of the London house into apartments at every chimney might well be reflected in the Jamestown remains. Hamor's earlier document, then, adds to the evidence that the rows were constructed sometime after July 15, 1610, when Strachey apparently describes the town without them, and 1611–14, when Hamor describes his houses and the Company mentions the governor's residence. As for the other of Hamor's two rows of houses, either this was an exaggeration, or he really meant that two rowhouses, or their remains, lie somewhere yet to be discovered.

Excavation at about the geometrical center of the triangular fort found a line of three postholes, ten feet apart. Their size, depth, and post molds indicate they once held massive structural timbers, apparently signs that one of the larger public buildings Strachey wrote about was located in the middle of the fort: the storehouse, guardhouse, or church. The holes are oriented along a line that would almost divide the fort triangle in two and thus

A number of decorative Delft tiles found in the Civil War earthwork fill in the vicinity of the governor's residence, perhaps evidence of the fine quality of the building from the time of occupancy by Governors Argall and Yeardley.

be perpendicular to the south wall. This almost certainly indicates the building was part of the James Fort design. Future excavations may discover whether or not these are the early signs of such significant structures, but there are also indications that post-fort construction of a building with a sizable cellar and the digging of a deep moat around the 1861 Civil War earthwork may have destroyed more signs of these early buildings (see the opening illustrations).

Another building site possibly related to the fort is among the Jamestown Rediscovery archaeological finds. Digging through the plowzone just north of the factory revealed a cellar-like pit. The artifacts inside suggest that the pit may have been one of the earliest parts of an expanded fortified town. It first appeared beneath the tilled soil as a circular discoloration about eight feet in diameter, possibly another backfilled well. The upper three feet of fill held trash-laden layers containing apothecary jars (one complete jar and many nearly complete), sheet-copper waste, jettons, fine glass buttons, a case bottle, fish hooks, ammunition and small powder flasks known as bandoliers, traces of cloth, a Scottish James VI coin of 1597, and a Groningen (Netherlands) token dated 1583. The fill also contained many Virginia Indian artifacts, including related (i.e., "mendable") pieces of pots, a section of reed matting, and arrow points accompanied by stone flakes from their manufacture.

Excavations have recovered more than 350 such projectile points inside the footprint of the fort, along the palisades, around and in the bulwark, and in the bulwark ditch. Their shapes and sizes date them primarily to two periods: the Archaic, 8000–1200 BC (30 percent), and the Late Woodland, AD 900–1600 (68 percent).[53] Of course, ancient Indians living or hunting on the island left the Archaic points. But the Woodland-period points

Late Woodland Virginia Indian pot, digitally reconstructed. This type of pottery makes up an average of half the total quantity of pottery found in ca.-1607–11 deposits in and around the fort. This and evidence of the manufacturing of stone tools and shell beads indicate much cultural and perhaps social interdependence of the English and the natives.

Artifacts laid out by upper (*foreground*) to lower levels (*background*) of deposits in an outlying house cellar. Fill taken together appears to comprise one of the earliest deposits yet found in the expanded fort/Jamestown site.

Some of the more than 350 Virginia Indian stone projectile and knife points found in historical deposits at James Fort. There is evidence of the manufacture of points within the fort.

predominate and comprise a unique assortment of shapes, sizes, and stone types, suggesting that they came from a wide area of coastal Virginia and North Carolina. The great number found buried with 1607–10 European artifacts suggests that the arrow points were being used by Indians taken into the fort or else reused by the settlers themselves. Smith reports that in exchange for bells, the Massawomeks gave him "venison, beares flesh, fish, bowes, arrows, clubs, targets, and beares skinnes." Some of the arrows must have arrived in the fort during battle. A few of the points may even be from the rain of forty arrows Archer witnessed flying into the fort.[54]

What is most remarkable about the arrow points found in the pit north of the factory is that the stone type of one of them is identical to that of some of the numerous stone flakes found with it. This debitage, or stone flakes, tells us that the manufacturer—a Virginia Indian—was producing the points in the fort itself.[55] It is very doubtful that settlers took up that craft; after all, they had metal-pointed bolts for their crossbows, and they had guns.

Nor are the arrow points from this pit and elsewhere across the fort site the only signs of the Indians' presence. The reed matting found in the pit was of the sort mentioned by Smith and others as important objects in the material world of the Virginia Indians. Made of marsh grass held together with bark fiber cord, the mat survived because it had been buried immediately under copper waste and ammunition bandoliers. The copper salts had acted as a sterilant, fending off organisms that normally would decompose the reed fibers. Thanks to this chance layering of deposits, this object is the only surviving example of a Virginia Indian mat yet found—

and a further witness to the close involvement of the Jamestown settlers with their Indian neighbors. The mat joins with the arrow points, with finds such as the quarter time capsule, and with evidence in the west bulwark ditch of the native manufacture of shell beads (raw materials, partially made beads, and shaping stone) to contradict the belief that the English and the Indians were uncompromising mortal enemies. Although Smith would report the native view that the English were all there to destroy them—"a people come from under the world to take their world from them"—it is improbable that any Indians who believed that would have voluntarily lived in the fort and befriended the colonists.[56]

Part of a native mat made of reeds fastened together with bark cord, preserved because of the presence of a fragment of copper above it.

This is not to say that in the earliest weeks of the 1607 summer there was any love lost between the settlers and their immediate neighbors, the Paspahegh. Captain Gabriel Archer reported almost relentless attacks at the fort. On the day Archer counted the forty incoming arrows, he also reported the death of a dog at the hands of the Indians. On four other days, he mentioned that long grasses and reeds stood along the fort palisades and bulwarks, noting that the Indians would hide in them and take aim at the colonists: "Sunday [May 30, 1607] they [Indians] came lurking in the thickets and long grasses, and a gentleman one Eustace Clovall unarmed straggling without the fort, shot 6 arrowes into him." Clovill died a week later. Soon after, Archer wrote that "3 of the [Indians] had most adventourously stollen under our bulwark and hiden themselves in the long grasses." Amazingly, it seems that the Indians themselves offered a solution to the long-grass sniper problem: "He [Indian] counselled us to Cutt Downe the long weedes rounde about our fforte."[57] Apparently, Powhatan's war policy of attrition was not a unanimous decision within his chiefdom. In any case, by August 1607, cutting grass must have become a low priority for the sick and dying soldiers.

Below the top three feet of the object-rich fill, the shape of the pit north of the factory changed from circular to rectangular. Finally, beneath a concentration of oyster shells, the shaft bottomed out onto a fairly level earth "floor." Mere pits do not have floors, so this feature is likely yet another trash-filled cellar. The cellar would also have likely lain beneath yet another tented-over cellar structure or mud-and-stud-type building, constructed on the same axis as the factory, west of north. No other evidence survived, however, of a superstructure. Probably the many seventeenth- to eighteenth-century churchyard grave shafts surrounding the cellar had destroyed any related building postholes. In any event, through the artifacts it contained, the pit not only showed the important relationships between the colonists and the Virginia Indians, but it also revealed the presence of another early building just outside of the extended palisade. This location may tell us more about the meaning of these artifacts: might the cellar and the building above it have lain in an area reserved for Indians, thus keeping the triangular section of the town separate and more secure? Future excavation to the north of the pit may determine that this structure came to be inside the extended fort, attaching to an as-yet-undiscovered wall line turning east from the churchyard. If that was so, the close relationship between the English and some Virginia Indians would seem an even more indisputable fact.

A Fort Well

Another important goal of Jamestown Rediscovery was to find the fort well. Why? First, the discovery of the well would offer an opportunity to understand more clearly why so many people died at Jamestown. On that subject documents disagree. Captain John Smith reported that the well he ordered dug in 1608 held "sweet water." The same reference implies that this well was the first to be dug at Jamestown, presumably ending the practice, during the preceding years, of drinking the slimy and brackish water directly from the James River. Strachey, however, tells a completely different story of the well and its water. He blamed the rash of deaths in 1609–10 directly on the same well, which he claimed was "Six or seven fathom deep, fed by the brackish river oozing into it; from whence I verily believe the chief causes have proceeded of many diseases and sicknesses which have happened to our people who are indeed strangely afflicted with fluxes and agues and every particular infirmity."[58] Apparently Strachey would not have called those 1609–10 months the "starving time": he suspected another cause for the deaths of that winter. Which of the conflicting descriptions of the well should we believe? Was Smith's and Strachey's well "sweet" or "poison"? Finding and testing the fort well water could answer that question, a critical step toward recapturing the reality of Jamestown's health challenges.

Locating the fort well had other potential attractions. Wells can be particularly valuable archaeological finds. When objects accidentally fall into the shaft of a working well, the water cushions the impact; as a result, unbroken artifacts accumulate at the bottom. The water also acts as a preservation agent. Permanently wet environments inhibit the rusting of metallic objects and can preserve organic materials such as wood, leather, and plants in a waterlogged state. These objects rarely survive in the alternating wet and dry conditions characteristic of other archaeological deposits, such as pits and cellars. Also, once wells are abandoned, they often become a convenient place to get rid of garbage and trash, usually over a short period of time. So well excavation can present an opportunity to recover unusually preserved artifacts in a time-capsule-like state.

Brick-lined well with surrounding construction shaft showing an early seventeenth-century iron breastplate as found in the abandoned well fill. Artifacts from the construction deposit dated the building of the well to the later fort period, ca. 1615.

Excavations have indeed discovered a well as old as James Fort, in the plain known as Smithfield outside the west bulwark. Since this well was found fifty feet outside the protection of the west wall, it cannot be the well Smith built in the fort in 1608–9 or likely the contaminated well Strachey described in 1610. Nonetheless, the Smithfield well turned out to be the hoped-for time capsule.

Located in an area heavily scoured by Civil War grading, the top of a brick-lined well shaft had been discovered during the misdirected search for the west wall. The well's brickwork was partially intact at ground level and enclosed within a larger surrounding backfilled hole made at the time of construction. Backfilling of this builder's basin was part of the construction process: courses of the original circular brick lining below ground, built with rectangular bricks and brick wedges, required the force of the exterior basin backfill to hold it together. Such construction physics was

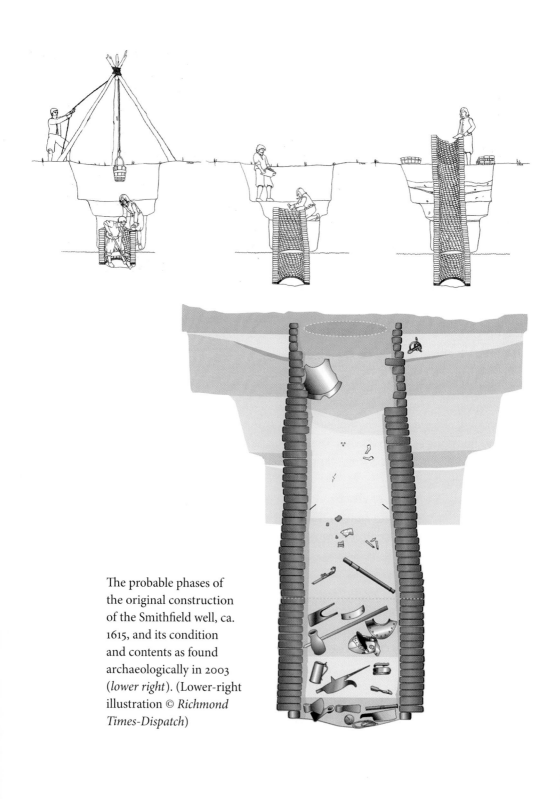

The probable phases of
the original construction
of the Smithfield well, ca.
1615, and its condition
and contents as found
archaeologically in 2003
(*lower right*). (Lower-right
illustration © *Richmond
Times-Dispatch*)

essential not only to building the shaft but also to keeping it open to the water table, reached at a depth of nine feet. The lining remained intact below the water table, where it finally rested on a wooden curb at fourteen feet below grade.

Artifacts that inadvertently made their way into the fill in the builder's basin reveal that the Smithfield well was built during the first fifteen years or so of the Jamestown settlement. Ceramics and pipe bowls in the collection are types known to have been made as early as the beginning of the seventeenth century, such as Spanish earthenware ceramic costrel (handled jug) fragments. Although remains of other such costrels found in Virginia have been dated no earlier than 1619, the Jamestown fragments do not necessarily share this date since no other site yet excavated in Virginia is as old as Jamestown, and Spanish costrels are known to date as early as 1600 in Europe.[59] Fragments from an Italian-made bowl, a type made as early as 1600, and pieces of a tobacco pipe thought to be made in Virginia, possibly by the 1608 immigrant pipe maker Robert Cotton, both suggest a fort-period construction date for this well. Another pipe with a distinctive octagonal bowl also wound up in the builder's fill (see illustration on p. 84). All that is known about this pipe's manufacture date is that an identical example was found on the mainland north of Jamestown Island, at a site believed to have been occupied in the first quarter of the seventeenth century. Taken together, these dates put the construction of the Smithfield well comfortably within the James Fort years. Documents narrow the well chronology even more.

After Strachey's indictment of the unhealthy well—possibly Smith's fort well gone bad—other references to Jamestown wells suggest dates but unclear locations. For instance, the strict martial laws put on the books by the new governor, Sir Thomas Gates, in 1611 include rules intended to keep certain well-polluting activities, such as washing dishes, away from "the olde well" and clear of the vicinity of the "new Pumpe" (a new well with a pump?). Undoubtedly the old well is the Smith-Strachey well and therefore located in the fort. But the location of the newer well is not specified.[60]

A further reference to this later well with its new pump may be Governor Sir Thomas Dale's report that when he came to Jamestown in May 1611, he put in a new well. The reason given for Dale's action was "the amending of the most unwholesome water which the old afforded."[61] It is possible that Dale's new well went into a central place in De La Warre's 1610 "perfected"

Jamestown, and that the Smithfield well and Dale's new 1611 well are one and the same.

Another new governor, Captain Samuel Argall, arrived at Jamestown in 1617 to again find "the" well of freshwater "spoiled." As part of his many fort repairs, he either cleaned out the existing well or replaced it altogether.[62] Is the Smithfield well the spoiled well possibly abandoned by Argall? The answer again lies in context and date. If Argall did abandon the spoiled well, it typically would become a trashcan, quickly collecting artifacts in 1617–18. However, while the discards in this well contained no precisely dated object like a coin to set a solid date, documents and contemporary artwork can help date certain artifacts in the trash—revealing them to be too late to have been rejects from Argall's time.

The shaft held nearly 1,400 objects in seven distinct layers: two near the bottom, almost certainly containing objects accidentally knocked into the water when the well was in use, and five containing artifacts purposely thrown down the abandoned shaft during and after the lining had partially collapsed.[63] The objects from these layers can therefore provide dates for both the use of the well and its abandonment. Certain recovered drinking vessels, arms, apparently one full suit of armor, tools, and even a shoe together likely set the demise of the well in the fort's final years, 1622–25. An intact, lidded pewter drinking flagon found almost at the bottom of the shaft can be dated roughly by its style but perhaps more precisely by the monogram stamped on the lid thumb piece. The vessel shape appears in English illustrations predating 1620. Three initials on the thumb piece— *R E* under a *P*—may identify the owners as Richard and Elizabeth Pierce, a couple who arrived at Jamestown in 1618 and lived just off the island on a tract known as Neck of Land by 1625. If these are the Pierces' initials, it follows that the well was in use after 1618, the year of their arrival in Virginia. Another pewter vessel, a standard-measure baluster form dating to the second half of the sixteenth century, although a rare find of the usually perishable pewter, is not a particular help in dating the well. But two broken German ceramic drinking jugs in the collection do help: a molded blue-and-gray stoneware baluster jug, bearing a scene telling the story of the Prodigal Son, and most of a brown stoneware jug known as a Bartmann. The paneled baluster jug with the biblical scene closely matches a museum piece dated 1618, suggesting that the jug was made at about the same time. A medallion embossed on the sides of the Bartmann included enough armorial symbols to suggest that it displayed the arms of three Ger-

Some of the hundreds of objects found in the Smithfield well before and some after conservation.

man principalities that existed as united states only during the period 1521–1609. The Bartmann may date later than that, however, because a similar jug was found on the 1629 wreck of the Dutch ship *Batavia,* but potters are suspected of using outdated molds to make the medallions.[64] It would be safe, however, to assume a 1609–29 date for the vessel—again well within the late fort period at Jamestown.

The well fill also contained a pole arm known as a "bill" and a breast-plate, with a very datable alteration, from a suit of body armor. After the Indian uprising in 1622, a thousand bills, deemed obsolete in England, were sent to the colonies, probably half to Virginia. The breastplate is of an early seventeenth-century style with ridged belly, made to accommodate the popular vests of that time known as doublets. This breastplate is also datable by a tab of armor attached to the right shoulder, a feature of two other breastplates found in Virginia, one at Jamestown and the other at an

Video image of a pewter flagon at the moment of discovery.

Late sixteenth- to early seventeenth-century pewter drinking flagon from the Smithfield well after conservation. The thumb piece was monogrammed *R E* under *P,* possibly identifying the vessel as the property of Richard and Elizabeth Pierce of neighboring Neck of Land, located on the mainland north of Jamestown Island.

upriver site, Jordan's Point, first occupied 1620–35. Seven axes and two hoes found at the bottom of the well are of types dating to the early seventeenth century. Most of these artifacts were found in serviceable condition, so it is likely that they were accidentally lost as they broke free from their duty as makeshift counterweights for well buckets.[65] Such counterweights would have been unnecessary baggage, however, if the well bucket came equipped with the massive iron handle found near the bottom of the shaft. This handle would not only have acted as a swivel to keep the rope from untwisting but would have tipped the bucket by its own weight. The handle's broken condition, however, suggests that the makeshift counterweight became its replacement.

The most surprising find in the well fill was a full suit of armor—a helmet known as a burgonet, front and rear gorgets to protect the neck, a breastplate, and a number of tassetts, or frontal hip and thigh protective plates—scattered through the well fill from top to almost bottom. The armor may have been discarded in favor of the lighter and less restraining "jackets"—an adaptation to the Virginia climate—or perhaps out of a false sense of security brought on by the years of peace with the Virginia Indians before the 1622 uprising. Finally, a child's shoe, of a style datable to the 1610s, was also found in the waterlogged well deposit.

Although this well was not the one about which Smith and Strachey disagreed, it did provide a chance to evaluate their different judgments of wells in 1609 and 1610. Strachey seems to have been correct in his estimate of the depth of Jamestown wells: the Smithfield well would appear to have been six ancient fathoms (eighteen feet), the figure Strachey gives.[66] The shaft stood only fourteen feet as found, but the missing four feet would probably have disappeared during the Civil War grading in 1861. Testing has shown, however, that Strachey's other assertions were more disputable. Later excavations located at least two of the missing wells.

THREE

RECOVERING JAMESTOWNIANS

When an emergency rescue squad arrives at an accident scene, medics immediately search for signs of life in the victim. If the vital signs are not evident, the medics' job is over. The remains of the body become the responsibility of forensic scientists, legally required to identify the body, if unknown, and to determine the cause of death. In the course of their physical inspection of the remains and of biological tests, these scientists can find signs of life in a different sense: they can reconstruct much of a person's life story. Through such efforts, the dead inform the living.

Archaeologists, too, search for signs of life, although their subjects are only skeletal remains. At Jamestown, burial recovery, meticulous examination, and careful analysis have led to a richer understanding of the colony's population. Thanks to these methods, we need not be restricted to written facts and artifacts to come to know seventeenth-century Jamestown: we can actually come face-to-face with Jamestown people of the past, getting to know them personally from the signs of their lives still held in their skeletal remains.

Scores of unmarked burials were recovered at Jamestown during the course of the first decade of the Jamestown Rediscovery excavations. Five were found and studied in what turned out to be the place where the victims of the first trying summer and early fall were laid to rest. The interplay of archaeological/scientific facts and documentary reference have led to identifying one of these burials with something approaching probability. Excavations within the Civil War earthwork in search of the western 1607 fort wall not only turned up the outer well but also another unmarked grave.[1]

The very siting and soil composition of the burial shaft immediately brought great attention to this grave. The burial was aligned with the predicted (and eventually discovered) west wall of the fort—a compass direction that only made sense in light of the sought-for triangular plan of the original James Fort. In addition, part of the discolored soil outlining the shaft was found to be under a circular, well-like feature jammed with seventeenth-century brickbats. Since the brick deposit had to postdate the burial, this group of circumstances, too, suggested an early seventeenth-century interment.

Removal of the brickbats and about a foot of fill containing domestic trash exposed the bottom, not of a well, but of a shallow pit. The mixed clay in the burial fill was still visible at the bottom of the pit, as was an outline of a posthole, which slightly penetrated the shaft. Artifacts from the pit fill, notably tobacco pipes including a local coarse-ceramic type probably first made at Jamestown after 1630, indicated the date of deposit: these undisturbed strata were at least as old as the

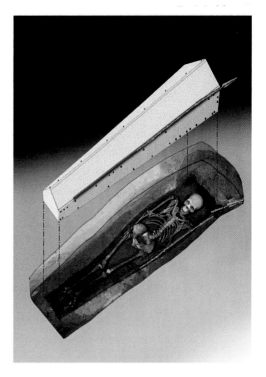

A European man in his mid- to late thirties buried with a captain's leading staff, laid along a gable-lidded coffin. (Reconstruction based on nail patterns and wood stains in the soil.)

1630s. This inadvertent sealing of the forgotten grave created a time lid on the age of interment—a date, circa 1630, before which the burial must have taken place. This dating, the location adjacent to the fort, and the alignment of the grave with the wall of the original fort pointed to the possible discovery of the most important of lost burials at Jamestown, that of Captain Bartholomew Gosnold.

When a decorative iron captain's leading staff appeared at the excavation level of the coffin lid, finding Gosnold below seemed inevitable. The superbly preserved skeleton lying within the coffin outline offered more reason to hope. The well-preserved pelvis enabled our steadfast forensic anthropologist, Dr. Douglas Owsley, to determine that this five-foot, three-inch European man died in his mid- to late thirties. It is known that Gosnold was thirty-six years of age at his passing on August 22, 1607, the day when George Percy reported that, after a three-week illness, "there died Captain Bartholomew Gosnold, one of our council; he was honorably buried, having all the ordinance in the fort shot off with many volleys of small shot."[2]

Finding Gosnold was a goal for the Jamestown Rediscovery project from the beginning. Why? His vital importance to both the planning and reality of the Jamestown adventure was unquestionable but not widely known. The discovery of his remains might help inspire a more careful reading of the record of initial English colonization. We already know that Gosnold's success as a mariner and privateer led him to briefly colonize one of the Elizabeth Isles and explore and name Cape Cod and Martha's Vineyard.[3] This exploration was a prelude to Gosnold's planning, fund raising, and recruiting for the Virginia colony of Jamestown, transporting the settlers, and laying the colony's foundations. Upon Gosnold's passing, even the self-promoting Captain John Smith and his archenemy Edward Maria Wingfield, the colony's first council president, agreed on Gosnold's value. Smith named Gosnold the "prime mover" of the planting of Jamestown. Wingfield, in an apologia after his removal from office, lamented, "divers of our men fell sick . . . amongst whom was the worthy and religious gentleman, Captain Bartholomew Gosnold, upon whose life stood a great part of the good success and fortune of our government and colony."[4] In the absence of Gosnold's support, Wingfield felt it inevitable that he would be deposed as council president—a strong statement about Gosnold's great value to the colony.

Gosnold's death so early in Jamestown's history robbed him of a chance to produce his own memoirs. The loss of his gravesite further helped relegate him to historical obscurity. But just as the archaeological discovery of James Fort has offered posterity a chance to reassess the Jamestown experience, so the probable discovery of the lost Gosnold grave brings to the forefront the significant accolades of Smith and Wingfield.

The high status accorded to this burial is established by the captain's leading staff or half pike found in the grave. Only the metal parts survived: the decorative point fashioned into a cruciform, and two metal fastening straps (lanquets). However, the decay of the pike's wooden shaft left enough of a dark stain in the ground to reveal its original length, five and one-half feet. During excavation, the corrosion on the metal point disguised its true

"Drill Postures," a detail from an engraving by T. Cockson (English, 1615–20), showing a leading staff identical to the Jamestown burial staff. (© The Trustees of the British Museum)

shape, but laboratory X-rays left no doubt that it was the head of a captain's leading staff. A search in the collections of European military staff weapons and period illustrations produced early seventeenth-century examples of officers' half pikes.[5] A 1615–20 woodcut shows an identical pike, describing it as a type of captain's half pike intended to be deployed in combat.[6] Examples remain of more decorative ceremonial captains' staffs, but such staffs would have stayed in England, while the more weapon-like half pikes went to the Jamestown frontier.

The presence of the wartime staff at Jamestown might seem to contradict the Virginia Company's instructions to the colonists not to appear menacing to the Virginia Indians. Following these instructions, at first Gosnold and the rest of the council even delayed constructing the fort. It is apparent, however, that Gosnold (or whoever the buried captain may be) had a more realistic understanding than the London-based Virginia Company of the situation they would face at Jamestown. The captain seemed to have known that no matter how peaceful the settlers tried to appear, sooner or later relations with the natives would indeed require the combat version of his leading staff. In fact, combat followed upon first contact at Cape Henry, and as we know, after only a few days of incoming arrows at Jamestown, Gosnold and the rest of the council "contrived" and directed construction of James Fort.[7]

Whether or not this burial is Gosnold might be further determined, we knew, by comparison of its skeletal DNA with that of a known relative, dead or alive. The challenge would be to find the right relative, which means only a maternal descendant. Why? Cells contain two kinds of DNA: nuclear and mitochondrial. Mitochondrial DNA—that contained in the mitochondria of the cell—preserves well in bones, is relatively stable, and can be compared across several generations.[8] Mitochondrial DNA is only passed along the maternal family line, so in order to compare a sample from the bones of a deceased individual, a sample from the mother, or from any of the female siblings who share the same sequence of mitochondrial DNA as the mother of the deceased, would have to be found.

To find a living relative, documentation of about sixteen generations of maiden names going back to Gosnold's mother, aunts, or sisters needed to be researched. Such research has proven that no living maternal line relative can be found. The other option was to find the burial of a female relative of Gosnold and sample it for comparison.

This option appeared to be possible through genealogical research.[9] In fact, with skillful deduction from evidence found in various wills and church records, two possibilities were located in England: Elizabeth (Gosnold) Tilney, Bartholomew's sister, buried in All Saints Church, Shelley, near Ipswich; and Katherine (Bowtell) Blackerby, Bartholomew's niece, buried in St. Peters and St. Marys Church, Stowmarket. Elizabeth married Thomas Tilney Esq. of Shelley Hall around 1598.[10] Her husband died circa 1618 (will dated 1618, proved 1620). Their son, Philip Tilney, sold Shelley Hall circa 1627. Elizabeth lived on at Higham St. Mary, and in 1646 she made her will. In that document, she commended her "body to the earth to be buried in decent maner in Shelly chauncell by Thomas Tylney Esquier my late husband." There are no Shelley parish registers for burials for this period, but luckily the Higham St. Mary register records that on April 10, 1646, Elizabeth, widow of Thomas Tylney Esq., died "and was buried in Shelley chauncell the day followinge."[11]

There is more to suggest Elizabeth's burial place. In the later seventeenth century, Shelley church was visited by William Blois (or Bloys; 1600–1673), an antiquarian from Grundisburgh in Suffolk. He saw and recorded:

An Isle in the church built by the Tilnys. Their coat in stone. And stools.
    1) A monument for a Tilny

All Saints Church, Shelley, Suffolk, England, where Bartholomew Gosnold's sister, Elizabeth, was buried in the chancel in 1646. This is the site of the 2005 excavation to obtain bone samples and thus DNA from the remains, hoping to further link the captain to the remains found at Jamestown.

St. Peters and St. Marys Church, Stowmarket, Suffolk, England, the burial place of Bartholomew Gosnold's niece Katherine Blackerby. This was another predicted site to obtain bone samples with DNA to identify the Jamestown captain's remains.

Choir pews in All Saints Church, Shelley, are located upon the likely burial site of Elizabeth Gosnold Tilney.

2) Another for Dame Margaret wife to Philip Tilney Esq., whose son Freder. Tilny Esq. by Anne, da. of Francis Framlingham of Debenham, had issue Charls [sic] that dyed without issue Anno 1595.

3) A stone. Hie iacet Wm. King fil. Joh. King, Do'o huius ville circiter 1500. His coat (not there) a lion ramp &c.[12]

Then, in 1825, Shelley church was visited by another Suffolk antiquarian, David Elisha Davy (1769–1851), who recorded the following information:

The church . . . consists of a Chancel, Nave and Isle on the S[outh] side.

The chancel is 19ft 10 ins long, & 18ft 3ins wide, covered with tiles, and ceiled. The Communion Table is not raised, but railed around. . . . On the north side was a large opening into what was probably a chapel or burial place for the family residing at the Hall [originally the Tilney family], but now used as a vestry, the entrance to which is through a narrow modern door.

The whole floor of the church is paved with white brick, and the church is kept in very neat and clean order.

Monuments, inscriptions etc.

In the chancel . . .

In the floor below the rails, on a small slab of Purbeck stone, were brasses . . . On another small one [stone], near the Vestry door, was a brass of this shape [Davy sketches a simple narrow rectangle]

In the Vestry

Against the north wall is fixed a square frame of stone, in the centre of which is the following shield of arms:

Tilney quartering Thorpe. Over it: crest: from a ducal coronet, a double plume of 5 and 4 feathers, and arising thence a griffon's head.

Supporters: two griffons, but broken.[13]

From the descriptions given by Blois and Davy, it was possible to identify and locate some of the graves in the chancel. Through the process of elimination, a possible occupant of the grave marked by the slab with the rectangular brass (now missing) can be identified. Members of the Tilney family unaccounted for by Blois and Davy include Philip Tilney (who died in 1602)[14] and his wife, Anne Framlingham. There are no burial records at Shelley or wills to identify where they were living when they died. Another unaccounted-for Tilney is Emery (brother and heir of Philip; died 1606) and his wife, Winifred Davis. Again, there are no burial records at Shelley or wills to identify where they were living when they died. Emery had lived in London and also had a house at Syleham in north Suffolk, so his burial at Shelley is unlikely. So the best candidates are Thomas Tilney (son of Emery) and Elizabeth Gosnold, his wife, as both are known to have been buried in Shelley church.

In 1882–83 Shelley church was "thoroughly restored," having been "very much in need of repair." The restoration included the removal of the old pews and their replacement with solid oak benches. The restoration also involved the tiling of the chancel, during which, documentary research suggested, the stone with the missing brass, likely marking the Thomas and Elizabeth Tilney burials and lying directly in front of the Tilney Chapel, was paved over.

Katherine Blackerby's genealogy also created a likely trail to her grave, although a bit of a leap of faith is required along the way. In a *Heralds' Visitation of Suffolk* in 1665, Thomas Blackerby named her as his wife and stated that she was the "daughter of Francis Sawtell of Parham Hall."[15] In his will, dated 1687, Thomas's marriage to a Sawtell is also established, as he mentions his deceased "brother" (in-law) Sawtell and his children.[16] The children's names match with those of Barnaby Sawtell Esq. (1609–1684) of Parham Hall, confirming that he was Katherine's brother. Barnaby himself was baptized in 1609 at St. Matthew's, Ipswich, the "sonne of Francis Sawtell and Marie his wife." A record of his marriage to "Marie" has not been found; however, there is good reason to believe that she was Mary Gosnold, Bartholomew's sister. But this is where the leap of faith comes into the picture. Davy, the Suffolk antiquarian, recorded this about Bartholomew's family in his manuscript *East Anglian pedigrees*:

Gosnold of Otley:
     Anthony Gosnold of Grundisburgh and Clopton married Dorothy, dau. of [blank] Bacon of Hessett.
     Issue: [all given without first names]
     [blank] Gosnold, married Thomas Tilney of Shelley, living 1606; [blank] Gosnold married Edmund Goldsmith; [blank] Gosnold married [blank] Bowtell of Ipswich; [blank] Gosnold married Zachary Norman of Dunwich; Capt. [blank] . . . Gosnold; Ursula Gosnold, buried at Grundisburgh 10 July 1688 [*sic*]; Bartholemew Gosnold, son and heir, of Virginia . . . Captain of a vessel, died in Virginia 1607.[17]

Combining Davy's list with information gleaned from family wills and other sources, the following list of Gosnold daughters can be drawn up: Elizabeth (married Thomas Tilney), Margaret (married Zachary Norman), Dorothie (married Edmund Goldsmith), Anne, Mary, and Ursula. From this list it can be deduced that the daughter who married a Sawtell was named either Anne or Mary—but which? Probably Mary, because the name Sawtell is uncommon in Suffolk, and the only gentry family of the name is the one descended from Francis and Mary of Ipswich. The dates match well for Francis to have married Mary Gosnold. Unfortunately, there is no known will for Francis or Mary, his wife. Here is where the slight leap of faith is required to draw the conclusion that Katherine Sawtell Blackerby's mother was, in fact, Mary Gosnold.

In any event, Katherine's husband, Thomas Blackerby (ca. 1612–1688), was a wealthy and influential man. Although a native of Suffolk, he had spent much of his life as a merchant in London, rising to be an alderman in 1667 and "Master of the Skinners' Company" in 1668. In Suffolk he served as sheriff in 1668–69. He also purchased the lordship of Stowmarket. Katherine is named as his "deare and loveing wife" in his will, dated 1687.[18] Combining these specific connections with one assumption, it can be concluded that Katherine Sawtell Blackerby at Stowmarket is very likely to have been the niece of Bartholomew Gosnold, being the daughter of his sister Mary. While all these fairly complicated relationships do not seem to get us to her exact burial place, they did make a ledgerstone in the floor in a Stowmarket church, St. Peters and St. Marys, a possible key to locating Katherine's grave.

The Stowmarket church parish registers record the burial of Katherine's husband on November 4, 1688, and her own burial on December 22, 1693. In 1811 the antiquarian Davy visited Stowmarket church, where he recorded the monuments, including, "In the chancel within the communion rails, on the south side, Memorial to Thomas Blackerby, died 2 November 1688, aged 76." The Rev. A. G. H. Hollingsworth (vicar of Stowmarket, 1837–59) in his *The History of Stowmarket* states that Thomas Blackerby was buried "under the altar steps—the most distinguished place in the church, and chosen expressly to mark the high estimation in which his character and person were held by the townsmen."[19] Stowmarket church was repewed and beautified in 1840.[20] A further restoration was carried out in the 1860s under the direction of architect R. M. Phipson. Despite the renovations, a black floor slab commemorating Thomas Blackerby lies in the center of the chancel. The extreme eastern end of the slab appears to go under the Victorian altar step. The slab carries a long inscription in praise of Thomas:

Esq. who was elected ALDERMAN of the City of LONDON
in the year of our Lord 1666
fined for the same and for Sheriffe
of the said City. He was HIGH SHERIFFE
of this County in the year of our Lord 1669

He was a man of very great TEMPERANCE
of exemplary CHARITY of profound
HUMILITY and strict PIETY very ZEALOUS
in the discharge of his duty both as a
MAGISTRATE and as a private person
He did much good both in this Town
and other places whilest he lived
and is gone to receive his Reward
He dyed 2 Novr 1688 Ætat Suae 76

There is no mention of Katherine. However, it seems very unlikely that Katherine would have been buried separately from her husband. Her absence from the inscription could be due to a lack of space on the stone or could indicate that, as a childless widow, at her death she left no relatives behind to see to it that the stone was properly inscribed. So there was a chance that Katherine could lie with Thomas under his ledgerstone. True, the central position of the stone today does not agree with Davy's description of the grave slab as being on the "south side" of the chancel. It is possible, however, that the stone was relocated during one of the Victorian restorations. At any rate, in light of the wealth and prominence of Thomas Blackerby, together with the date of the burial, he and his wife would likely be laid to rest in either a brick-lined shaft or an actual vault beneath the stone or nearby. That type of interment for people of prominence was common in the late seventeenth century.

Having exhausted the possibility of a living relative and theoretically located the place of burial of Bartholomew's sister, Elizabeth Tilney, at Shelley and his niece, Katherine Blackerby, at Stowmarket, the next steps were to uncover the remains, identify them more precisely, then obtain bone samples for DNA profiles. This was not to be as simple as it sounded.

First of all, official permission had to be in hand before there was any hope of excavation. These Gosnold relatives are buried in consecrated ground, both inside churches, and therefore under the legal and spiritual care of the Anglican Church of England.[21] The churches are also protected from any damage to structure by the Council for the Care of Churches. This protection is all the more strict because of the dangers posed elsewhere to the evidence of England's past: because England is such a tightly packed treasure chest of archaeological sites stretching over many millennia, and land development is always putting this valuable legacy at risk, the country's archaeologists must concentrate their efforts on rescuing sites in harm's way. Research archaeology, especially any studies of burials in an otherwise "safe" environment—that is, inside churches—has to be of paramount significance and well planned in order to obtain permission, in this case permission from the Church of England, to proceed. It was also vital that the parishioners in both churches be convinced that the work would proceed with a minimum of disruption to church fabric and worship services and would be done with the utmost respect for the deceased. In the end, all of these conditions were met, the authorities convinced, and for the first time in the history of the Church of England, permission was granted. Why? The international significance of Gosnold won the day. This was not to be just a case of some individual trying to prove relationship to someone famous by violating a church grave for DNA. Identifying Gosnold was part of a project with great educational potential.

More precisely identifying Gosnold held the potential to illuminate the experience of the British in the New World in a special way. This burial outside the fort—and therefore in plain view of Indian adversaries—flew in the face of Virginia Company instructions not to show any signs of illness or death to the native population. If the DNA comparison proved positively that the buried captain was Gosnold, however—a man particularly respected by the other leaders as the moving force behind the success of the American colony—the motives for breaking that rule would become clearer, shedding light on the human side of the Virginia story: such a burial with full honors would be a prime example of how, in a difficult situation, the leaders of the colony did their best to maintain British religious and social order even as they adapted to their circumstances in Virginia.

In addition to a clear statement of the purpose the project would serve, the church authorities needed to know how the project would be executed. Indiscriminate digging through the church floors, disrupting grave after grave in the hope of finding a likely candidate for Gosnold DNA, could never be allowed. To assure that such destruction would not occur, the process had to include fail-safe controls along the way. The digging would

be done in phases, with repeated reassess-
ment of the chances of finding the right
grave without irreversible damage to the
churches. That analysis would be performed
by a committee of individuals representing
the church, the church archaeologists from
the Suffolk County archaeological unit, and
the two sponsoring institutions, the APVA
and the National Geographic Society.

Digging would be preceded by ground-
penetrating radar (GPR) reading of the
chancels, which would have virtually no
physical effect on the churches. That testing
could proceed even without a full sanction
by the church. An electronic device was
rolled across the chancel floors, emitting
electrical pulses and recording the echoes
they produced as they encountered different densities of material beneath, such
as masonry walls and voids in burial vaults.

Diagram of the ground-
penetrating radar test at
Stowmarket showing the
existence of burial vaults (*in
yellow*). The largest signal
was from the area beneath
and beside the ledgerstone
marking the burial of Thomas
Blackerby.

Two strong signals were found at each church. The two at Shelley were not
in the most likely burial place for Elizabeth Tilney. At Stowmarket, however, an obvious sign of a vault lay under and to the right of the Blackerby
ledgerstone. But despite the apparent mixed success of the GPR testing, the
decision was made by the churches at both the parish and diocese levels to
grant permission, known as a faculty, to begin the phased operation.

At Shelley, the pews and a wooden floor had to be removed to conduct
the ground radar test. This revealed part of the ledgerstone with the now-
missing nameplate seen by Davy. So far, so good. The committee agreed
to remove the stone, along with a surrounding unmortared eighteenth-
century brick floor, both of which lay in a few inches of bedding sand.
Delicate dusting of the soil beneath the sand revealed discrete patches of
soil discolorations, signs of filled-in burial shafts. There were indications
of at least three grave shafts, one clearly cutting through all the rest—proving it to be the most recent interment. This finding was encouraging, since
Elizabeth Tilney's grave would likely intrude upon the space in which her
husband, Thomas, had been buried twenty-eight years before her. So to
move on, only one grave would be disturbed.

Careful brushing of the dust found beneath an unmarked ledgerstone at Shelley exposed the outline of a burial shaft with no apparent postburial disturbance of the ground.

Digging began, and five feet below the ground surface signs of a decomposed coffin holding the skeletal remains of what appeared to be a woman were discovered. If Elizabeth's nameplate were found on the coffin, or if the remains were those of a woman who died in her seventies, Elizabeth's estimated age at death, we would have the needed assurance that the right grave had been located and would proceed to the bone-sampling. But the complete clearance of the remains had to be left for the next day.

Meanwhile, work continued back at Stowmarket. At St. Peters and St. Marys Church, workmen had removed two floor stones next to the Blackerby ledgerstone, which revealed the domed roof of a brick vault lying beneath loose rubble used to raise the chancel floor in the Victorian-era renovations. This was a good candidate for a Blackerby vault, likely containing both Thomas and his wife, Katherine. But the bricks and mortar appeared to date to the Victorian time, well over a century later than the burials of Thomas and Katherine in the late seventeenth century. Nonetheless, the decision was made to drill a small hole in the roof of the vault and insert a fiber-optic viewer to look for two coffins. The fiber-optic viewer, a five-foot-long cane-like device with a tiny swivel video camera on the end, sent images of the vault interior to a viewing monitor. The monitor image clearly showed that the vault was completely intact and contained what appeared to be a stone shelf, possibly an inner tomb. This was encouraging enough to justify the enlargement of the excavation, which revealed the walled-up vault entrance. The subsequent removal of a few bricks opened a hole large enough to permit flash photographs to be taken of the vault interior.

At that point the committee halted the work to assess the photographs and to reconsider how much excavation would be required to gain access to the room. If there was any reason to believe that there might be two burials

A photo taken through a test hole in the Stowmarket vault showed an inner stone tomb that was wide enough for two individuals as well as brickwork that could be as old as the Blackerbys' interment, 1688, and revealed a decaying wooden brick mason's mallet left by mistake or perhaps by design before the vault was sealed.

Fiber-optic inspection of the inside of the possible Blackerby sealed burial vault distinctly showed an intact room and an inner tomb.

Smithsonian forensic anthropologist Dr. Douglas Owsley (*left*) and Suffolk archaeologist and historian Edward Martin inspect the wooden coffin and plate found in the Stowmarket inner tomb. The style of the plate and the age of death, seventy-four, still legible on the plate established this to be the tomb of John Boby, who died in 1817 at the age of seventy-four, and, next to him, his wife, Ann, who died in 1834.

in the vault and that the vault itself had been rebuilt during the Victorian renovations, then there would still be a good chance that the Blackerbys lay inside, and we would push on. The photos did in fact show that there was a stone tomb inside, exactly wide enough to hold two side-by-side coffins. Some of the bricks in the wall farthest from the camera appeared to be the color of seventeenth-century bricks, a possible sign of a rebuild.

Masons proceeded to open the vault entrance just enough to provide access to the vault. They then lifted one of the stones that sealed what appeared to be one part of a double stone tomb. This revealed a collapsed wooden coffin originally covered with black cloth fastened with decorative rows of large brass tacks. Resting on the wood in a chest-high position was an elaborate but very rusted sheet-metal plate known as a depositum plate. The plate was in the form of a tracery crown below angels, and at the center was a mostly illegible epitaph. Only the scrolled hand-painted letters "-ed" and the partially legible number "74" could be read. This appeared to be the last line in the epitaph, which traditionally records the person's age at death: "aged—." This man had died "aged 74." According to his ledgerstone, Blackerby died at seventy-six. So this was not our man. Also, the depositum plate was of a style much more recent than the 1688 date of Thomas Blackerby's burial.

There still remained the possibility that an earlier burial, possibly of a woman, lay next to him in the unopened side of the inner vault. The masons returned and removed another stone, opening enough of the remaining tomb to reveal its contents. There lay another collapsed but smaller wooden coffin with a depositum plate, but this time made of lead. The lead was cause for one last flicker of hope, until a closer look at the plate revealed eighteenth- to nineteenth-century-style angels with no epitaph. Indeed, both plates could be no older than circa 1770.[22] But it turned out the burials were not even that old. The final evidence came from high up on the south chancel wall. There a ledgerstone clearly stated, "Near this place are deposited the remains of John Boby, Gen: (late of Stowupland) who died 7 April, 1817 aged 74 years Also Ann, relict of John Boby, Gen: who died 25th of January 8, 1834, aged 84 years." So there was no need to expose any of the bones beneath the wooden coffin lids. Instead, we made a hasty retreat from the vault, leaving the Bobys once again to rest in peace.

Another avenue remained to be pursued. When the archaeologists had cleared space at the Boby vault entrance, a dome-covered vault with brick and mortar of a much older appearance was found. Unfortunately, a fiber-optic peek into that vault dashed hope once again. The monitor clearly showed what had to be scattered broken coffins, probably disarticulated bone among them, and brick rubble spilling down the entrance. It was wisely decided that even if this was the Blackerby vault, chances of coming up with a reliable sample were not worth the expense and damage that entry would cause. At that point it was extremely comforting to know that the possible remains of Elizabeth had already been found at Shelley. The Stowmarket venture had ended.

Back at Shelley All Saints, the Suffolk archaeologist, donning his sanitized suit, gloves, and mask to prevent his own DNA from contaminating the

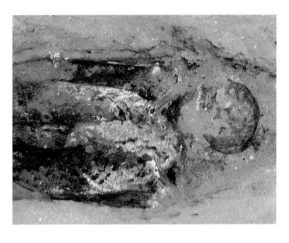

The Shelley woman, Elizabeth Gosnold Tilney (?), in the remnants of her hexagonal wooden coffin. The remains were only partially uncovered, minimally disturbed, and respectfully and quickly reburied.

woman's remains, proceeded to uncover as much of the skeleton and trace of the coffin as the deep, narrow shaft would allow. At that point, Dr. Owsley arrived to assess more precisely signs of sex and age. After an agonizing hour, there were great sighs of relief when he concluded that this was indeed a woman of advanced age. But the fact that she had almost all of her teeth and that they were not overly worn cast some doubt in Owsley's mind that this was a woman old enough at her time of death to be Elizabeth.

Again, Elizabeth's birth date is unrecorded, but her age at time of death can be estimated by reviewing other documented family history. Her first child was born in 1600 and the last in 1612. Therefore, one can assume that she married Thomas Tilney in the late sixteenth century, perhaps at age twenty to twenty-six, the latter being the average age that women married at that time. Therefore, she would probably have been between sixty-eight and seventy-four when she died in 1646. Owsley could not determine in the field whether the Shelley woman was as old as her late sixties to early seventies, so he took additional bone samples for future laboratory age testing. The grave was left otherwise undisturbed. Following this sampling procedure, the All Saints vicar offered a eulogy and prayer, and the burial shaft was refilled.[23]

DNA does not always survive in buried remains, and because more than three and a half centuries had passed since Elizabeth Gosnold Tilney died, there existed the possibility that no DNA would be found in the Shelley samples. Fortunately, that was not the case; scientists were able to extract a DNA sequence. And although the sequence was considered "minimal and degraded," there was enough of a DNA signature to compare with the sequence from the Jamestown captain. So far, so good.

The results of the comparative test proved as surprising as they were disappointing. The disappointment came in that the comparison soundly "excluded" the possibility that the Jamestown captain and the Shelley woman were maternal relatives.[24] That would seem to rule out Bartholomew Gosnold as the Jamestown captain. But at the same time, that could only be true if the Shelley woman was in fact Elizabeth Gosnold Tilney. Failure to find a coffin plate positively identifying the Shelley woman as Elizabeth and the less-than-certain determination made at the church that the Shelley woman could be as old as sixty-eight to seventy-four left the DNA mismatch inconclusive.

Further testing of the Shelley burial samples to more precisely determine age provided the surprise. Analysis of the samples for calcium and a closer inspection of her teeth convinced the specialists that the Shelley woman was thirty-eight to forty-six when she died.[25] She was far too young to be Elizabeth Gosnold Tilney. Consequently, it appeared that after all the months of historical research and negotiations with the church officials, the Shelley burial might be of no help at all in identifying the Jamestown captain.

But the case for proving that the Shelley burial is not Elizabeth Gosnold Tilney may not be as ironclad as it appears. Some of the tests that determined that the Shelley woman was too young to be Bartholomew's sister were called into question by the Advisory Panel on the Archaeology of Christian Burials in England (APACBE).[26] That organization is made up of a group of archaeologists and scientists who work regularly on burial issues in England. They concluded that the possibility that the Shelley burial was Elizabeth Gosnold Tilney cannot be ruled out, basing their decision on what British archaeologists had learned by aging burials removed by archaeologists in 1984 to 1986 from tombs at Christ Church in East London.[27] There were records of the age at death of many of these burials. The Christ Church archaeologists submitted selected skeletons to anthropologists to determine each burial's age based on standard macroscopic and microscopic methods. But the archaeologists also made sure the tests were not influenced by prior knowledge of the recorded ages of the deceased. As a rule, the scientists aged the older burials as much as fifteen years younger than their historically recorded age. Based on the results of the Christ Church study, the Advisory Panel concluded that the Shelley burial age determined by testing in the United States plus the likely fifteen-year error factor brought her close to the known age of Elizabeth, sixty-eight to seventy-four years. If this were true, of course, the failure of the DNA from the Shelley woman and the Jamestown captain to match would indeed rule out Bartholomew Gosnold as the Jamestown burial.

But the American and British scientists did then agree that other tests besides determining age at death could add to the evidence chain. Because the chemical composition of people's bones can reflect what they ate during their lives, and because what people ate in the seventeenth century derived mostly from local sources only, tests to recover certain bone chemistry can determine where people came from. Of particular interest in the bone chemistry is the relative presence of two types of stable carbon isotopes: the C_3 isotope, found in the bones of people who primarily eat wheat, and the C_4 isotope, found in the bones of people who primarily eat corn. The scientists agreed that a reading of the Shelley burial's stable isotopes should give similar dietary statistics to those of the Jamestown captain, that is, if he was in fact raised in the wheat-rich county of Suffolk, England. Also, a carbon-14 dating reading of the Shelley sample could pin down the date of the burial, which would give additional evidence to determine if the Shelley woman is Ann Framlingham (who preceded Elizabeth Gosnold Tilney as lady of Shelley Manor) or Elizabeth, who died more than fifty years later. The isotope test showed similar C_4 readings for the Shelley woman and the Jamestown man, suggesting at least that the Jamestown man, like the Shelley woman, could have been raised in Suffolk. This can be considered one more shred of evidence that the Jamestown burial is Bartholomew. The carbon-14 reading of the Shelley samples turned out to be the year 1690, plus or minus fifty years, which tends to rule out Ann, who died in 1590, but offers the possibility that the Shelley burial is Elizabeth, who died in 1646.[28]

So is the Jamestown captain Bartholomew Gosnold or not? Obviously, a final, unequivocal conclusion is not possible to attain without a perfect DNA match. There was no such match. There are certainly good reasons to doubt that the Shelley woman is Elizabeth Gosnold. If she is not Elizabeth Gosnold, of course, the mismatch identifies no one. Nevertheless, one can still review the other evidence to determine the most likely identity of the Jamestown man: the captain's staff, the well-constructed coffin, the age at death, the orientation of the burial, the record of Gosnold's ceremonial August 1607 interment, his English and possible Suffolk diet, signs of a healthy gentlemanly lifestyle, the dates of artifacts covering his grave—and of course, the DNA comparison with a nonrelative has to be a mismatch if the Jamestown captain is Bartholomew Gosnold.

Remember that the Jamestown burial's location, outside the fort, could be testimony against this captain's being Gosnold. Discovery of the twenty-four 1607 graves inside the west wall of the fort seems to establish that the colonists did strictly follow the Company's directive to hide any sickness and death from the Indians. Why, then, would the settlers break the rules and advertise the death of anyone, especially a leader like Gosnold, by burying him in plain sight outside the fort wall? One possible explanation is that the burial ceremony, with all its pomp and gunfire, could have been intended as a sign of strength rather than of weakness; that is to say, a feigned show of force outside made to disguise the rash of deaths within could still point to Gosnold.

Looking from another perspective, if this burial is not Gosnold, then who could it be? If this man expired after 1607, the year Gosnold died, then he did so at a time when it is likely the Indians knew full well the Englishmen were mortal. In that case the unknown captain might be none other than the chronicler of 1607, Gabriel Archer, who died during the 1609–10 "starving time."[29] But anyone of that status dying after the 1608 church was built would likely be buried in the fort and in the church or near it. The same holds true for another prominent settler who died at Jamestown in 1610, Sir Ferdinando Wenman, appointed "Master of the Ordinance" by Lord De La Warre.[30] But it is unlikely that Wenman, a knight, would be buried with a captain's leading staff. And the presence of the captain's leading staff rules out any possibility that the Jamestown burial is that of the most prominent of all the settlers, the Lord De La Warre, who died en route to Jamestown in 1618 and whose body was brought to Virginia (undoubtedly Jamestown) for burial.[31] The royally appointed Governor De La Warre, a lord, would certainly have been buried in Argall's new church, even if the church was not completely finished by the time his body arrived in 1618.

But back to our earlier question, Is the Shelley woman Elizabeth Gosnold Tilney? On the one hand, she is identified by the same type of circumstantial evidence identifying Bartholomew Gosnold: documents (ancestry,

Full-body reconstruction of Captain Bartholomew Gosnold based on forensic and documentary evidence. (National Museum of Natural History, Smithsonian, Studio Ice)

burial place, and "older" age at death), archaeology (gravestone, undisturbed condition), and forensic anthropology (sex and field assessment of age). On the other hand, the combination of the anthropological tests (teeth and calcium minus the possible fifteen-year error factor, stable isotopes, carbon-14 dating) tends to establish that she is not Bartholomew's sister. As it stands, then, while the results are not incontrovertible, the evidence leans strongly toward the conclusion that the Jamestown burial is that of Captain Bartholomew Gosnold.

Regardless of any definitive conclusion, the Shelley-Jamestown DNA research process itself is a significant achievement in historical archaeology and anthropological science. The fact that DNA could survive in burials more than three centuries old and survive to the degree that it was even possible to compare samples from two graves separated by an ocean is a milestone. Perhaps of more significance yet, the exercise in DNA detective work managed to rescue from historical obscurity Captain Bartholomew Gosnold, the overlooked principal figure in the planting of the Virginia colony.

DEPARTED GENTLEMEN, 1607

Near the captain, removal of the plowzone that lay over the longest fort rowhouse revealed more signs of burials. Twenty-four soil stains the size of single graves and two apparent multiple graves were found aligned parallel or perpendicular to the fort wall. The position of one of the apparently double-sized shafts suggested that it might possibly be a backfilled cellar in front of the building hearth instead of a burial site. The other apparent double shaft seemed to have been disturbed at one corner by the construction of a chimney in the long rowhouse. Since there was every reason to believe the rowhouse was built in 1611 or earlier, this construction above them would indicate that these were very early graves. Datable objects in the shafts might also help date the burials and provide the date after which the rowhouse was built.

In order to establish the nature of the ambiguous shaft and the date of the possible double graves, both features were excavated. Digging proved that the shafts were in fact double burials holding the skeletal remains of four European men. The two men who lay partially beneath the chimney died in their late teens or early twenties. One of the two men in the other grave died in his mid-twenties, the other in his mid-forties. No artifacts were

Excavation of two double burials, likely to date to the summer of 1607, beneath the foundations of the James Fort rowhouse and surrounded by twenty-one other single burials.

recovered from the burials or the grave-shaft fill except for a few fragments of Virginia Indian pottery and flakes of rock from Indian manufacture of stone tools or weapons. The absence of European artifacts in colonial deposits like this grave shaft suggests that the men died very early in the James Fort period. It might be asked why early burials were allowed to take up useful space within the fort—unless the dwellers were hiding death from their Virginia Indian adversaries. If this was the explanation for the location of the graves, it could be likely that these burials were the final resting places of the twenty-one gentlemen, a surgeon, and two "others" George Percy listed as dying between August 6 and September 19, 1607.[32] In that case, the ages at death could be clues to their identities, especially those of the two men with the great difference in age. On August 24, 1607, Percy recorded that Edward Harrington and George Walker died and were buried on the same day. English church records of christenings established that an Edward Harrington would be twenty-five and a George Walker would be

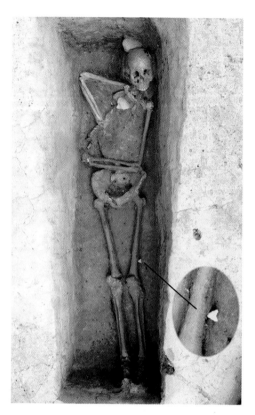

Skeletal remains of a boy in his mid-teens found buried just inside and along the fort's west wall show how he met a violent death: an arrow wound in his left leg and apparent injuries to his shoulders.

forty-five in the year 1607. If these are our men, and as they have such common English names there can be some doubt, then it is likely that the other double grave and the single graves about them are the resting places of those unfortunate colonists of that late 1607 summer.

One of the first to fall in the fateful 1607 summer was the boy who was killed during an assault on the colonists by the Virginia Indians on May 25. Excavation of a single burial of a male in his mid-teens, oriented and adjacent to the fort's west wall, revealed what may well be the remains of that boy. There could be little doubt what killed him: a wound to the leg, caused by an arrow tipped with a stone point that was found next to his leg. Preliminary analysis also determined that he had injuries to his shoulders and had his jaw bone eaten away from an abscessed tooth.[33] Four boys were among the first settlers: Samuell Collier, Nathaniel Pecock, James Brumfield, and Richard Mutton. There is some evidence to suggest that Collier and Pecock were alive in the 1610s, but there is no record that Brumfield or Mutton lived that long. Either Brumfield or Mutton could well have been this arrow victim.[34]

Signs of life and death in bone at Jamestown have not all come from burials. Fill in the west bulwark trench, almost certainly thrown there after 1611 and maybe as late as Argall's 1617 rehabilitation of the town, contained not only the rich evidence of Anglo-Indian presence in the fort but also, and surprisingly, a third of a human skull. Enough of the complete skull was there to determine that it came from a middle-aged man who, before apparently dying as a result of a violent blow to the back of the head from a stone implement (like a stone axe), had undergone attempted surgery.[35] Two circular cuts into the skull before death indicate that the "chirurgeons" at Jamestown attempted to cut a nickel-sized hole in the victim's head, a process known as trepanning, apparently in order to relieve the pressure of a swelling brain. The drill never made it through the skull in either attempt; in fact, two cuts were made at one location, perhaps indicating that the patient could not be restrained enough to finish the job. The patient may have died in surgery, since there are signs that the surgeons decided to perform an autopsy, presumably to inspect and learn from the injured brain. The upper edge of the fragment had been sawn, the marks indicating the complete removal of the top of the man's skull. Forensic analysis was able to determine that the man was a European. The bone fabric was full of lead absorbed unknowingly through life by someone probably eating from lead-laden pewter or lead-glazed

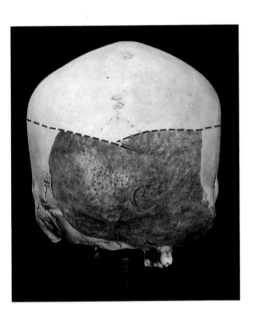

Left: Fill in the west bulwark trench yielded this rear section of a human skull amid discarded garbage and trash of ca. 1610. Forensic analysis determined this to be from a mature European man who may have died during a surgical procedure known as trepanning—an attempt to save the injured man by drilling a hole in the skull. Saw marks indicate the procedure was unsuccessful and that an autopsy was performed. *Right:* Eighteenth-century drawing illustrating the trepanning procedure initiated on at least one Jamestown colonist. (Science Museum Pictorial/Science and Society Picture Library, London)

plates with pewter spoons and drinking from pewter or lead-glazed cups. A person carrying so much residual lead in his bones, and dying during the first years of the colony, would have to be an immigrant and certainly not a Virginia Indian.

Excavation of the rest of the ditch failed to reveal any more parts of a skeleton, so the single skull fragment must represent the medical waste of one of the surgeons. The rest of the body may well lie among the fourteen burials found beneath the nearby governor's house. This partial skull underscores again the great risk of living at Jamestown. It shows, too, that the chirurgeons were hard at work not only in trying to save the injured but also in trying to improve their own skills.

The clear archaeological indications of death throughout the site of early Jamestown underscore the enormous courage it took to come to Jamestown from England during those first few years. There was danger from every quarter: salt in drinking water from the river, well water fouled from unsanitary use, disease from insects, empty food stores, accidents, warfare with the Virginia Indians, and, of course, jealousy and political battles within ranks. After the first few months of settlement, it is unlikely that the great risk for an "adventuring person" who wanted to join the Virginia colony was totally unknown back in England. One can only conclude that even the slim chance for a better life in Virginia outweighed the prospects of death amid the foul marshes at Jamestown or simply staying at home.

FOUR

REANIMATING JAMESTOWN

By studying the documentary records left behind by the Jamestown settlers, the four-hundred-year-old footprints of the fort the settlers built, and the remains of the settlers themselves as well as the artifacts they created or brought with them, we have been able to generate images of the built landscape of Jamestown and of those who dwelled in it. These varied remnants have also deepened our understanding of many episodes in Jamestown's history. These artifacts—especially the more than 2 million individual objects so far discovered at Jamestown—can also shed light on the states of mind of those who came to Jamestown. The things the settlers brought with them and the things they created while at Jamestown are the most literal as well as symbolic embodiments of what the adventurers thought they would find in Virginia and how they adapted to what they did find. Perhaps even more than the documentary, architectural, and skeletal evidence the colonists left behind, these artifacts enable us to trace a process that began the transformation of Englishmen into Americans. All of these remnants of Jamestown life yield the most meaning when juxtaposed to a document that states explicitly the intentions and preconceptions of the Jamestown colonists—the Virginia Company shareholders' instructions to the settlers. This juxtaposition can help us take a fresh perspective on the colonists' anticipations as well as their accomplishments, leading to a more complex story than the simpler tale of poor preparation and incompetence.

It is undeniable that the Virginia Company officials and the adventurers made some big mistakes. Wearing body armor in the blistering Virginia summer certainly could take a far greater toll on the population than the

The Jamestown Rediscovery collection includes more than 2 million objects, at least one-third found in undisturbed deposits dating to the early James Fort period (1607–10).

best Powhatan archer. Whatever food made it to the colonies must have quickly spoiled in the heat and humidity. And, again, the crew that had to deal with these inappropriate supplies was one John Smith described as "poor gentlemen, tradesmen, serving men, libertines . . . ten times more fit to spoil a commonwealth than either to begin one or but help to maintain one."[1]

But we have already seen that poor preparation and incompetent management are hardly the whole story of what went on at Jamestown; they do not even suffice as explanation for the hardships the settlers suffered. We know, too, that Jamestown was not wholly a failure—that a permanent English presence in America did, in fact, take hold. Careful study in particular of artifacts great and small testifies to the level of skill and knowledge of both the Virginia Company leadership and its Jamestown adventurers, offering a new and potentially more objective way to learn what the colonists did, driven by the Virginia Company plan, for the well-being of themselves and their sponsors.

The Virginia Company crafted the instructions for settlement with which the colonists arrived on the Virginia shore before the would-be colonists even left England. This survival manual speaks most directly to the preparation the colonists received. Richard Hakluyt (1552–1616), a geographer, clergyman, translator, collector and editor of adventure narratives, and advocate for the westward expansion of English power, was most likely the author. He edited, translated, and inspired many volumes of firsthand narratives of adventure and discovery, the most notable of which are his *Divers Voyages* (1582), *Principal Navigations, Voiages, and Discoueries of the English Nation* (1589), and its second edition, much enlarged, *The Principal Navigations, Voiages, Traffiques and Discoueries of the English Nation* (three volumes, 1598, 1599, 1600). Thanks to Hakluyt, although the English at Jamestown were late in New World colonization, they would not face Virginia without benefit of the experience of those who went before them. In 1606 Hakluyt was likely one of the chief promoters of the petition to the king for a patent to colonize Virginia. When the ships, supplies, and men set sail from Blackwall for the voyage to Virginia, Hakluyt and the Company made sure they carried the "instructions to the colonists from the Virginia Company shareholders 1606" with them. These directives laid down precise rules for locating, defending, feeding, supporting, and ruling the Virginia colony. The list was well drawn, and, as it turned out, much of it was crucial advice.[2]

In the following summary, the Virginia Company's instructions can be organized by category:

Location

The strongest, most wholesome and fertile place is to be chosen, on a river that has a safe entrance harbor and is navigable farthest inland.

For defense, a town site is to be chosen one hundred miles from the sea, if possible, or, if nearer, on an island; at a point on the river narrow enough to protect the settlement from ships by musket fire from both banks; and with no natives living between the site and the seacoast.

For trade, the town site should be near the river channel, providing easy access between ships and the shore.

For cultivation, the site should already be cleared of trees and undergrowth.

Defense

Scouts should be stationed at the river mouth.

Twenty men should be assigned to fortify the settlement.

Above all else, any death or sickness should be hidden, lest the Indians discover the settlers are mortal men.

Indians should never be allowed to carry the guns.

Cultivation

Twenty men should be assigned to clear, cultivate, and plant.

Planting should not be done in low or marshy ground.

The Indians should not be offended, but traded with for corn, in order to conceal the colonists' own planting until it can be determined if the English corn will grow in Virginia.

Economy

Forty men under Newport and Gosnold should be assigned to seek precious metals inland.

The high value of trade goods should be protected by prohibiting the wage-earning sailors or any other unauthorized persons from trading with the Indians.

Governance

Sails and anchors should be taken off the ship to stop anyone from escaping the colony.

Official reports of the colony's progress should be sent to the Company.

No unauthorized person should be allowed to return to England.

All letters should be censured, deleting any discouraging words.

God should be served and feared or the colony will fail.[3]

Did the colonists follow these orders? And were the orders wise? As to the first question, the buried record of Jamestown makes a strong case that the settlers most often did obey the instructions. When they did not, it can often be established that they had good reason for diverging from the rules; in such cases, we can see these early English settlers beginning to transform themselves into Americans. On some occasions failure to honor the Company rules—whether by negligence or simply the inescapable facts the settlers confronted—attested to the wisdom of those rules by leading to regrettable consequences.

The exact location of the fort itself, as determined by archaeological excavation, indicates that the directives for choosing a settlement site were taken seriously. The James Fort site was, in fact, the strongest location for the settlement: an island defensible by its natural water hazard. The site also followed instructions in being located on a Virginia river that had a safe entrance harbor, reached the farthest inland, and had a deepwater channel close to shore. And the settlement was built on an abandoned, open Indian field.[4] But Jamestown was not one hundred miles from the sea, was not built at a narrow point in the river, and was certainly not lacking in native neighbors. How to account for these features of the island that should have disqualified it by Company standards?

The answer is simple. Rather than ignoring those qualities, the leaders, faced with the actual Virginia geography that confronted them, threw out the unrealistic terms of the shareholders. There simply is no Virginia river with a deep channel between banks that are musket-range apart (two hundred yards), one hundred miles from the sea. Nor was there any site up any river with no Indians living between it and the sea.

Unfortunately, meeting the first Company priority directive—a secure location—did lead the colonists to compromise on the second Company priority directive: a "wholesome" location. Swampy James Island is definitely not wholesome. The threat of attack from the Spanish and the reality of the initial Virginia Indian assaults appeared a greater threat to survival than any difficulty getting freshwater and fresh air. Still, the concern for a wholesome location was not jettisoned entirely. The Jamestown marshes were interspersed with enough rich and elevated ground to build a fortified town and to plant crops. The fort was built, as archaeology has discovered, on the island's highest ground. In addition, the river must have appeared fresh enough during that May landing time to make the lack of a freshwater spring on the island seem a minor drawback. So in choosing the location for their settlement, the colonists did follow some of the Company's wise advice while reasonably adapting the rest of it to the realities of the Virginia geography.

As to the Company's other instructions for achieving security, the signs in the ground make clear the men's attempt to follow the Company directive to "fortify." A bulwark made of tree branches went up at once. Virginia reality struck quickly, however. The Indian assault of May 25 made it quite clear that a brush fort would not do. There followed a frantic construction program that archaeology shows was nothing short of Herculean. Consider the following: If the council followed the Company directive to assign just twenty of the men to build the fort, then in just under three weeks' time, according to archaeological evidence, these few men, some likely even gentlemen, cut, hauled, divided, and sometimes split at least 610 four- to eight-hundred-pound trees, then dug a trench at least 1,030 feet long and two and a half feet deep to seat them in. That meant each of the twenty men had to fell, haul, dig, and plant one or two trees a day, and so a total of twenty to forty, for nineteen days straight (May 28–June 15, 1607) in what would likely have been a hot, humid Virginia early summer.[5] For comparison purposes, it might be noted that the contractors who built the Jamestown set for the New Line Cinema film *The New World* in 2004 also constructed a triangular palisaded fort, slightly smaller than the original, with trees of the same size, in about three weeks—using power equipment. And at the same time, the settlers split trees for enough clapboards (rough planks) to load the three ships returning to England. Little wonder that by August, Percy listed exertion from carrying palisades as one of the causes of the rash of deaths afflicting the new outpost. Although at a great cost, the men were successful at least in this: they had fortified themselves against Indian attack. Arrows do not seem to account for many of the losses.

Archaeological investigation has also made it clear that whoever did perish very early on was buried inside the fort. The settlers' losses would be out of sight, just as the Company directed. There was one exception, however: the burial of Gosnold, the captain. His grave, outside the fort walls, looks like a big mistake, a refusal to follow the Company's overarching rule never to let the enemy see death and sickness. Advertising weakness, especially the death of a leader ceremoniously buried, could indeed convince the Indians that the English were not immortal—that they were, in fact, in dire straits behind the walls. There is a plausible explanation for Captain Gosnold's very visible funeral, however. Perhaps the funeral with all its pomp and gunfire was meant to be not only a proper farewell to the Jamestown prime mover but also a feinting show of force to the enemy. In any case, someone as revered as Gosnold had to get the full traditional twenty-one-gun salute and the traditional space of honor outside the fort/town walls in Smithfield, the military parade ground. Still, even if the honor shown Gosnold was strategically unwise in the New World context, all of the other twenty-four graves located so far that can be dated to the very earliest fort occupation are located within the fort walls. As the Company had advised, deaths were hidden from the enemy—or, at least, they were for a while. Discovery of a circa-1610–30 mass burial ground on the high ground far west of the fort shows that the Indians soon enough would have learned not to buy the immortality charade.

Even relatively minor experimental attempts at cutting, hauling, and seating palisade posts have given Jamestown Rediscovery archaeologists insight into the Herculean efforts the original colonists undertook to build James Fort in only nineteen days.

The New World movie set, based on some of the Jamestown Rediscovery architectural evidence, accurately depicts the James Fort of 1607 and its early shelters. (*The New World*, © MMVI, New Line Productions, Inc. All rights reserved. Photo courtesy of New Line Productions, Inc.)

An iron scupper found in the east bulwark, a special seventeenth-century tool for digging the narrow, deep trenches required to seat palisades.

Of course, the best way for the Company to hide from the Indians any physical problems was to make sure there were none. In preparation for fighting health hazards, the Company sent medicines, physicians, pharmacists, and surgeons. These professions combined to make up the healing arts of the time: the surgeons cut, the physicians collected and philosophized, and the apothecaries drugged.[6] There are archaeological signs of the presence and the practice of these healers at Jamestown. Drug jars (albarellos) are the most numerous of pottery vessels in the artifact collection, and they are commonly found among the oldest deposits. Used by apothecaries—two of whom were named among the first supply—these vessels were designed as containers for medicines and salves. It is likely that the settlers had access to whatever medicines were considered helpful against the known diseases of the times. The Company also sent a leading university-trained physician, a plant and herb specialist named John Fleischer. He likely searched the alien Virginia wilderness for new miracle cures, but there is no record that he succeeded before dying himself in 1608. Still, it is logical to assume that some of these albarellos were intended to double as containers for the export of any new medical discoveries. As it turned out, however, great quantities of sassafras, thought to be a cure for syphilis, are the only documented Virginia medicine sent back to England.

Medical instruments and what can be considered medical waste from an operation testify to the presence of surgeons and their practice. The spatula mundani, an iron tool used to cure constipation, and part of a boring instrument used to extract bullets were found, both surgeon's instruments that could have come from a surgeon's tool chest sent to the colony in 1609. The most graphic archaeological sign of surgery, however, was the human skull fragment found in the fill of the west bulwark ditch, circa 1609–12 (see chap. 3). The two circular marks on the bone are clear signs that someone, likely one of the surgeons, attempted to heal the man by performing

Delft drug jars, made to hold medicines and salves, are the most common
European pottery form recovered from James Fort–period deposits.

trepanation (drilling a hole in the skull to relieve pressure and remove bone
splinters) before he finally died. Death did not stop the surgeons, the saw
marks on the upper edge of the skull fragment indicating an attempt to
study the effects of the injury by an autopsy. The surgeons were actively
pursuing their practice even in the harsh conditions under which they had
to operate.

Did the settlers follow the Company regulations by keeping guns out of
the hands of Indians? There is no archaeological evidence to speak to that
question. But from hints in the documents as well as from the discovery of
great numbers of contact-period Indian artifacts (like pottery) and signs
of the Indian manufacture of stone tools, weapons, and shell beads, we
do know that some Indians were inside the palisade walls. Weapons were
surely within their reach at any time. John Smith complained about the
"Dutch" glassmakers instructing the Indians in the use of firearms. Smith
wrote as well of two Indian brothers stealing pistols and of an Indian who
accidentally turned into a suicide bomber when he tried to dry out powder
on a breastplate over an open fire. So the arms restriction, an obviously
key Company directive, seems to have been ignored in the long run by
the colonials, if not at first, then eventually. That was a tragic mistake. In
the 1622 Indian revolt, some of the Indians living in close contact with English settlements in the Virginia hinterlands actually used the colonists'

own weapons and iron-cutting tools against them.[7] On the other hand, the Jamestown home base was spared by an Indian forewarning. In the end, despite the neglect of this particular rule, James Fort itself never fell to an enemy during its lifetime.

As for the colonists' attention to Company rules relating to cultivation, archaeology gives some clues. The discovery of palisade lines branching out from the triangular footprint of the fort suggests the existence of protected spaces outside the fort, likely locations for gardens. The flag-shaped enclosure on the Zúñiga map is probably one such garden, located on easily secured high ground near the fort. The choice of such a location indicates an effort by the twenty assigned farmers to avoid clearing and planting in low marshy ground, just as the Company advised. The garden depicted on the Zúñiga map also seems to include carefully divided rectangular planting beds. This evidence lends credibility to Percy's report that the colonists had planted two mountains (ridges) that by mid-July produced corn that "sprang a man's height" despite the late planting in the middle of May.[8] Crop failure must have followed, however. Famine is the primary culprit Percy cited in his listing of the deaths of twenty-five gentlemen in August and September.

The 1606–12 drought, recently discovered by archaeologists, must have gone against any chance of success for the late planting.[9]

Artifacts discovered in the fort attest to the colonists' effort to obey another of the Company's rules regarding cultivation, that early gardening attempts be hidden until the viability of the English seeds in Virginia soil had been determined. These artifacts— European beads of glass and copper, jettons, and squares of sheet copper, all undoubtedly traded to the more accommodating Indians in exchange for corn—show the colonists' attempt to conceal their own efforts at self-sufficiency. Indian-made bowls found among the colonists' rubbish and trash possibly were the means of getting the corn into the fort.

Among the artifacts that tell the most about the colonists' efforts to fulfill the

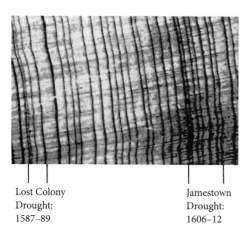

Lost Colony
Drought:
1587–89

Jamestown
Drought:
1606–12

Bald cypress growth-ring stress indicates two droughts, each during the very difficult years of English attempts at Virginia settlement. (The University of Arkansas Tree-Ring Laboratory)

Samples of the collection of copper found in ca.-1607–10 fort deposits. Captain John Smith reported on the great value of copper and glass beads in the earliest trade for food between colonists and Powhatan's Tsenacomacans.

A variety of trade beads.

This late sixteenth-century painting depicts copper pendants worn by the coastal Virginia Indians. There is evidence that the colonists at Jamestown brought great quantities of copper with them to Virginia to trade for food. (From *The American Drawings of John White*, vol. 2; © The Trustees of the British Museum)

charge of the shareholders are the many signs of manufacture for profit.[10] After all, Jamestown came into being for one overarching reason: to make money for the Virginia Company investors. Fortification and self-sufficiency were to be achieved primarily so that the settlers could turn their attention to generating whatever Virginia had to offer for export. The artifacts unearthed at Jamestown give plentiful proof of the colonists' focus on this mission.

Again, the first ships home carried the most readily available commodity for export, split planks. Well-used iron axes and wedges found in the early deposits are evidence for the production of these rough boards. Excavations also uncovered signs of early pit sawing. Just short of the point where the west fort palisade line met the now eroded shoreline, digging revealed a rectangular pit containing what appeared to be decayed sawdust at the bottom. This regularly shaped and backfilled hole lay beneath a ditch parallel to the fort—the latter apparently the beginning of a bulwark ditch, since its shape mirrors that of its sister defensive outwork at the south corner of the triangle (see illustration on p. 60). The fact that the sawdust-filled, squared pit lay beneath the bulwark ditch shows that the saw pit was set up very early in the fort's life. Pit sawing was a simple way to produce wainscot (fairly dressed planks), another timber product to send home. These pits were operated by two men, one at the upper and one at the lower end of the saw, who alternately pulled down and pushed on the saw handles to carve boards from logs laid between their stations. Toiling with timber for export was certainly in keeping with Company policy.

Site of a saw pit at the west bulwark.

The fort was also meant to serve as the base from which forty men under the command of Christopher Newport and Bartholomew Gosnold could probe inland for precious metals—especially for gold. The president and council did indeed send men upriver, probably to conduct the Company-directed "mineral search." Voyages to the hinterlands of the Chesapeake and its rivers followed. No gold turned up, although "gold refiners" and mineral men came to Jamestown in 1608–10, probably bringing with them the metallurgical equipment found during the excavations of the earliest deposits.[11] These included the lower ceramic boiler (cucurbit) and the upper glass-collecting cover (the alembic) from a still (possibly intended to create the nitric acid required for separating gold from silver), distilling dishes, dippers, and melting crucibles. Whether this equipment was ever used or was just broken and tossed away as the dreams of gold proved unfounded cannot be known. Still, the colonists arrived equipped for prospecting, however unrealistic their hopes.

Another of the Company's hopes for getting rich quick lay in the discovery and export of precious stones. While diamonds and rubies were not to be found, among the artifacts datable to James Fort's first three years are a number of colorful semiprecious stones such as amethysts, garnets, and quartz crystals. These were possibly appraised—undoubtedly to great disappointment—by the jewelers the Company sent to Jamestown in 1608.

Another scheme for exploiting minerals was the making of brass, which required copper and zinc. Certain Company shareholders were connected with the English copper industry, and thousands of strips and shavings of English copper were found on-site, most in 1607–10 contexts.[12] There is no doubt that some of the copper was there to trade with the Indians for corn, venison, fish, and fowl, a plan that quickly fell apart when the sailors flooded the market with copper, leading to its devaluation. The Company's explicit warning against such an eventuality apparently either went unheeded or was out of the colonists' control, but the wisdom of that warning was demonstrated by the event. The devaluation of copper seriously added to the food shortage. However, much of this hoard of copper scraps was likely sent to Jamestown to be processed with Virginia zinc into brass for export. Crucibles with copper residue and a plug of copper from a crucible show that these scraps were used in experiments in the colony. Was brass produced? There is no processed brass in the archaeological collection, implying that this hope, too, proved false. A report by Don Pedro de Zúñiga as early as August 22, 1607, confirms that the colonists hoped to find the material to make the copper alloy "bronce" (brass).[13] In any case, archaeological evidence demonstrates that the colonists made a concerted effort to live up to the Company's industrial expectations.

Documents and artifacts also give hard evidence of the Company's hope for profit from another industry: glassmaking. In 1608 "eight Dutchmen and Poles"—the "Dutchmen" probably Germans—arrived at Jamestown at Company expense, sent there to make "trials" of glass as well as pitch, tar,

An alchemist surrounded by his metallurgy equipment; similar pieces have been found at Jamestown. (*The Alchemist,* Cornelis Bega, 1663, J. Paul Getty Museum, Los Angeles; digital image courtesy of the Getty's Open Content Program)

Evidence of copper smelting, which may have been used in attempts to produce brass.

Below: Ceramics made for metallurgy found at Jamestown, including a distilling dish (*left front*); earthenware dipper (*center*); and German crucibles.

and soap ash. Evidence of glassmaking at the fort site abounds. Among the collections are heat-resistant clay crucibles and melting pots containing melted sand and glass residue, glassmaking slag (froth), and more than 7,000 pieces of European window-glass cullet (broken fragments typically used during glass manufacture)—all clear signs that the Germans practiced their craft. In two short months, enough had been produced for a "trial of glass," probably ingots, to be sent back to England. It does appear, however, that the industry was short-lived: the "Dutchmen" eventually threw their lot in with the Indians and smuggled weapons. This life of espionage ended with the death of the imported glassmakers at the hands of the natives by late 1609. Apparently no other attempt at glass production was made until the Company sent Italian glassmakers to Virginia in 1620. A site of glass furnaces made of cobble was found on the mainland next to the Jamestown Island isthmus by National Park Service archaeologists in the 1940s.[14] They concluded that this effort was also short-lived; no evidence was found that this operation produced anything more than glass ingots.

The recovery of a multitude of locally made clay tobacco pipes and pieces of a broken ceramic vessel (a sagger) used in pottery firing indicates more efforts to live up to the Company business plan. Pipe maker Robert Cotton was sent to Virginia with the second supply in 1608. There is every reason to believe that the distinctive pipe type found everywhere in deposits dating to the early fort period—made of local clay and impressed with a multiple fleur-de-lis diamond-shaped mark—was molded by Cotton and fired in his small saggers. These pipes, along with bricks found in the same early deposits and in fort building hearths, must represent the first successfully mass-produced, finished commodity of Anglo-America. The pipes were also apparently exported, for an identical example was found in the English city of Plymouth.[15]

Virginia-grown tobacco, of course, eventually came along to fill the colonial pipes and to give the Company and individual settlers a return on time and money.[16] But it was years before a tobacco strain was discovered that would produce sufficient bulk for export. That might be why hoes are conspicuously absent in deposits dating before 1610, although the circa-1620s well held three, all of them narrow grubbing hoes suited for tending tobacco fields.

The colony's economic viability required a number of support industries, and the Company accordingly sent out a number of skilled men—carpenters, blacksmiths, brickmakers, bricklayers and masons, coopers, tailors,

Evidence of glassmaking at James Fort includes crucibles with melted sand and glass in them and broken fragments of English window-glass waste (cullet), brought over to aid in the glassmaking trials at Jamestown.

These distinctive tobacco pipes and fragments of a pottery-making device known as a sagger suggest that the 1608 colonist Robert Cotton, "tobacco-pipe-maker," made these, one of the first commercial Jamestown products.

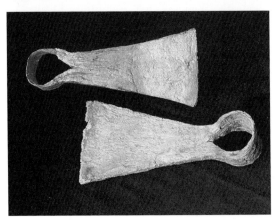

Two hoes, perhaps for tobacco cultivation, from the Smithfield well, which was filled during the beginning of the Virginia tobacco boom.

hunters and fishermen—many of whom left their mark on the archaeological record.[17] Felling axes, hatchets, and gouges, all tools of carpentry primarily for the gathering, dressing, and joining of timbers and boards, were found. Blacksmithing left its traces in slag, waste iron, and some finished products. The "clinker" (waste) that appeared in practically every 1607–24 deposit is another sign of working iron. The smiths also adapted standard body armor, such as breastplates, to the Indian guerrilla warfare they faced. The plates were cut up to make more flexible arrow-proof jackets, and gun support tabs riveted to breastplates made them more fit for the musketeers. Smiths hammered one breastplate into a bucket or kettle, and the recovery of a horseshoe from one of the earliest contexts on the site, the store cellar, indicates that one blacksmith typically doubled as a farrier. Waste nail rod suggests that the local smiths produced some of the more than 125,000 nails recovered during the excavations as well.

Fragments of brick in every early site, including at least five hearths in the earliest buildings, suggest the two bricklayers listed among the original settlers also made bricks. While no evidence of brick firing was uncovered, these bricks were likely to have been made in Virginia. Space in the ships' holds was far too valuable to waste on inexpensive bricks. Virginia clay is ideal for brick manufacture as well.[18] On the other hand, the mason who arrived with the original settlers must have been frustrated by the lack of natural stone in the immediate environs. He and his successors did find enough by 1610–11 to build the cobble-footed rowhouses dating to that time found along the fort's western wall—one, probably the governor's residence. The presence of a probable medieval building block in that footing does, however, show that ballast from England could wind up as building materials at Jamestown.[19]

Excavations also recovered evidence of barrel making—likely for domestic as well as export use—and tailoring. One cooper left in the ground his croze iron, a special type of plane that carves out the locking-groove for barrelheads, and the handle of a bunghole drill. Other wood-shaping devices such as a broad axe and an adze could be signs of the cooper's craft. Tailors left their mark on the site by losing more than nine hundred straight pins, fifty-five sewing needles, fourteen brass thimbles, and two hundred buttons made of brass, iron, and glass. One cluster of eight buttons attached to a thimble was once apparently part of a tailor's kit. Although these particular copper buttons must have dropped from the tailor's own supply, another elaborate button of blown glass must have come from the

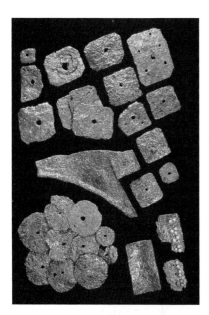

Blacksmiths were busy at Jamestown making body armor known as jacks of plate out of the more rigid and less maneuverable breastplates (*center*).

A breastplate recycled into a basin.

attire of a very high-status person, perhaps from a councilor's doublet (vest). More than seventy-six lead bale seals are further evidence of tailoring. These seals were clinched to rolls or bales of cloth for a variety of reasons, such as to identify place of manufacture or of dyeing, tax status, or length of the roll.

There were no Company directives concerning hunting or fishing. That obvious survival strategy needed no urging since instruction in sport hunting and fishing was standard for gentlemen in England.[20] Artifacts from the excavation include not only the gear required for hunting and fishing but also butchered bones of native Virginia animals and marine life. Although the guns colonists brought were primarily heavy weapons, intended for defense, they undoubtedly were used to acquire some of the fourteen species of wild birds and eight species of wild mammals whose butchered bones were identified in the earliest archaeological deposits.[21] Marine bones and shells abound as well in the garbage deposits of early Jamestown, including twenty-five species of fish and reptiles. While there is much complaint in documentary sources about the lack of fishing skill and equipment, the variety of fish hooks, net weights, and line sinkers in the Rediscovery collections is evidence that the Company did at least supply the colonists with the means to exploit the marine resources for survival. In fact, to judge by representation in one circa-1610 deposit, wild sources made up over half the meat diet. These signs of a wildlife menu seem to contradict Smith's complaint that "[t]hough there be fish in the sea, fouls in the air, and beasts in the woods their bounds are so large, they so wild and we so weak and ignorant we cannot much trouble them."[22] Or was all of this food from the wild acquired by trade with the Indians?

As the Company directed, Newport was in charge until the settlers touched land, at which time a sealed box was opened to identify six governing councilors. These six plus the ex-officio Newport elected a president for a one-year term: Edward Maria Wingfield. The real power, however, lay in the council in England, and the all-powerful final vote belonged to James I. This reality left the resident leader, Wingfield, with unclear authority, subject to removal at the whim of the council. Wingfield was indeed removed, on the charge of hoarding food, after the disastrous summer of 1607, when about half the original settlers died. Archaeology has opened a window on that chaos, revealing the gravesites and burials of the gentlemen who perished by that first September.

Tools for barrel making including a croze iron used to make barrelhead fastening grooves.

The Company's decision to transfer the seat of power from far-off England directly to Jamestown—another accommodation to New World realities—also left its signs in the ground. Transfer of power came to the fort in the form of the first substantially constructed timber-framed cobble-based rowhouse, one likely fit for a true resident governor. Such a building undoubtedly was intended to command more respect from the men and the Virginia Indians alike. Construction of the substantial church described in 1608 also showed that the settlers took seriously their charge to colonize "in the name of God." It is curious, however, that almost all the religious artifacts in the Rediscovery collections are Catholic. One sole exception is the hardware from a very thick book, likely a Bible in Robert Hunt's library, burned in the fire of 1608.

Documentary sources prove that the colonists, as required by the Company, sent home periodic official reports. Archaeological discoveries from

Collection of carpenters' tools recovered at James Fort, including dividers, a felling axe, a hatchet, a socket chisel, and two files.

the early years of Jamestown include the means for writing such reports: an inkwell, pencils, seals, and signet rings. A ring with a crossed eagle, possibly the family crest of William Strachey, is the most dramatic of all of the signet rings for stamping wax seals. Whether discouraging words were censored is harder to establish from documents alone. Certainly, some of Strachey's prose as well as Percy's gruesome reports suggest that the Company directives to paint Jamestown in the best possible light were ignored at times—probably to the detriment of the colony. Still, the negative reports never seemed to stop immigration. All the archaeological signs show the growth and expansion of Jamestown throughout the Company's existence and beyond, until the end of the century.

Documents, architectural remains, and especially artifacts recently recovered at the site of early Jamestown reflect a very busy place, as the settlers, following the instructions they were sent with, sought to make the Virginia Company a profitable enterprise—primarily by establishing a secure colony from which to export whatever Virginia had to offer that would turn a profit. That security almost immediately required the construction of an armed camp. From this fortified town, supported by domestic industry and trade, materials for export were manufactured or searched out by explorers. Security, exploration, and trade required soldiers, manufacturers, merchants, and craftsmen, all of whom were numbered among the settlers. This military and industrial trading center was above all else supposed to become an English colony, literally and figuratively a "New England." Little wonder then that the artifact collection found among the ruins of earliest Jamestown is rich in evidence of a robust, multifaceted community.

Eyewitness descriptions of life at early Jamestown detail other activities that kept the colonists busy. For instance, the men collected sassafras roots and "gilded" soil (soil they thought contained gold) to stock the homeward-bound ships. Settlers also built two blockhouses near the fort.[23] The church and the store seemed to be continually repaired or rebuilt. On special days the colonists attended church or court or entertained a visiting emissary from the Powhatan chiefdom. When a supply ship was in port, colonists bargained with seamen for food and whatever luxuries they could get their hands on. The English drilled with their arms, took target practice, stood watch, and mounted ordnance.

All this activity attests to the careful preparation and the hard work of the Jamestown settlers. If that preparation and that work did not always suffice to meet the original objectives of the Virginia Company, the cause for such

A number of religious objects found at the fort site in a variety of time contexts, including a jet (hard coal) cross depicting a curious stick-figure crucifixion, rosary medallions, and a silver seal with the scallop sign of St. James.

Signs of literacy at Jamestown include (*from left*) two wax seals—a portcullis (castle gate) and a standing lion—and a seal chain; two rings—a merchants' sign and a "displayed eagle" signet; and a lead inkwell. The eagle ring may well have belonged to William Strachey, secretary of the colony in 1610–11.

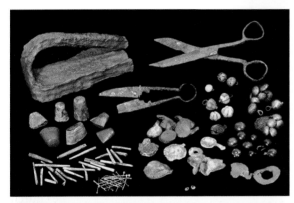

A collection of objects used by tailors, including (*from left to right and top to bottom*) an iron, thimbles, decorative copper aglets for laces, straight pins, scissors and shears, lead cloth seals, and glass and copper buttons.

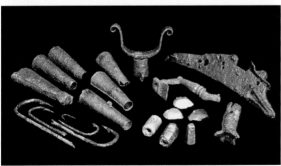

Hunting and fishing tools were plentiful at Jamestown despite Smith's claim that many gentlemen were not skilled with them.

failures was sometimes negligence, but perhaps most often facts of the New World the settlers found—facts of climate, geography, geology—were to blame. In observing the adaptations made both by the settlers and by the Company in the effort to accommodate these facts, we are witnessing the birth of the first Anglo-Americans.

It is also true, however, that some of the failures can be laid at the feet of the settlers themselves. Not all of Jamestown's gentlemen acted for the greater good: some spent their time black-marketeering and living high on the hog. These were "the saint-seeming worthies of Virginia."[24] But research has demonstrated the undeniable presence of devoted and diligent men, dedicated to the purposes of the colony. These were the truly saintly worthies of Virginia. As a result of their efforts, Jamestown would live on to become the first permanent English settlement in the New World.

Part II
MORE BURIED TRUTH

FIVE

HOLY GROUND

On April 5, 1614, after her conversion to Christianity, Pocahontas married the tobacco planter John Rolfe. The wedding took place in the Jamestown church built by Captain Christopher Newport's sailors in January or February 1608.[1] They had the time to do this because they stayed far too long at Jamestown (fourteen weeks) before sailing back to England for more, and desperately needed, supplies.[2] Mariners could easily repair a ship, or even build one, but a church was an odd assignment, and it did not turn out well, according to John Smith, for in a mere fourteen days the church had "melted away."[3] After the ship and its crew did sail for England, Smith reports that the church was repaired in mid-April. The new and supposedly improved version did not last long either. By 1610 the building again needed major repairs. These were carried out that June by Lord De La Warre's men. After the renovation William Strachey described it:

> In the middest [of the fort] . . . is a pretty chapel. . . . It is in length threescore
> foot, in breadth twenty-four [60' × 24'] . . . [and it has] a chancel in it of cedar
> and a communion table of black walnut, and all the pews of cedar, with fair
> broad windows to shut and open . . . of the same wood, a pulpit of the same,
> with a font hewn hollow, like a canoe, with two bells at the west end.[4]

This repaired church had more staying power. But it too was no permanent sanctuary. Although it was standing for Pocahontas's wedding in 1614, Samuel Argall described the church as "down" when he came to Jamestown as lieutenant governor in 1617. Rather than rebuilding Smith's church yet again, Argall built a smaller one nearby.

Our excavations in the southeastern sector of the James Fort triangle pinpointed the remnants of the earlier, 1608 church. Miraculously, archaeological evidence survived from this first formally built structure, the "pretty chapel" so thoroughly described by Strachey. Fifteen unusually large and deep structural postholes and four ceremonially aligned burials escaped destruction during the construction of the Civil War earthwork. The postholes formed a rectangular pattern measuring 24' × 64', very close to Strachey's "threescore by twenty-four." All the burials were found at the east end of the footprint, the traditional space in the Anglican church known as the chancel, which was reserved for the graves of high-status people. The probable identification of the chancel, the measurements of the post pattern, and the fact that the structure was located in the fort precisely where the "+" appears on the Zúñiga map (see illustration on p. 47) are compelling evidence that these are the remains of the very church that the sailors built, Smith finished, Strachey described, Argall replaced, and in which Pocahontas was married.

Systematic removal of the overlying soil on the church site revealed that it had been seriously disturbed, but not completely destroyed, by the deep digging in 1861. But the extreme depth of the main structural postholes, in most cases six feet below the early seventeenth-century grade, assured that a portion of all of the holes survived this Confederate earthmoving operation. Deep postholes offer telling evidence of the church design, indicating that the main structural support posts were intended to withstand the outward pressure of the high, wide, heavy roof of a typical vaulted church ceiling. Church ceilings were symbolic gateways to heaven, but they also had an acoustical purpose. In contrast to the melodic Catholic chants in Latin, Reformation English sermons were intended to be heard word for word.[5] The vaulted ceiling served as an amplifier for a message that the Virginia Company was dedicated to making loud and clear.[6]

The posthole pattern revealed more about the church design. A center post in the west end wall ruled out a central door in that location. The door must have been on the south wall near the west end, a typical location for doors in Anglican churches. Wall posts, detected by post molds within the surrounding posthole fill, were enormous: a foot in diameter. They were also exactly in line with, but not exactly at right angles to, their counterparts on the north wall. This reveals the construction process. The precise alignment of the wall posts suggests that builders framed the long axis walls on the ground and then raised them on each side as a unit. Each side

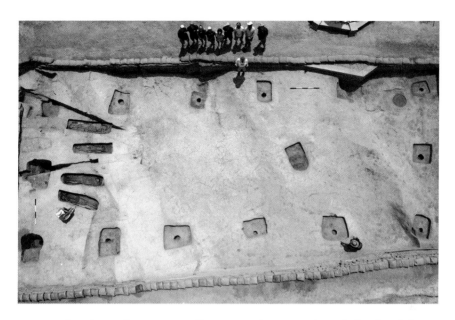

1608–16 church site showing partially excavated structural postholes that define the 24' × 64' building. Note belfry (?) support posthole (*center right*) and the four chancel burials A–D (*left, bottom to top*). These are the oldest remains of a Protestant church yet found in America.

assembly of a rigid-framed wall would show archaeologically as a neatly linear alignment of postholes, but it would not be necessary for the main posts to align from side to side. They did not. Timber sills between posts just above ground level would have made the frames even more rigid, another reason why the posts became so perfectly aligned down the line. The existence of sills, in turn, could indicate that the church had a wooden floor. Smaller supporting studs to hold the mud walls between major support posts would have completed the pre-assembly.

One puzzling extra main post was found twenty-one feet from the west end of the rectangle, centered exactly on both the long axis of the building and the nearest four main structural posts (see illustration above, center right; the west side is to the right). It was seated as deep as the wall posts and the hole held the same-sized post, strongly suggesting that it, too, was part of the early original construction. Why it was there is puzzling since it would have stood directly in the center of the church aisle. However, Strachey's description may explain this singular post. The "two bells at the west end" might have required another central post to support their weight within a timber-framed belfry. Thick fragments of brass bells have been found elsewhere in the fort. If they are pieces of the 1608 church bells, then the weight of two of them plus a timber belfry might have required the extra support post in the main church aisle.

That explanation for the mystery post is not without its problems, however, assuming that the structure had a traditional gabled roof. The location of the post, at some distance from the west end of the building, would put a belfry in an unusual position. On the other hand, the peak of a hipped roof would have been farther east and possibly above the mysterious post. The question remains, however, Why would a central support post be seated as deep as the side posts if its sole purpose were to support weight directly overhead? Like the sidewall posts, perhaps this post was also meant to take lateral stress. The roof design and the builders might explain the depth. The mariners had been in port at Jamestown since January, and presumably they began putting up the church frame as soon as possible. They would soon have learned that there was an incessant prevailing west wind at Jamestown. Their response to its force may have been to forgo putting a tall, vertical church gable wall facing the west wind and to construct a lower-resistance hip roof instead.[7] In other words, not only would the extra post have supported the weight of the belfry, but it would have acted as an extra lateral support against pressure from the incessant west wind. Apparently, a church design by mariners was not without some merit.

Numerous prehistoric artifacts were found in the fill around the posts. This is not surprising given the early date of construction, January–February 1608. Why? Consider the frame seating process. The mariners first dug through the topsoil and then through some natural clay, down as far as a shovel could reach (three feet). Again, unless they accidentally dropped any English artifacts as they dug, the excavated soil, the spoil, would likely contain only the Indian occupation artifacts that were already in the topsoil before the English arrived. Then, from the three-feet-deep hole, the excavators had to dig down another three feet to reach the six-feet depth through natural clay that was never exposed on the surface and therefore could not contain any artifacts at all. Finally, once the frame posts were set in the deep holes, the spoil went back in to firm up the posts, basically in the same order as it came out. In that case, the prehistoric Indian artifacts from the topsoil went right back near or close to their original position. A church built in 1608 should have that exact artifact signature.

Had there been any doubt that the posthole pattern was in fact the foot-

A conjectural main frame superimposed on the 1608–16 church postholes.

print of the 1608 church, our excavation of the burials put it to rest. Over-all, the subsequent intrusions into the site, such as later ditches, the Civil War earthmoving, and twentieth-century utility trenches, did only nominal damage to the actual skeletal remains. We decided to totally excavate the burials for a number of reasons. One was to determine whether or not the burials were all of high-status individuals, as would be usual in a church and in the church chancel. We also hoped to gather enough historical and forensic evidence to identify the individuals and scientifically learn as much as possible about their lives. The final goal was to rememorialize each grave with an appropriate marker.

Even before we uncovered the burials, we knew the names and something of the biographies of five people who died during the relatively short time the church existed, were likely buried at Jamestown, and were high enough in rank to qualify for a chancel burial: Captain Gabriel Archer (1575–1609) was trained in the law, an experienced mariner, author of a detailed account of the events during the construction of the 1607 fort, and the Jamestown magistrate. Captain William West (1586[?]–1610) was killed by Indians at the Falls of the James and almost certainly would have been brought back to Jamestown by his close relative Thomas West (Lord De La Warre) for burial in the chancel. Captain Peter Wynne (1560[?]–1609), described as "a valiant gentlemen and old soldier" and "a tall black fellowe," gained his rank fighting on both the English and Spanish sides during the Dutch Wars, was on the Jamestown ruling council, and was appointed posthumously lieutenant governor of the colony by Gates. Sir Ferdinando Wenman (1576–1610), Knight, was a cousin of Lord De La Warre and held the prestigious post of Master of the Ordinance. Finally, the Reverend Robert Hunt (1569–1608) was instrumental in getting Captain John Smith appointed to the council and was a humble but steadfast peacemaker among the colony factions.[8] Although all of these high-status individuals played short but seemingly significant roles in the formative years of the Jamestown colony, they are relatively unknown today. Despite their relatively brief mention in historical documents, forensic and archaeological evidence found in the graves could provide an unprecedented opportunity to connect their names with individual burials and to bring to life their contributions to establishing Jamestown.

The four aligned graves (labeled for analysis A, B, C, and D) were indeed found to hold the remains of four high-status individuals, all Englishmen.[9] Besides burial in the prestigious church chancel, other signs of high standing were apparent. Nail patterns and signs of decayed wood found in the graves established that B, C, and D held coffins. Coffins were expensive, and the coffins of B and D especially so in that they were anthropomorphic in form (human-shaped), much like an Egyptian sarcophagus. They would have required special cabinetmaker's skills to produce and therefore would have been extremely expensive, a sure sign that these two individuals were men of means. Surprisingly, two of the individuals, C and D, were buried with ceremonial objects. Remnants of a silver-fringed and spangled silk garment were found with burial D, and part of a captain's leading staff and a small silver box with burial C. These artifacts without a doubt indicated that the men were elite, for with the exception of the graves of the very rich or well born, it is rare to find any objects in English burials.

Despite the fact that more than half of the skeleton of burial D had been damaged when the twentieth-century power-line trench cut through it, meticulous archaeological work on the surviving left arm and a section of the chest exposed a very fragile fabric, which turned out to be a military sash. Sir Ferdinando Wenman, the knight and cousin of the high-born governor-for-life Lord De La Warre, could have been buried with such a prestigious item. But he died at Jamestown during the summer or fall of 1610 at age thirty-four, while the condition of the teeth and long bones forensically established this person was in his mid-twenties when he died,

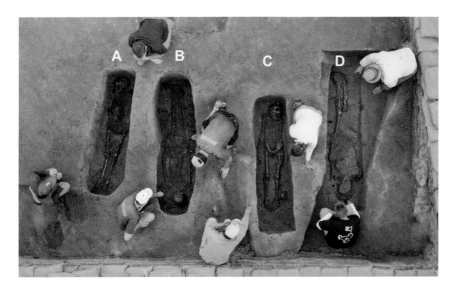

The chancel burials.

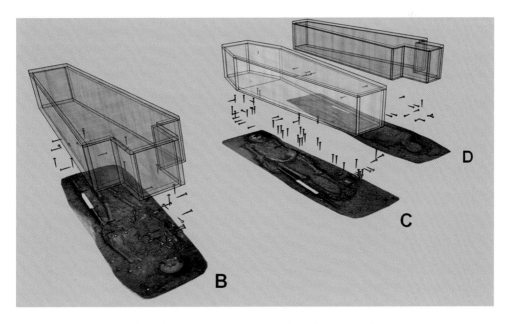

The three chancel burial coffins reconstructed from digitally recorded nail positions showing that B and D were anthropomorphic, or human-shaped, and identically constructed (likely by the same cabinetmaker), and C was a traditional hexagonal form. (David Givens)

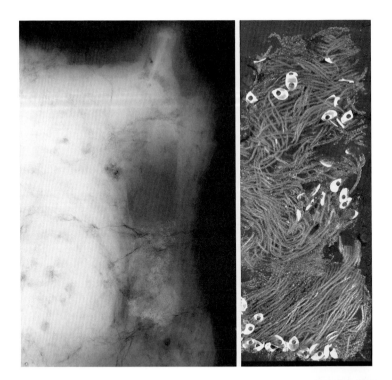

Left: X-ray of the left arm, shoulder, and chest section of burial D. *Right:* An enlarged CT scan of the silver bullion fringe adorned with silver sequins and silk fabric, likely an officer's sash. (Emily Williams, Colonial Williamsburg Foundation; Mark Riccio, Cornell University)

Captain's leading staff point base found in the 1608 church chancel burial C, compared with the captain's leading staff found in the James Fort parade ground (2002) in the burial thought to be the grave of Captain Bartholomew Gosnold.

Seventeenth-century officer (*left*) holding a captain's tasseled leading staff that has a point identical to those found on the Gosnold and burial C coffins. Note the silver or gold bullion fringe on his sash of rank, similar to the fringe found with chancel burial D. (*Officers of the White Banner*, Jacob Willemsz Delff II, 1648, Museum Prinsenhof Delft)

too young to be Wenman. Captain West, identified by William Strachey as De La Warre's "nephew" and named by George Percy as De La Warre's "kinsman," would rate a burial with a silver sash for two reasons: his rank and the fact that he was related to Lord De La Warre. More importantly, West's age at death (determined by some record of his English life) was twenty-five, which is consistent with the forensically determined age of the remains.

While West's age at death is documented in genealogical records and forensic analysis, the section of the captain's ceremonial leading staff socket and the silver box turned out to be more vital clues to the identification of burial C.[10] It is significant that the leading staff is almost identical to the more complete one found on the coffin of the burial thought to be Captain

Gosnold. Again, that staff and other compelling evidence led to the most likely identification of that burial as Gosnold. So the leading staff socket found on yet another coffin in James Fort is strong evidence that burial C was indeed another captain. In any case, if burial D is Captain West's grave, then by the process of elimination it is likely that burial C is the grave of one of the two remaining captains who died during the life span of the church: Gabriel Archer or Peter Wynne. The silver box found laid on the burial C coffin proved to be the key to identifying this person as Captain Gabriel Archer. How so? First, X-ray fluorescence testing (XRF) determined that the box was made primarily of silver, certainly a sign of high status. Further, as the box was removed from the grave, a rattling sound left no doubt that some metallic things were in it. Speculation about the contents ran rampant among the crew, with wishful guesses ranging from coins, which might date the burial, to armorial signet rings, which might identify the individual. But it could not be opened without damaging it, as the sliding lid was corroded shut. How to have our box and open it too seemed a dilemma.

The investigation had to turn to nondestructive technology. First, X-rays indicated that there were probably two dense metal objects inside, but they both looked like shapeless globs, probably lead. It took 3-D images produced by powerful micro-computed tomographic (CT) scans to identify the contents.[11] The dense metal objects appeared to be two parts of what is very likely a small hollow lead vessel known as an ampulla, which according to religious tradition would hold holy water, blood, or oil. The scan also detected seven splinters of human bone. The combination of bone, ampulla, and silver box established that this tiny container is a spiritual object known as a reliquary, in which case the bones would have been revered as those of a saint. Because reliquaries are traditionally, though not exclusively, part of Catholic practice, the presence of the reliquary suggests that the individual laid to rest in burial C was Catholic.[12] Although the reliquary may offer a clue, it is important to point out that coffin wood found beneath the silver box indicates that object was *on* and not *in* the coffin. If it was a personal possession, then why was it not in the coffin with the deceased? Perhaps it was just overlooked until the last minute, or perhaps a Catholic placed it on the coffin in the grave shaft in a final reverent gesture.

The box lid itself is a possible clue to the identification of either the man in the coffin or the person with the grave offering. A crude initial is scratched on it that appeared to be a capital *W* or a capital *M,* depending

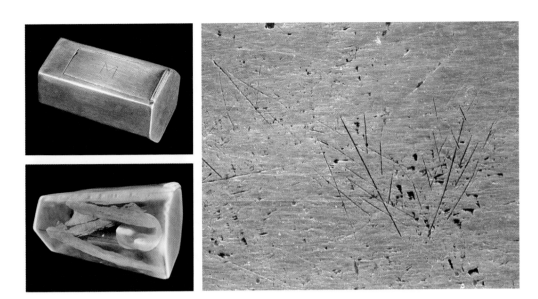

Top: The monogrammed silver box (reliquary) found in burial C. *Bottom:* Micro-CT scans showing the broken-open lead ampulla and fragments of human bone inside the unopened silver box. *Right:* The sketched arrows. (Michael Lavin, Jamestown Rediscovery, micro-photonics; Mark Riccio Cornell and Scott Whitaker, Smithsonian)

upon how the container was held. At first it seemed logical to assume that the initial was the first letter of a captain's last name, in which case there was good reason to conclude that the initial was intended to be read as a *W* for Wynne, West, or even Wenman. But it was curious that the outer lines of the *W* were parallel to each other and not splayed like a normal *W*. It took intensive magnification (scanning electron microscopy) to prove the letter to be an *M*.[13] The magnified lines revealed precisely how the letter was made. Oriented as an *M*, it was clear that the inscriber made the letter naturally with downward strokes. If the letter was a *W*, the incised pattern of the lines would determine that the letters were formed by pushing up from the bottom, an odd and almost impossible way to form the letter.[14] *M* it is. Properly reading the letter, however, did not seem to be much help in identification of the buried man. During the 1608–16 church period, there was no known death of a captain with a last name beginning with the letter *M*.

The fact that the box is a reliquary is more helpful. It seems likely that at least one of the captains was devotedly religious and possibly Catholic. Wynne did once serve with the Spanish in the Low Countries and might well have been a closet Catholic among the Jamestown Anglicans. But Wynne died in his mid- to late forties, while forensic evidence sets the age at death for burial C as early thirties. Archer died at age thirty-four, and we know that Archer may have had very strong Catholic leanings, for court records show that his father, Christopher Archer, refused to attend mandatory Anglican church services in his hometown of Mountnessing, Essex. Such objectors were Catholics who were known as recusants and were often branded as "outlaws."[15] It seems reasonable to assume that the son, Gabriel, may have adopted and kept steadfast the family faith.

Still, it remains to be explained how a reliquary labeled *M* wound up in the grave of man whose last name began with an *A*. There is a possible explanation, as speculative as it may be. First, the reliquary may not have belonged to the deceased, as it was found resting on the closed casket. Perhaps this last-minute ceremonial offering (like the captain's leading staff) came at the hand of a friend and fellow soldier. If burial C was Archer, that soldier and colleague could be Captain John Martin, who, in league with Archer and John Ratcliffe, together overthrew the presidency of Captain John Smith in September 1609. Soon after that, the Indians tortured and killed Ratcliffe, and the "starving time" claimed Archer. So Martin, the last of the three captains left standing, could well have put the staff and the box on the coffin of his fellow conspirator just as Archer was laid to rest. In that case, it is even tempting to conclude that the reliquary marked *M* was Martin's. On the other hand, Martin was the son of Sir Richard Martin, the Master of the Royal Mint, who had been active in radical Protestant causes, including an effort to encourage Queen Elizabeth to more strictly enforce Protestantism. As Archer may have become a staunch Catholic following in his recusant father's footsteps, so too Martin may have chosen the ardent Protestant faith of his father.

Another possibility is that the *M* was not a monogram for the owner but rather a reference to a saint whose bones were packed inside the box. If the *M* stood for St. Mary,[16] perhaps the reliquary was not a personal possession at all but rather a "public reliquary"[17] that may have adorned the church altar, placed there either openly or secretly as part of the consecration of the church.[18] It is possible that someone, maybe Archer or even Martin, brought the reliquary to Jamestown as an act of "translation," that is, bringing it from the English mother church to establish the Jamestown sanctuary. If that were the case, then the questions become, Why was it buried, and why buried with Archer? One possible answer comes from *when* he died, almost certainly during the "starving time," when things looked so hopeless at Jamestown. Perhaps the last survivors buried this sanctified object in Archer's grave to make sure it would not fall into Powhatan hands.

Had Archer become the de facto leader at Jamestown during the "starving time," a stand-in for the governor, George Percy? His leadership role was not mentioned in accounts from the period, but what we know about his Jamestown years seems to show that he could have taken over during Percy's illness. Archer had come to Virginia with the original settlers and survived the horror of that first devastating summer when 60 percent of the group of 104 died. Then he had struggled through but survived the extremely cold winter of 1608 during which fire destroyed much of the fort and many more of his colleagues perished. By the fall of that year Archer, Martin, and Ratcliffe had created a political vacuum by successfully removing the severely injured Captain John Smith from the presidency. As a consequence, Smith went back to England. Archer followed and remained there for a year, but he came back in 1609 as the captain of the ship *Blessing*, with its cargo of men and families. One must wonder why, after seeing most of his fellows die so horrifically during the first few months of settlement, anyone in his right mind would return. What was in it for him? One possible answer could be that he was on a religious mission, perhaps a Catholic plan to take over Jamestown for Spain. Had he become a lay Catholic priest while in England for that year, during which he became an agent in league with the aforementioned disgruntled English Baron Arundell, who claimed he could get rid of Jamestown without firing a shot? A Catholic takeover from within might have been the plan, no guns required. Another fact that supports this conspiracy theory is that Archer was buried with his head to the east, the traditional orientation for a clergyman's burial. Could he have been an Anglo-Catholic priest who, while filling the void created by the death of Hunt, planned to turn the Reformation on its ear in a place far from Anglican authority?

Speculative conspiracy theories aside, there is perhaps more physical evidence that connects the reliquary to Archer. A series of yet more roughly engraved lines on one end of the reliquary appears to be a tiny sketch of a number of arrows forming a V-shaped cluster. The Archer family armorial shield includes stylized arrows. While the symbol on the box is minute and faint, when viewed through the electron microscope the overall pattern is more than incidental scratches. So, disregarding the *M*, the arrow inscription, the Catholic reliquary, the leading staff, and the age at death together determine that Gabriel Archer is indeed the best candidate for burial C.

If burials C and D are indeed Archer and West, then by process of elimination burials A and B are the graves of Hunt, Wenman, or Wynne. But who is the odd man out? Hunt died at age thirty-nine, Wenman at thirty-four, and Wynne likely in his late forties. The forensic age estimate of burial A is 35.5, and burial B, 35, which seems to eliminate Wynne altogether. A contemporary description of Wynne also refers to him as a "tall black fellowe," which does not jibe with the forensic stature estimate for burial A of only five foot two inches.[19] The question then becomes, Which grave is Wenman and which is Hunt? There is every reason to conclude that A is Hunt and B is Wenman. Wenman is close to the right age at death of burial B, and just as West, a kinsman of Lord De La Warre, rated one of the two expensive anthropomorphic coffins, Wenman, the knighted cousin of De La Warre, was likely buried in the other. It is also significant that nail patterns of those two specially made coffins indicate they were indeed built by the same artisan. This may mean that these individuals died close together after the "starving time." West and Wenman died a couple of months apart in the late summer and fall of 1610, while Hunt and Archer died at least a year and a half apart in 1608–9. The coffin maker, like almost everyone else, would have been dead before he could make another special coffin for Archer. It may also be significant that both Wenman and West were De La Warre relatives and that the governor, who was at Jamestown when they both died, saw to it that they were laid to rest with great pomp and circumstance. The specially made human-shaped coffins would certainly add prestige to their ceremonial funerals.

It is likely that Hunt died very soon after the January 1608 fort fire that destroyed all his personal belongings and his library. But all we can know for sure about when he died is that he was dead by the time his will was read in England, July 15, 1608.[20] The news that he had died likely reached England by way of Captain Christopher Newport, who sailed from Jamestown on April 15. This means that Hunt died when the chancel first existed (even though it was left to Smith to refinish the sailors' church after Newport left). The fact that burial A was the only shroud interment is consistent with Hunt's reputation as a humble man, a peacemaker, one who might not have wanted a pretentious coffin; and securing a coffin during the harsh winter of 1608 may well have been impossible.

Another consideration with the potential to help sort out the identities of those buried in these graves is that, like burial C, burial A was laid in his grave with his head to the east, while the other two lay with their heads to the west. Elizabethan Christians did traditionally bury clergymen with their heads to the east in the belief that at the Resurrection they would rise and face their congregations. Everyone else would be buried with their heads to the west so that when they arose, they would be facing the rising sun. The silver-box burial (C) and the shrouded burial (A) both have a clerical orientation. But does that mean they were both clergymen? Not necessarily. Many other burials so far studied at Jamestown seem to disregard the compass altogether. If we assume that formal chancel burials would follow convention, however, this in its own right might argue that burial C is not Archer and is, in fact, Hunt. But could the orientation be a mistake? Probably not. The coffin nail patterns found in burial C indicate that the coffin had a traditional hexagonal shape, which basically conforms to the human body with the head-and-shoulder section obvious even after the lid is closed. So there could be little likelihood that the pallbearers would mistakenly lay the coffin with the head to the east. Again, orientation is another reason to conclude that Archer was in some way a man of the cloth and another reason to conclude that burial A is Hunt, who was the only clergyman named in records who died when the church was open for service. It should be acknowledged, however, that there is an outside chance that burial A could possibly be some other unknown pious individual. Strachey wrote that by 1610, "every Thursday" other "true preachers" took their weekly turn to offer sermons.[21] Their names are not recorded.

More evidence about the identity of the chancel burials can come from chemistry. Stable isotopes in the chancel bones produced readings of carbon, nitrogen, and oxygen that suggest high status and the region in England from where the chancel burial men came. The bones of all but the shrouded burial (A) were in a condition to produce the isotopic readings. Preliminary results from the others indicated that burials B, C, and D ate well and probably all came from the coastal plain regions of England. While this is consistent with records that already very clearly indicated that all four of these men were of high status and from the English coastal region or very near it, it is not much help in identifying the individual burials. Testing for lead content in the bones proved more useful. Again, high lead values correlate with status, for the rich could afford to dine on and drink from pewter. Burial B, Wenman, and burial D, West, scored very high in lead value, and the readings were almost identical. That was not surprising, since again, they were almost certainly two prestigious Lord De La Warre relatives. Burial A, Hunt, had the lowest lead reading, as one would expect of a cleric.[22]

If Hunt is burial A, as it seems, and the first to be buried in the new chancel, could the position of the rest of the graves have any correlation with the chronology of their deaths? If they were buried one by one south of Hunt, then theoretically they would be interred in this sequence: (B) Archer, died in the fall of 1609, (C) Wenman, died in the late summer of 1610, and (D) West, died in the fall of 1610. But that burial order simply does not square with the identities based on the preponderance of other evidence. After Hunt died (burial A), Archer was buried south of the center line of the chancel, with Wenman next between Hunt and Archer, and then West along the south wall, a spatial pattern that does not fit any overall burial chronological order.

Rather than helping with identity, however, the locations of the burials could reveal details of the interior plan of the chancel itself. All the graves were located off center to the south and a little distance from the east end of the church. Is that meaningful? In this sense it may be. There is a record that space in the chancel was reserved for the chair of Jamestown leader De La Warre, who "hath his seat in the choir [chancel], in a green velvet chair."[23] It seems likely that the post-1607 council presidents including John Smith all sat in the vacant space near the north wall of the church. Hence Hunt was buried far enough to the south to leave a vacant place for the leader's chair, while the other vacant chancel space to the east of the burials was undoubtedly reserved for the altar.

In sum, we are fairly certain who is who: burial A is Reverend Robert Hunt; burial B, Sir Ferdinando Wenman; burial C, Captain Gabriel Archer; and burial D, Captain William West. But what does this knowledge add to the Jamestown story? First, the lost 1608 church, its lost chancel, and its lost chancel burials all have been found. Second, the biographies of four practically anonymous Jamestown leaders have come to life. We now know that Wenman and West, both relatives of De La Warre, were held in high esteem at Jamestown. Third, while written records confirm the leadership roles of Hunt and Archer, the documents are all but mute about most of the activities of West and Wenman. Their archaeological discovery in the prestigious chancel in some way fills that void.

Finding the first church itself adds to the Jamestown story in other ways. It underscores how thoroughly the rigid English social hierarchy was transported to Virginia. As we have seen, the church was the center of the James Fort's society, spiritual and secular. It stood from 1608 to circa 1616, which was before, through, and at least six years after the "starving time" (1609–10), when perhaps as many as 90 percent of the thousands of Virginia immigrants died. Yet between 1608 and 1616, which included the "starving time," there is written evidence and now a physical record of the deaths of only four high-status people. With the exception of one, Captain Archer, who died during the "starving time," the rest of the "better sort" must have used privilege to stay alive during times of life-threatening conditions. In addition to having first claims on food during times of famine, they mostly lived in the better-built houses while the lower-class settlers and soldiers dwelled in tents and "holes in the ground." In these temporary shelters the commoners must have lived like refugees: exposed both to the winter cold and the brutal summer heat, relegated to survive as best they could in their "places." For them, even survival cannibalism had been an option.

As we have seen, some of the reformed traditions of the church also survived the ocean crossing. The church design and the reservation of the chancel for the burial of upper-class people certainly carried over. Even Catholic symbols like the reliquary, although banned in Reformation England, can be considered holdovers from England as there are many examples of Catholic iconography hidden behind church walls and buried in the ground in late sixteenth- or early seventeenth-century Anglican churches.[24] And Captain Archer may have been among many who, at the very least, outwardly accepted the Reformation but steadfastly clung to familiar Catholic spiritual practices and objects. But, again, he obviously could not put the box on his own coffin, and whether or not it was deposited there secretly or openly is unknown. But it is telling that the reliquary was somehow linked directly to a man of high status. Clearly the Catholic rosary beads and medallions found at Jamestown in the past now cannot be explained away as merely shiny trinkets for the Indian trade or simply lost by the few Spanish captives held at the fort (see illustration at the top of p. 163). These other Catholic objects are now strong evidence that Captain Archer and his friend were probably not the only practicing Catholics at Jamestown.

Identifying the 1608 church by matching it with Strachey's precise dimensions and by finding the high-status chancel burials also positively identifies, again by another process of elimination, the brick-on-cobble foundation first discovered during the APVA digging in 1897. One of the founders of the organization, Mary Jeffery Galt, reported that she had dug into this foundation "with her own hands" and identified it as possibly the footing of the church of 1608. Finding the actual 1608–16 site proves that Galt's discovery had nothing to do with the 1608 church. Our work confirms, rather, that she found the remnants of the church reported to have been built during Argall's renovation of the fort in 1617. Conclusively identifying that particular Jamestown church is a significant archaeological discovery. America's first democratic representative assembly met there two years later.

SIX

JANE

In the summer of 2012, a mutilated human skull and severed leg bone were found in a trash deposit that partially filled an early seventeenth-century James Fort cellar/kitchen. Archaeological context, forensic science, and historiography together determined that this was incontrovertible evidence that a girl, whom we came to call Jane, had been cannibalized during the 1609–10 "starving time" winter. This grim discovery illuminates beyond all others how desperate and how close to ruin the Virginia venture became.

The discovery happened this way. All indications were telling us that we were excavating layers of backfill thrown into a 1608–10 James Fort cellar, probably a structure attached to the storehouse cellar/well complex. All we knew so far was that before it was abandoned, the underground room had been used by the original colonists as a kitchen, and when it was abandoned, De La Warre's cleanup crew threw more "starving time" material in this cellar and the cellar/well nearby. More butchered horses and dogs were in the debris as well as sherds of broken pottery that fit together, or mended, with those from the other cellar, establishing that the life of this structure also ended in June 1610.

One Friday at the end of the day, Jamie May, a senior archaeologist, came to me and in hushed tones said that one of our interns was beginning to uncover a row of what she thought looked like human teeth. I was not all that surprised. We had found human teeth, and even partial skulls, in other early seventeenth-century deposits. Most of those remains were mixed with other discarded artifacts after the settlers had accidentally dug into one of the hundreds of unmarked burials that were practically everywhere across

1608 cellar/kitchen showing (1) entrance wall postholes; (2) entrance stairs; (3) the ash- and sturgeon-bone-laden floor, and (4) two brick-faced ovens.

the fort site. Nonetheless, Jamie's whisper was a reminder that we needed to show respect for the dead by figuring out some way to keep these remains out of public view.

I climbed down into the cellar to see the find for myself. Just beginning to show were indeed human teeth, encased in a stratum of butchered animal bones and artifacts dating to 1609–10, the "starving time."

I immediately wrote this discovery off as yet more fragmented remnants from accidental grave disturbance. But whenever human bones were found apart from formal graves, I could not help wondering if they were physical evidence of the numerous historical references to "starving time" cannibalism. However, the end of the week was upon us, so with those tantalizing thoughts, we carefully reburied the teeth.

The ensuing excavation proved extraordinary. As we began a meticulous effort to clear soil away from around the teeth, they quickly proved to be just the tip of an iceberg. We found half a human skull and other fragmented cranial remains. There seemed to be signs that the skull had been chopped in two. Was this the cause of death, and, if so, was this evidence of a four-hundred-year-old murder? Or was this, in fact, evidence of cannibalism? Because the remains were so delicate, the work had to go slowly.

Left: A German Bartmann jug medallion dated 1[5]99 from the abandoned cellar/kitchen fill. *Right:* Bartmann sherds from the "Jane" layer and the central cellar/well fill mended (fit together), evidence that this and all the rest of the backfill in these two deposits came from a common trash pile, likely debris thrown there during the "starving time" of 1609–10.

Discovery of the skull of a teenage girl (later called "Jane") next to an Indian pot in a layer of trash partially filling the abandoned cellar/ kitchen.

Partial excavation of the abandoned cellar/kitchen showing a cross-section of fill: (1) the kitchen work floor; (2) the collapsed mud superstructure wall; (3) the trash deposit that held Jane; (4) the clay that finally filled the abandoned cellar cavity with enough soil to reach the surrounding early seventeenth-century elevation.

Soon a crowd of visitors congregated at the edge of the trench. To distract them, I came up out of the cellar and began a monologue about the details of the kitchen cellar room while others feverishly continued the removal process. As I spoke, the remains, still in a block of dirt, were securely placed in an artifact tray, well away from the crowd, and whisked away to the lab for a more controlled final excavation.

Once the soil surrounding the bones was removed in the lab, we could see the entire surface of the skull and the mostly complete upper row of teeth. Clearly there were two or three chop marks to the back of the skull and four distinct cuts to the forehead, all signs of extreme trauma. Before jumping to any conclusions about the cause of the injuries, we needed the analysis of an expert forensic anthropologist. We immediately sent the specimens to our project-long collaborating expert, Dr. Douglas Owsley, at the Museum of Natural History, Smithsonian Institution. He confirmed our suspicions. There was no evidence of murder, but the remains had been, as he put it, "processed."

Owsley determined that the skull and leg bone had undergone sustained blows, chops, and cuts from several sharp, metal implements, reflecting a concerted effort to separate the brain and soft tissue from bone. Months of intensive scientific testing—including high-magnification technology, stable isotopic tests for oxygen, carbon, and nitrogen, and tests for lead—determined that the bones were the remains of a fourteen-year-old English girl of lower status, probably raised in southern England. Owsley concluded that the rigorous postmortem cuts to the skull and jaw, and the way the leg was severed, were clear evidence of cannibalism.[1]

Forensic analysis offered these details:

"Although incomplete, enough of the cranium was recovered to determine the individual's age, sex, and ancestry. Its size and shape, small and elongated with a vertical forehead, are characteristic of an early seventeenth-century English female. The girl's unerupted third molars with partially formed roots indicat[e] that she was fourteen years of age when she died. The bones' stable carbon and nitrogen isotopes indicate that she lived on a European,

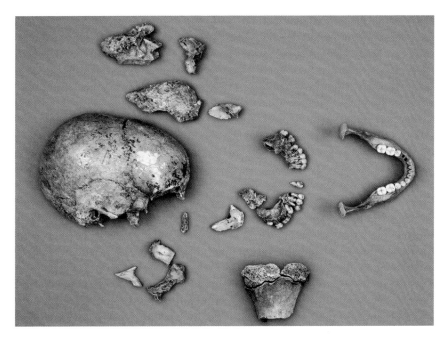

The cannibalized remains of Jane—more than a dozen parts of a female human skull, jaw, and butchered shin bone—found among discarded trash from the "starving time" cellar/kitchen fill. (Smithsonian)

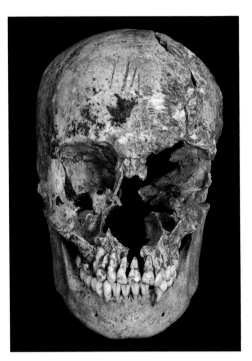

Jane's skull shows forensic evidence of more than fifty after-death chops and cuts from a knife and cleaver, or small hatchet. Four chops to the forehead represent a tentative, failed attempt to remove the brain after death. Sawing motion with a knife made its mark as all soft tissue was cut from the face and mouth. (Smithsonian)

wheat-based, and not an American, corn-based diet, and that she was a recent immigrant. Examination of the girl's skull identified multiple chops and cuts from three different sharp, metal implements, such as a knife and cleaver, or small hatchet. The pattern of blows and cuts reflects a concerted effort to remove soft tissue and the brain. Four chops to the middle forehead represent a tentative, failed attempt to open the cranium. Bone in the back of the head shows a series of deep chops. These forceful blows fractured the cranium along its midline.

"Bone below the right eye socket (maxilla) has a series of small, fine cuts from a knife. These cuts were made while removing the cheek muscles. Numerous small knife cuts and punctures in the mandible reflect attempts to remove soft tissue from both the inside and outside of the lower jaw. The left temporal bone was punctured by a small, rectangular tool. The narrow tip of the tool caused a compression fracture as it pried the bone from the side of the head to gain access to the brain. The right tibia's growth plate at the knee was just beginning to fuse; another sign that the girl was in her middle teens. The bone also has a chop halfway through its shaft. The blade entered the leg bone below the knee and from behind, partially breaking the bone. Then it was snapped in two exposing the marrow. Fine cuts indicate a sharp knife was also used to remove flesh."

There are six references to cannibalism at Jamestown, ranging from eyewitness recollections to hearsay accounts. Before finding the physical evidence, there was good reason to doubt them all, even though five out of the

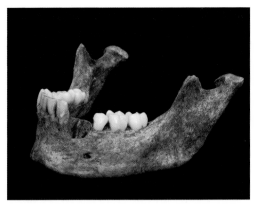
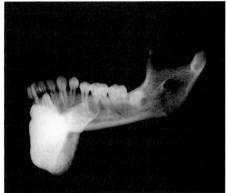

Jane's jaw with only slightly worn teeth and her unerupted third molars, visible in the X-ray, provide evidence that she was probably fourteen years old when she died. The bones held stable carbon and nitrogen isotopes that indicate she had lived primarily on a European (English), wheat-based diet, rather than on an American, corn-based one, which identifies her as a recent immigrant. (Smithsonian)

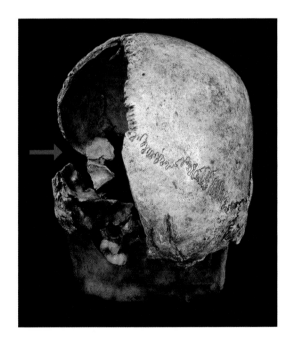

The brain was removed by inflicting deep chops to the back of the head, fracturing the skull along its midline, and then prying with a knife at the left temple (*red arrow*). (Smithsonian)

six tell essentially the same story. They read like exaggerations and political finger-pointing at John Smith or George Percy. George Percy, president of the council at Jamestown during the entire "starving time," provides the only real eyewitness report, although it was written as late as 1624 as a rebuttal to John Smith's account implying that Percy was responsible for tragic circumstances that led to cannibalism. Percy recalled in his *A True Relation* that the living dug up and ate corpses, and that a husband killed his wife and then butchered her, preserved her with salt, and ate parts of her before he was caught. When the man was discovered, Percy tortured him until he confessed and summarily executed him for his grisly deed. In his own words:

> And now famin beginneinge to Looke gastely and pale in every face, thatt notheinge was Spared to mainteyne Lyfe and to doe those things w[hi]ch seame incredible, as to digge upp deade corpes outt of graves and to eate them . . . Thatt one of our Colline murdered his wyfe Ripped the Childe outt of her woambe and threwe itt into the River and after Chopped the Mother in pieces and sallted her for his foode. . . . For the w[hi]ch Crewell and unhumane factt I adjudged him to be executed the acknowledgm[en]t of the dede beinge inforced from him by torture haveinge hunge by the Thumbes w[i]th weightes att his feete a quarter of an howere before he wolde Confesse the same.[2]

Captain John Smith, who left the colony before the starvation took hold, tells the same basic story about cannibalism and the "salted wife," blaming Percy and adding speculation about how she was cooked and how she tasted! He also added that the "poorer sort" dug up, cooked, and ate an Indian:

> Nay, so great was our famine, that a Salvage we slew, and buried, the poorer sort tooke him up againe and eat him, and so did divers one another boyled and stewed with roots and herbs: And one amongst the rest did kill his wife, powdered her, and had eaten part of her before it was knowne, for which hee was executed, as hee well deserved; now whether shee was better roasted, boyled or carbonado'd, I know not, but of such a dish as powdered wife I never heard of. This was that time, which still to this day we called the starving time.[3]

In another report from 1624, eight men, referring to themselves as "Ancient Planters," signed a document that reportedly was comprised of recollections of the early history of Jamestown and the "starving time." "A Breife

Declaration of the Plantation of Virginia" states that the settlers did live on dead Englishmen and an Indian; how many is unclear. It, too, recounted the tale of the murdered and salted wife, significantly adding to it that the husband ate all but her head:

> driven through unsufferable hunger unnaturallie to eat those thinges which nature most abhorred, the flesh and excrements of man, as well of our owne nation as of an Indian, digged by some out of his grave after he had laien buried three daies & wholly devoured him; others, envyinge the better state of bodie of any whom hunger had not yet so much wafted as there owne, lay waight and threatened to kill and eat them; one amonge the rest slue his wife as she slept in his bosome, cut her in peeces, powdered her & fedd uppon her till he had clean devoured all partes saveinge her heade, & was for soe barbarouse a fact and cruelty justly executed.[4]

Two official Virginia Company reports also described cannibalism and the murder of the wife: *A True Declaration of the estate of the Colonie in Virginia, 1610,* which includes a testimony by the lieutenant governor, Sir Thomas Gates; and *The Tragical Relation of the Virginia Assembly, 1624.* Gates's account had to be secondhand, as his arrival with some provisions in May 1610 seemed to bring the "starving time" to an end. He does include the tale of the murdered wife, which basically jibes with the other accounts, but he makes it sound rather like a domestic quarrel gone bad, with cannibalism only the husband's transparent alibi. Unlike the other accounts, Gates's does not refer to any other instances of cannibalism for survival. Could this be an attempt to take the blame off the shoulders of the Company for holding back supplies as the settlers starved?

The Tragical Relation of the Virginia Assembly, 1624, takes the opposite tack, blaming the English suppliers for the lack of "sustenance," which "constrayned" the husband to kill and powder his wife. "Many" others, so the report goes, had no choice but to eat corpses, and one man reportedly had become so accustomed to eating the dead after the "starving time" that he had to be executed to make him stop. This seems to say that the practice of survival cannibalism was a forgiven act, only punishable when it continued after normal food supplies were at hand.

> Wee cannot for this our scarsitie blame our Comanders heere, in respect that or sustenance was to come from England . . . soe lamentable was our scarsitie that we were constrayned to eate Doggs, Catts, ratts, Snakes, Toadstooles,

horse hides and wt nott, one man out of the mysery that he endured, killinge his wiefe powdered her upp to eate her, for wch he was burned. Many besides fedd on the Corps of dead men . . . , and one who had gotten unsatiable, out of custome to that foode could not be restrayned, untill such tyme as he was executed for it.[5]

Finally, the Spanish ambassador to England, Don Alonso de Velasco, wrote to the king of Spain on June 14, 1610, that an Indian siege of the fort had starved out the colonists to the point that the "survivors" ate their dead as well as an Indian casualty. This is the only historic account of cannibalism that does *not* mention the murdered wife. Velasco implies that this information came from sailors who had lately arrived in England from Virginia, May–June 1610. These were probably the group of deserters commanded by Francis West, who made off from Virginia with a shipload of Indian corn as the "starving time" set in. George Percy reports West's desertion just before he describes the most severe effects of the food shortage and the cannibalism. It therefore seems logical that West had already left Jamestown to trade with the Indians for corn when the woman was murdered. West never came back to Jamestown in 1610, so he and his sailors could not have told Velasco about it. The point of Velasco's letter was obviously to relay to the Spanish king in the most graphic terms the extent of the trouble in Jamestown. How better to have made his point than by sensationalizing the story of the murdered wife, if he knew about her?

> Sire.—From Virginia there has come to Lyme, a ship of those that remained there lately, and those who arrived in it, report that the Indians hold the English surrounded in the strong place which they had erected there, having killed the larger part of them, and the others were left so entirely without provisions that they thought it impossible to escape, because the survivors eat the dead, and when one of the natives died fighting, they dug him up again, two days afterwards, to be eaten.[6]

In addition to these written reports there is one more "document" that might be vividly telling the same story in a different way. A writing slate found in the "starving time" fill in the cellar/well includes what seems to be a very provocative drawing. The sketch shows a soldier clearly wielding a sword, apparently about to slash a well-dressed woman whom he holds by the neck. Is this a sketch of the murder of the wife so consistently chronicled in the various accounts of cannibalism? Such a conclusion is, of course, a bit circumstantial and literally "sketchy." The process of reading the slate, especially the graphics, boiled down to an artist's eye discerning a pattern among the scratches into the slate. Despite the admittedly subjective interpretation, there seems no doubt about the two characters and the apparent violence about to happen. Could it be mere coincidence that the slate drawing seems to depict what all of the accounts of the cannibalized wife relate? Or does the drawing of the soldier about to kill a woman illustrate the fate of Jane? Probably not, but the records and the drawing at least raise the question, Was Jane the murdered and cannibalized wife?

There is conflicting documentary evidence. On the one hand, those five historical accounts (1610–24) of a married woman being murdered and cannibalized during the "starving time" are consistently strong, corroborated evidence that the crime happened. The remains of a female who had been processed for cannibalization was found in a "starving time" context. One account suggests "the severed head" of the butchered wife may have been already butchered and discarded when the husband was caught. Also, the story of the unnamed, murdered, butchered wife is the only known written record of a woman's death during the "starving time." Although the forensic analysis indicated that the woman was dead before the skull was "processed" and that none of the cuts and chop marks was the cause of death, it is possible she could have been murdered in any number of ways that left no telltale signs on the skull but rather signs of trauma on the rest of her skeleton. Other remains have not been found.

Of course, Jane could have been any one of the other women who arrived in 1609, although fourteen is a somewhat young age for marriage, at least among the upper classes.[7] But it is important to remember that Jane was likely among the 1609 "lewd company" that Percy considered lower-class people. In addition, the description of the crime scene reported to Percy by whoever caught the husband in the act could have meant that the man had eaten all of the wife "save" (except) the head. Did this mean that the man grimly processed and ate the brain first, then disposed of the head before he was caught with the remaining body parts? Might this account for the fact that the rest of the girl's bones, except for the jaw and the fragment of leg bone, were not found with the skull?

Jane's fate might itself be evidence of a lower-class status. We know the names of about half of the sixty to ninety survivors of the "starving time" by combining names in Percy's account with a 1623–24 muster that lists who was still alive among the earlier colonists.[8] They were primarily upper-class: captains and gentlemen. Only one laborer could be identified. At least five of the survivors were women, and, of course, Jane was not one of them. The high status of the survivors suggests that the leaders had the pick of whatever food supplies were around during the lean months, while the lower classes were left to starve. This reinforces Smith's comment that the "poorer sort" were the cannibals, and perhaps that Jane met her fate at the hands of one of them. If she was the powdered wife, it may follow that she and her husband were indeed of the "poorer sort." But her diet in her earlier years appears to have been good. Her stable isotope test, showing high levels of nitrogen (protein), may argue against her being among the lower-status people in England, unless she was a maidservant for a gentleman's household. On the other hand, the lack of a lead signature in her bones argues for her being a lower-status person because the "better sort" ate and drank from pewter, which leaves a high lead signature.[9] Ironically, those using the best tableware were slowly committing suicide.

What is Jane's real name? So far, it is impossible to know for sure. But there are possible candidates. It is important to note that a Richard Brislow (Bristow?), laborer, arrived in Virginia with the second supply in 1608, and there is a record of the marriage in Sisland of a Richard Bristow in 1606 to an Elizabeth Fields. She may be one of three women named Elizabeth Fields whose christening dates would make them fourteen to fifteen years old in 1610. Also, a number of men named Richard Bristow were recorded as living in southern England near the various women named Elizabeth Fields. Jane has an isotopic oxygen signature suggesting an origin in southern England. Is Jane really Elizabeth, a wife sent to join her husband with the Falmouth fleet of 1609? Possibly. One might question how a lower-class Elizabeth could afford the passage, but she could have been a maidservant of a gentleman's family on the same voyage. All is admittedly speculative, but at this stage in the genealogical research these are some possibilities.[10]

Whether or not Jane is the murdered wife, and what her real name was, essentially remains a mystery. But the story that the Jamestown colonists practiced cannibalism to survive during the "starving time" is now proven true. The James Fort 1609–10 archaeological context, the forensic identification of dozens of processing marks, and the historical accounts confirm that irrefutable conclusion. But how did conditions at Jamestown deteriorate to the point that cannibalism was an option? Both history and science can provide an answer.

In the summer of 1609, the nine-vessel fleet, led by the flagship *Sea*

Venture, cleared Henry VIII's Pendennis Castle as it made out to sea from Falmouth Harbor. For almost all of the 450 colonists—men, women, and children—that landmark would be their last glimpse of England. This was a well-funded and -equipped armada carrying a new charter for the Virginia colony and bountiful provisions, a major effort to ultimately rejuvenate Jamestown. The voyage did not go well. A hurricane separated the *Sea Venture* from the others and eventually drove it aground in Bermuda. Virginia's newly appointed lieutenant governor, Sir Thomas Gates, Admiral George Somers, and 150 other immigrants remained in Bermuda for nine months while two vessels were built to complete their journey to Jamestown.[11] The effects of the storm on the rest of the convoy were severe. When they limped into Jamestown, "Some had lost their Masts, some their Sails blown from their Yards; the Seas so over-raking our Ships, much of our provision was spoiled, the Fleet separated, and our men sick, and many died, and in this miserable estate . . . [we] arrived in Virginia."[12] But a greater disaster awaited them that following fall, winter, and spring. They were about to face the darkest months in Jamestown's history, after which only sixty people out of about three hundred would be alive.

In the fall of 1609, conditions at Jamestown were ripe for a perfect starvation "storm." Inadequate planning, overpopulation, faltering local leadership, desertion, hostile Virginia Indians, and a drought came into play practically simultaneously. From the original landing day, May 14, 1607, the colony faced a food deficit. As John Smith wrote, "we were all ignorant, and supposing to make our passage [from England] in two monthes, with victual to live, and the advantage of the spring to worke; we weare at sea 5 monthes where we both spent our victual and lost the opportunity of the time, and season to plant."[13] For the next three years, the colonists never could overcome the original food shortage on their own, with those who survived the first summer relying on food from the Indians. Reliance on the Indians for food was, of course, the plan from the beginning. The colonists would be the merchants, trading iron tools and copper for the Indians' corn. In reality, Smith acquired corn by firm negotiation or force.[14]

Not only did the August 1609 fleet bring spoiled stores and three hundred more mouths to feed, but the new arrivals included the kind of people who would hardly help the cause. Percy emphatically refers to them as "unruly gallants," "swarmes of idle persons, which having no means of labor to releeve their misery, doe likewise swarme in lewd and naughtie practices." Remember that, according to Smith, the new arrivals were "poor

Left: A child's silver whistle with a coral teether found in the "starving time" layer of the cellar/well. This likely came to Jamestown in the summer of 1609 with the huge influx of settlers that, for the first time, included some children. *Right:* The portrait shows young Charles II with a similar teether. (National Portrait Gallery, London)

gentlemen, tradesmen, serving men, [and] libertines . . . ten times more fit to spoil a commonwealth than either to begin one or but help to maintain one." In a matter of days, the new arrivals proceeded to devour what little corn the colonists had planted.[15]

The "lewd company" included women and children, whose presence had to raise a red flag for Powhatan. Clearly, he could figure out that the Tassantassas (English) were not just itinerant traders in his land but were moving in to stay. Then Smith, the only English leader whom Powhatan respected and with whom he would usually trade, was mysteriously wounded when a powder accident practically blew off part of his leg. In September Smith was sent home to England, and George Percy took over the presidency. But Percy proved no staunch stand-in. He was sick himself part of the time and not quite the strong character needed to weather the starvation storm.[16]

With Percy in charge, attempts to trade with the Indians horribly collapsed. He first "sent Captain Ratliefe to Powhatan to procure victuals and corn." But the Indians would have none of it anymore. "[T]he sly old king . . . surprised Captain Ratliefe alive, who he caused to be bound unto a tree naked with a fire before, and by women his flesh was scraped from his bones with mussel shells . . . so for want of circumspection [Ratcliffe] miserably perished."[17]

Then Percy sent "Captain West . . . to Potoamack with about thirty-six men to trade for maize and grain, where he in short time loaded his pinnace sufficiently, yet used some harsh and cruel dealing by cutting off two of the savages' hands and other extremities." This was not a particularly wise way to pave the way for future food trading. But that was not the end of the story. When West's ships were "coming by Algernon's Fort, Captain Davis did call unto them, acquainting them with our great wants, exhorting them to make all the speed they could to relieve us, upon which report Captain West . . . hoisted up sails and shaped their course directly for England, and left us in that extreme misery and want."[18] Off they went to England with piracy on their agenda.

Meanwhile, better leadership than Percy's was delayed in Bermuda until May 1610. The 150 travelers on the flagship *Sea Venture,* in contrast to the "lewd company" of "unruly gallants" that had made it to Virginia on the other ships, included the next lieutenant governor, Sir Thomas Gates; the admiral of the fleet, Sir George Somers; future knight and would-be governor of Virginia George Yeardley with his wife and family; William Strachey, experienced with foreign English mercantile outposts; and a host of gentlemen and wives and maidservants.[19]

William Strachey, the new secretary to the colony, did not blame Percy for the "starving time." Remember, he reported that it was the warring Powhatan and disease that sealed the settlers' fate: "And it is true, the Indian killed as fast without, if our men stirred but beyond the bounds of their blockhouse, as famine and pestilence did within."[20] The besieged colonists could not even get any fish from the James River: "The Indians . . . endanger and assault any boat upon the river or straggler out of the fort . . . they shot two of our people to death."[21]

Another major cause of the "starving time" was beyond human control: the drought. One of the staples on which Jamestown colonists relied between "starving times" (summer of 1607 and 1609–10) was sturgeon, which were so abundant at one point that John Smith proclaimed he could catch as many as could be "eaten by dog or man" in one casting of the net.[22]

These corpulent river creatures migrated up the James in the spring and fall, passing by the island to reach the freshwater they needed for spawning. As we have seen, the river at Jamestown Island is naturally brackish where the salt water from the ocean meets the freshwater flowing from the interior, a zone known now as the salt ledge. But exactly where the ledge forms varies according to rainfall. It moves downriver during rainy periods and upriver during drought. We have also seen that the period 1606–13 was the driest period in Virginia in the preceding 770 years.[23] This being the case, when Smith reported that the sturgeon failed to appear in the fall of 1609, the drought probably was the reason. The freshwater had moved far enough upstream that the sturgeon raced past the island undetected by the colonists as they sought the salt ledge in the interior reaches of the river.[24] The drought also accounts for the meager Indian corn crop in 1609–10. Smith wrote that at one point the werowance of Quiyoughcohannock "entreat[ed the President of the colony] . . . to pray to my God for raine, for their Gods would not send them any."[25] And Strachey also reported that "The Indians were themselves poor, they were forbidden likewise . . . at all to trade with us."[26]

The discovery of Jane raises the broader question about what seventeenth-century Western culture thought about anthropophagy, the scientific term for cannibalism. There is no doubt that western European society viewed the practice as taboo and labeled those who practiced it as barbarians. According to the historians James Horn, Douglas Owsley, and Beverly Straube, however, "[s]ocieties across the world from prehistoric until recent times have adopted the practice of cannibalism either for ritualistic or other purposes. Powdered human bones and human blood, for example, were widely believed to have medicinal benefits throughout Europe in the 16th and 17th centuries." The consumption of human flesh at Jamestown was neither ritual nor medicinal; it was for survival. Suffering and psychological trauma caused by prolonged starvation together with the will to survive induced some settlers "to do those things which seem incredible, as to dig up dead corpses out of graves and to eat them."[27]

While the physical evidence of cannibalism in the colonial world is unique to Jamestown, accounts of its practice are not. Percy himself prefaces his account of the "starving time" winter by an apparent attempt to minimize the taboo nature of what happened on his watch in 1609–10: "The Spaniards plantations in the River platte and the straits of Magellan suffered [from hunger] insomuch that having eaten up all their horses to sustain them . . . mutinies did arise . . . for which Diego Mendoza, caused some of them to be executed [hanged] . . . others secretly . . . cut down their dead fellows from off the gallows and bury [buried] them in their hungary bowels."[28] There are other incidents recorded in the Spanish colonial world. In 1568, Florida Indians drove Spanish colonists into a garrison at Santa Lucia. The besieged settlers eventually resorted to survival cannibalism: "There they [Indians] held the path by which the Spaniards went to draw water, killed a large number of the colonists, and drove the survivors to take refuge with the garrison at Santa Lucia. This unexpected increase in population created so great a famine at Santa Lucia that the unfortunate colonists had been driven to the practice of cannibalism."[29] Stories of the French effort to settle in modern-day South Carolina also include an instance of anthropophagy. In 1562, after abandoning their aborted colony at Port Royal, adrift in the Atlantic in a makeshift boat, a number of starving Frenchmen drew straws, executed the loser, and cannibalized his body.[30]

Nor was Jamestown the only scene of cannibalism in Virginia. In 1649, a marooned and starving group of would-be Virginia immigrants lived off dead men and women: "Of the three weak women before mentioned," wrote Henry Norwood, "one had the envied happiness to die about this time; and it was my advice to the survivors, who were following her apace, to endeavor their own preservation by converting her dead carcass into food, as they did to good effect. The same counsel was embraced by those of our sex: the living fed upon the dead; four of our company having the happiness to end their miserable lives."[31]

What does Jane's story say about the Jamestown venture? There are records of at least eleven failed European attempts to establish a colony in the New World before Jamestown managed to succeed. Discovering the truth about the cannibalism stories leaves no doubt exactly how close Jamestown came to joining the other aborted settlements. Barring the timely arrivals of Gates and De La Warre, American history could have taken a much different course. The English might have given up on Virginia and focused their colonial settlement in the West Indies. Had the English failed to colonize the mainland, Spain may have spread north, or the French south, imposing different social, political, and economic traditions on the Atlantic coast.

That is not to say that living off the dead saved the day. Rather, it appears that those who survived, the "better sort," lived on some food source other than the remains of those who had already died. Cannibalism appears to

Forensic sculpture reconstruction of Jane's face on an exact digital resin copy of her skull. (Studio EIS)

have ended when Gates arrived in May 1610—with the exception of the survivor who became so addicted to eating human flesh that only his execution could break the habit.

So the horror of Jane's discovery spotlights what can be considered a profoundly significant moment in the history of the future United States.[32] And perhaps the recovery of Jane from the trash, examining her mutilated remains, and reconstructing her appearance somehow atones for her untimely demise and her body's grim post-mortem history.

Finally, the unexpected discovery of Jane's remains taught us one more thing about the abandoned cellar/kitchen fill, proving that the kitchen operated before and possibly during the early weeks of the "starving time," but no longer.

Further, the cellar/kitchen was almost certainly part of the storehouse/cellar/well structure, as it was directly aligned with and exactly ten feet away from that complex, first appearing as an L-shaped, mixed-soil stain clearly visible against the background of surrounding yellow subsoil clay. Excavation of the mixed fill revealed that this was indeed the site of a cellar/kitchen/bakery. Two ovens were found carved into the clay cellar walls, and crudely mortared brick walls were found below the oven openings, probably supports for the oven doors. There was clear evidence that a set of crude wood-on-clay steps provided access to the kitchen from the original level of the fort to the north. Layer-cake-like strata had accumulated during the use of the cellar, and our excavation, layer by layer, told its chronological story. The lowest deposit on the clay floor indicated that originally the cellar had been used for ironworking. Strata above indicated that the ironwork quickly switched to baking. Wood ash littered the floor above the iron level. This was obviously ash waste raked out of the ovens when they reached their baking temperature. The uppermost layers of the ash contained turtle shells and scales (or scutes) from enormous sturgeon, the colonists' staple before the "starving time." A thick layer of variegated-looking mixed clay rested above the sturgeon level, almost certainly another deposit of fallen mud-and-stud walls from the collapse of the aboveground kitchen superstructure. Above that lay the De La Warre–redeposited "starving time" debris, and Jane's remains, all of which completely postdate the working kitchen.

There is some written record of the kitchen's history. Captain Christopher Newport brought the first resupply to the colony in early January 1608. Soon after unloading his cargo and one hundred men, fire broke out in the fort, possibly caused by the loading of gunpowder into the storehouse.[33] For some reason, Newport with his band of settlers, mariners, and sailors decided to stay at Jamestown until April 15. Smith lamented that "the ship staying 14 weeks when she might as well have been gone in 14 days" taxed the colony's food supplies.[34] To while away the hours when they were eating up the food stores, however, Newport directed his crew to improve the storehouse and to build a substantial church and a "stove," which in the seventeenth century meant a hot room. It is likely that that stove was, in fact, the cellar/kitchen in which Jane's remains were found. This reference establishes the date of the kitchen construction as the late winter or early spring of 1608, when Newport's crew was in port. We can also surmise that the kitchen went out of use and collapsed during the early days of the "starving time." Perhaps it was torn apart for firewood. After all, who needs a kitchen if there is nothing to cook?

SEVEN

COMPANY TOWN

It is important to emphasize that the Virginia "venture" was exactly that, essentially a risky scheme to turn a satellite English colony into a profit-making enterprise for the Virginia Company investors. So it stands to reason that the first fort building the settlers were instructed to construct was a storehouse, a shelter for the provisions to keep the men alive as well as a secure place to deposit all the precious metals and other riches the Company entrepreneurs expected they would find. It is not surprising, then, that the increasing number of sizeable postholes found dead center in the triangular fort almost certainly marked the location of the storehouse. These holes defined part of a sixteen-foot-wide and at least forty-foot-long structure. The rest of the long axis of the building was likely missing, erased during the construction of the 1861 Jamestown Civil War fort. In fact, it is remarkable that any of these postholes survived at all. The enormous amount of dirt moving required to produce embankments large enough to protect massive Civil War cannons wiped away much of the seventeenth-century remains. However, under the earthwork a fair number of storehouse holes survived both inside and outside the fortifications. The Civil War grading did go deep enough, apparently, to completely destroy any remaining storehouse holes toward the river, but the four surviving posts along the west wall plus a conjectured northern corner post establish the "at least" length of forty feet. This would be far too small for the numbers and ambitions of the colonists. It must have extended much farther south. In fact, there is enough space between the last surviving storehouse posthole and the projected fort wall line to accommodate a building one hundred feet long, still leaving enough space for the standard ten-foot "street" between them.

There is documentary record of this spacious storehouse. By 1611, Secretary of the Colony Ralph Hamor described it as being 120 feet long and 40 feet wide, built in three attached sections.[1] But the length and especially the width of the posthole-defined structure did not come close to a building that spacious. Still, there is some archaeological evidence that Hamor was not exaggerating, at least about the length and the sections. Traces of foundation trenches lying at right angles to the storehouse postholes, and basically aligned with the holes, were also found just north of a midcentury house cellar. Digging into the trenches revealed that this addition rested on horizontally laid timber foundations, which were replaced later with a cobblestone footing laid in clay. The same construction sequence turned up at the nearby 1611 governor's rowhouse site. The footing appeared to be remains of an addition to the storehouse, most of it subsequently destroyed by the circa-1650s cellar. Yet if this footing was once connected to the posthole building to the south, the surviving storehouse would have been at least 64 feet long even without including the hypothetical length toward the palisade. In this scenario, Hamor's description holds true. More evidence of size is suggested by comparison with the record of the storehouse at Jamestown's sister settlement, Fort Saint George in Maine. That building, also supported by posts in the ground, was 70 feet long.

Why are the identification and size of this building footprint so significant? This discovery is yet another manifestation of the Virginia Company's business plan, unrealistic as that turned out to be, and it comments again on the willingness of the colonists to rigidly follow Company instructions. How so? The central location, probable size, and early construction date prove that the Company's mandate requiring the colonists to build the storehouse first was taken seriously. This was despite the fact that they themselves had to live in tents and "holes in the ground." It probably did make sense that the storehouse building was so enormous and erected first to accommodate the promised "abundant" resupplies from England and to quickly provide a "bonded warehouse" for the anticipated rapid discovery of gold and silver. In reality, gold digging came up empty, and the supplies, if they showed up at all, were meager at best. Yet the colonists kept adding on to the building. Why expand space they did not need? Was this yet another waste of time in the face of the reality of their situation in Virginia? Probably so, but again, finding remains of such a huge central building at

James Fort is strong testimony to how adamantly committed the Company and colonists were to their entrepreneurial mission.

"A WELL . . . OF EXCELLENT SWEET WATER"

Even the large core section of the storehouse had two more additions: a structure to the east with a deep cellar above a barrel-lined well, and the subterranean kitchen next door. The well, in all likelihood, is the "well of excellent sweet water" to which Captain Smith alluded in 1609 that finally produced a freshwater supply and ended the colonists' suicidal practice of drinking from the brackish river.

Above the well, a close examination of the unlined cellar walls revealed corner notches in the clay where a rectangular timber footing once supported a wooden floor six feet beneath the surface. The walls and a floor that deep would produce a cool, dry-well storage space for perishables. Below that room lay the remnants of the barrel-lined well, which was built enough off center in the cellar to create usable cool storage space on the floor above it. It is important to note that the clay cellar walls found archaeologically were not severely eroded over time. This has to indicate that the structure over the cellar had an overhanging roof to protect the vulnerable walls from rainwater erosion. Once that protective roof collapsed, numerous cobblestones found at the bottom of the well show that erosion of the walls eventually did take place, which undercut a stone foundation at the surface that finally wound up falling to the well bottom.

It is significant that the well and cellar were attached to the storehouse. Having a significant store of provisions and a freshwater supply for the settlement was vitally important. It is clear from contemporary descriptions that food and good water were often scarce and had to be rationed.[2] This of course meant controlling access to both. Encased within the storehouse complex, the attached cellar/well could be secured merely by locking a single storehouse door. The well's central location in the fort also accommodated well surveillance. This underscores the power of the Company's cape merchant, who was in charge of the store. He could literally dictate life and death. The beginning of "freedom from want" in America would have to wait until the Company figured out that it had to offer more benefits to emigration than a chance to toil, die of thirst, or starve in the strange new land.

This unusual cellar/well combination had a short life. Strachey's 1610

Left: The central cellar/well showing the upper clay cellar walls above the partially excavated circular eroded well shaft. *Above:* Computer-generated cellar/well reconstruction adjacent to the south wall of the storehouse. (David Givens)

comment that the sweet water had gone very sour because it was "fed by the brackish river oozing into it" is almost certainly true. An initial testing of the water in the brick-lined well outside the fort triangle had indicated that the Jamestown groundwater is basically potable today. This positive test originally suggested that historical references to well contamination from the salty river water may have been exaggerated. It appeared that blaming salt poisoning from contaminated well water for many of the deaths during the winter of 1609–10 was a governor's attempt to mask the real killer, starvation. However, recent groundwater testing in a number of borings in and around the fort explains both the present freshwater currently found in the brick-lined well and the references to well-water salt pollution. Our study found that during wet periods the well water was basically salt-free, while in dry periods high levels of salt entered the groundwater table from two directions, on the north side of the fort from the nearby saltwater marsh and on the south side from the James River.[3] It is also logical to conclude that salt coming from both directions could wind up in the groundwater whenever constant drawing of well water depleted the surrounding freshwater, allowing salt-contaminated water to seep into the well shafts. In other words, the overworked well probably acted like a sponge, drawing in the brackish river and marsh water. Also, studies have found that in dry periods, the freshwater table disappears and the saltwater level rises. Remember the 1606–13 drought? Under these circumstances, the short lifespan of the storehouse cellar/well, and indeed of the many other wells dug at Jamestown in the seventeenth century, should be no surprise.

Like so many of the structural remains found at the fort site, the abandoned cellar/well lay below as much as ten feet of Confederate earthwork fill and the circa-1750–1861 plowzone. Our excavation of those soil deposits eventually exposed a rectangular dark soil stain, the top layer of a trash dump. When the surface of this fill was archaeologically leveled, the site looked like a target, with concentric dark bands encircling the bull's-eye. This was clear evidence that we had found a deep deposit that had been periodically filled and refilled as the soil in the center kept sinking into what proved to be the abandoned well below. Not unlike peeling an onion, our excavation of these colorful circular stripes of debris recovered artifacts indicating episodes of sinking and filling beginning in the third quarter of the seventeenth century. Removal of these more "modern" levels eventually reached the initial filling, some four feet below the surface. At that point to the bottom (fourteen feet below the surface) we recovered more than 500,000 artifacts dating from the period 1607–10. These included arms, ammunition, armor, gunlocks, swords, both European and Virginia Indian pottery, clay tobacco pipes, metalworking crucibles, bottles, jewelry, coins, Indian shell beads, glass trade beads, Indian bone needles, and an extensive collection of discarded food remains including more than 30,000 oyster shells and thousands of butchered animal and fish bones. The butchered horse, dog, rat, and snake bones found among these faunal remains were clear signs of a time when normal food was scarce. These sealed layers of trash, and the fairly uneroded condition of the clay cellar walls, indicated that this enormous deposit went into the abandoned cellar/well practically all at once. This begs the questions: Where did all this trash come from, and how did so much accumulate in what seemed to be so short a period of time? A logical answer lies in when the deposit was made.

Remember that upon arriving in June 1610, De La Warre ordered his men to "cleanse the town." Garbage and trash dating to that year went into many of the fort's building cellars and pits, clear evidence of a cleansing operation after the "starving time." The open and spoiled cellar/well must have been yet another convenient empty hole for getting rid of the fort debris. But where did the debris come from? Likely close by. More digging exposed an area free of substantial building remains in the southwestern sector of the fort. This was probably the marketplace Strachey described as

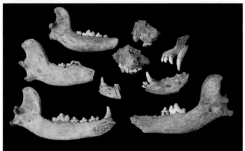

Butchered horse (*lower left*); dog (*lower right*); and thousands of extremely fragmented animal and fish bones from the timber-lined well, clear evidence of the scarcity of food supplies during the 1609–10 "starving time."

being in the "middest" of the fort. And clearly there was nothing to market, especially food, during the "starving time." This open space, then, certainly could have become the "starving time" dump. Here the settlers, if some were strong enough, could have thrown their waste onto a common pile that De La Warre's men wound up "cleansing," including the remains of the horses and dogs.

Fragments of pottery that fit together, or mended, from many deposits across the site, including the cellar/well, suggest a common source that likely accumulated during the "starving time." More than sixty Irish pennies dated 1601 or 1602 and a 1601 coin proof found in the cellar/well deposit strongly suggest that the deposit was made at a time when money had no buying power within the fort, especially to buy food—if indeed the

From the cellar/well: one of more than sixty Irish copper pennies dated 1601 or 1602 (*top*) and a voided copper plate for two 1601 halfpenny coin designs that never went beyond the trial stage in England (*bottom*) but were probably brought to Jamestown with the thousands of other copper scraps to make brass. One of the patterns was officially minted in silver as shown. (Private collection of Jamie May)

coins had any real monetary value at all. Add to that the Virginia Indian siege of the fort during the "starving time" and the ever-deflating value of copper from overtrading, and it is little wonder that so many of these coins would find their way into the town dump by the time De La Warre did his cleansing.

Two other types of objects are especially clear windows into the reality of the Jamestown venture: a slate tablet, and some curiously marked Robert Cotton clay tobacco pipes. The most unexpected was the 5″ × 8″ discarded tablet covered with faint inscriptions: words, symbols, numbers, and drawings of people, plants, and animals. This discovery was not unlike finding the proverbial lost letters in an attic trunk. Here was an object that was

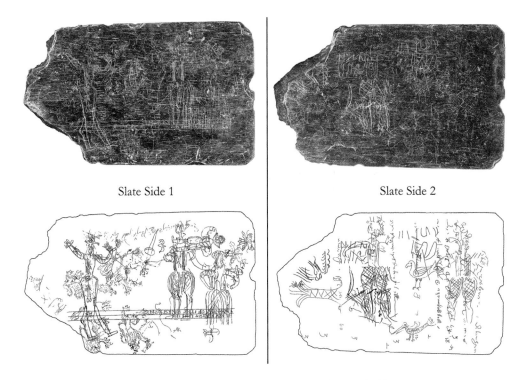

Slate Side 1

Slate Side 2

Above: Both writing surfaces of the cellar/well slate enhanced with chalk.
Below: Digital highlighting showing all drawings, inscriptions, art, and text.
(Michael Lavin, Jamie May)

inherently both an archaeological find and a historical document. But how to read it remains a challenge.

This much can be known. Prior to De La Warre's late spring cleaning, the owner(s) drew and wrote on the slate with a pencil made of slate and/or something more dense, making either chalk-like marks or permanent scratches. Usually the mark could be wiped off to make a "clean slate" for the next use or user. But whenever anyone pressed hard enough, the pencil left permanent scratches on the tablet that couldn't be erased either in part or completely. As a result, there are layers upon layers of inscriptions ranging in quality from mostly fragmented to mostly complete. But the real challenge in reading these inscriptions is more than their fragmentation. The overlapping use and reuse of the slate and the fact that the marks are basically the same dark-gray color as the slate itself have made the deciphering process even more difficult.

In order to understand them, we needed to enhance the slate inscriptions in some way. Our research turned logically to a variety of nondestructive analytical processes drawing on both art and science. Initially, white chalk dust was rubbed into the grooves that made up the inscriptions. This process created some contrast between the marks and the gray background. Then high-resolution digital images made of the slate were fed into a computer. Artistic highlighting of the chalked inscriptions brought out the drawings, words, and letters in varying degrees of clarity.[4] Other attempts at highlighting included three-dimensional X-rays produced by scientists at the National Aeronautics and Space Administration (NASA) laboratory using an enhancing program (a microfocus computed tomography X-ray system) in an attempt to look at the slate surfaces in micro "layers."[5] The NASA X-rays highlighted some of the inscriptions, but art and conservation work was much more successful in defining them. Nonetheless, more scientific "art" tests were conducted by conservators and scientists at the Smithsonian Institution's Museum Conservation Institute, which produced high-resolution photographs using different light sources and focal lengths.[6] This process, known as Reflectance Transformation Imaging, or RTI, exaggerated the grooves that make up the slate's inscriptions, producing high-resolution images where the grooves intersected. This made it possible to determine the time sequence of the various inscriptions. Like a micro archaeological site, where later ditches cut through fill in cellars, RTI began to determine which inscription lines overlapped and therefore were inscribed later in time than other inscribed lines.

Even the Federal Bureau of Investigation (FBI) got involved in the quest for a slate translation.[7] One FBI technique was simply to use a powerful microscope technology called Keyence to analyze the surface in great detail. This ultra–high resolution technique also began to sort out the sequence of the artwork and writing episodes even more precisely than the RTI technique. Another FBI process, laser profiling, produced a micro three-dimensional map, thus enhancing the grooves much like the RTI process. The profiling had promise, but it was complicated by the fact that the slate is not uniformly flat to begin with. This actually distorted the images.

In the end, we found that the really telling analysis came from a curator of manuscripts at the Folger Shakespeare Library, who read the artistically and photographically enhanced images by applying her expertise in Elizabethan/Jacobean-period alphabets and phrases.[8]

There are many clues to the number of users of the slate sorted out forensically so far: by orientation of the tablet, superimposition of the drawings and text, handwriting style, text type, and artistic style. On one side of the slate, an "author" holding the slate horizontally, with the broken end to the right, inscribed three straight lines to serve as a guide for two lines of writing. The first line consists of block capital letters and likely a date. This upper line does not seem to form an English sentence and may end in a date: "I" EL NEV FSH"I"HT LBMS I5o8 (or 1598, the more likely reading if it is a date). The lower line of text does compose an English sentence, also in block capital letters. It appears to read, "I AM NON OF THE FINEST SORTE" or "I A MINON OF THE FINEST SORTE." It is not clear if the author used the "I"-like symbol between certain letter runs, or if it stands for "I" or, in the case of the date, the number 1. Near the lower edge of side 1, there is a line of cursive text in Elizabethan secretary hand, a distinctive style often used in legal documents during the sixteenth and seventeenth centuries. This seems to restate the sentence, "I am non of the finest sorte," adding the letters "lyr sh p p" at the end.

On the side opposite the block lettering, someone wrote what appears to be eight or perhaps as many as twenty lines of text with the slate held vertically, the jagged end at the bottom. Along the right margin a column of arabic numerals appears, which may or may not relate to the text lines. There are five number 3s, two 2s, and what appears to be the number 18. Also, some words and symbols reveal that this was written in Elizabethan secretary hand.

The artwork includes sketches of three men, a woman, four lions, three flowers, and three fleurs-de-lis on one side, and two men, three birds, and a tree on the other. Judging by their dress, the images of the people include three men, possibly soldiers, dressed in early seventeenth-century trousers known as venetians. One of the soldiers appears to be wearing a cabasset-style helmet and wielding a sword, apparently threatening the woman he holds by the neck with his left hand. She is wearing a doublet vest, possibly with shoulder wings, a ruff about her neck, and an Elizabethan hair cover-ing known as a coif, all late sixteenth- to early seventeenth-century cloth-ing components. It is apparent that another and more accomplished artist drew one of the men on side 1, positioning the slate vertically. This man is wearing a ruff collar, a type that required a frame known as a supportasse to hold its shape, a decorative doublet, and venetians—all dress usually reserved for the elite.[9]

Based on style, it is very likely that as many as three different individu-

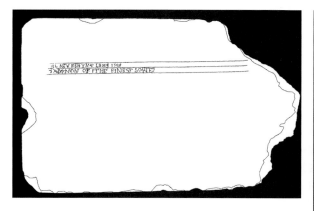

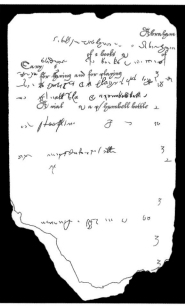

Left: The enhanced deeply scored text.
Right: "Abraham's" list with deciphered words in red. (Michael Lavin, Jamie May)

als drew the people. One person sketched the ruff-collared man on side 1; another person drew the two men on side 2 and the helmeted soldier and woman on side 1; and yet another produced the very crude sketch of another male on side 1. The crude figure is shown wearing a period-type hat with what appears to be an arrow stuck through it. Also on side 1 there appears to be a sketch of a man's profiled head crowned with an Elizabethan hat.

One side of the slate also includes a number of other drawings made with the slate in the same vertical orientation as the collared man—three flowers and three fleurs-de-lis—while four lions were drawn with a horizontal slate orientation. In the world of heraldry, lions in the depicted stance, known as the rampant position, are a common symbol on crests and shields. The flowers were drawn in some detail, perhaps enough to identify them. One very likely is a thistle, and two others may be daffodils.

The opposite side includes three fairly detailed pictures of birds. Two are obviously birds of prey: a pelican, tern, or short-legged heron (green heron), and above it an eagle, sea gull, or even possibly a cahow or petrel native only to Bermuda. There is also a small songbird pictured on the broken edge. Two were drawn when the artist held the slate in a horizontal position. A tree is drawn vertically on this side as well, almost certainly a palm (Palmea). It may also be a sketch of something the artist saw in Bermuda, the palmetto. There are, however, an estimated 2,500–3,500 species of palms, making a positive identification unlikely, even if the drawing were more precise. Based on what could be the depiction of a hanging blossom above or connected to the tree, it might instead be a banana tree.

The slate inscriptions raise the obvious questions: What is the meaning of the various lines of text and the sketches, who made them, and when were they made? There is evidence that suggests answers. The two block-lettered lines of text on side 1 are the most legible and offer the best opportunity to garner meaning. The top line contains sixteen letters, but only two vowels: "I" EL NEV FSH"I"HT LBMS. It does not seem to be a sentence unless it is shorthand using only the first letter of each word. If it is, then the odds of finding the right words based on the first letter alone are slim. Was this a schoolboy practicing block letters? One might expect someone practicing penmanship to include the entire alphabet. Or are some of these initials acronyms? If so, they do not appear to stand for any known English societies, although there were hundreds of them. Or is this a coded message? There are eleven different letters among the apparent sixteen characters, and thirteen letters from the twenty-four-letter Elizabethan alphabet do not appear. So one could conclude that the letters chosen likely do contain a message. One possibility is that these are initials of people. Who and why? Possibly this slate was once used as a cursing stone, a Welsh tradition. In Wales it was a custom to put a curse on someone by putting his or her name or initials on a slate and tossing it into an open well. But the Jamestown slate was found in the thick rubbish purposely dumped into the abandoned well, which does not seem to fit the Welsh cursing practice.[10]

The numbers in that same line can be read as an apparent date: "1508" or "1598." The "0," however, might be a backward "9." And the "1" may not be a number but rather the aforementioned spacer "I" symbol with strangely forked serifs and a line through the middle. Only the "5" and "8" cannot be in doubt. If the "1" is not the number "1," then this could be a tally of something, a record of as many as 508 or 598 of "LBMS," whatever they are.

The sentence below the individual letters on the marked line with the statement "I AM NON OF THE FINEST SORTE" or "A MINON OF THE FINEST SORTE" is somewhat more understandable. The use of the forked-serif "I" raises the question of how to read it: "AM NON" or "MINON." "MINON" could be a misspelling of the word "MINION," which can mean anything from a small cannon to a servant. The "MINON" statement is a rather upbeat translation compared to the more negative admission of the writer that he or she was not included among the "finest sorte" of people.

So who wrote these lines and drew these pictures? It is tempting to identify at least one author/artist as William Strachey, secretary of the colony in 1610–11. It was Strachey who wrote about his harrowing experience on the vessel *Sea Venture* as a hurricane drove it ashore in Bermuda, and about the nine months he spent there as two ships were built to bring him finally to his Jamestown destination. At Jamestown he describes James Fort, the desperate condition of the town right after the "starving time," and how the arrival of Lord De La Warre saved the colony in 1610. He may have arrived with his pocket slate, his "rough draft" notebook that he had used since 1598 and had lost during the aforementioned De La Warre cleanup.

There is a chain of evidence pointing to Strachey. The use of secretary hand on the slate may be one clue. It was commonly used by attorneys for legal documents, and Strachey trained in the law at the prestigious Gray's Inn. Also, Strachey's coat of arms includes a rampant lion and fleurs-de-lis. He may have been sketching a version for a document or an engraving on some of his pewter or silver. The mysterious paragraph could be lines of scripture since it mentions Abraham, and the lines may be numbered. Strachey apparently had a habit of writing scripture, if the biblical text in his signed Commonplace Book is any indication.[11] The book is miniscule, and the size of the letters is as tiny as the slate writing. Moreover, when he was marooned on Bermuda he could have made the sketches of what may be a cahow, a bird native only to those islands, and the native Bermuda palmetto, about which he writes in his book *The Historie of Travell into Virginia Britania*. Also, in 1598 Strachey was hobnobbing with London intellectuals and courtiers, who were "the finest sorte," but he was penniless at the time and brooded over the fact that he was not wellborn.

The name Abraham, however, could mean something besides scripture, and the lines of text and numbers seem to be all part of some kind of a list: there is a line listing some commodity, like "vial of" and "bottle" followed by its numerical value. This could possibly be a ledger or an inventory. Whose list? Abraham is not a common name among the known settlers. Nonetheless, a metals refiner, Abraham Ransacke, is listed among those who came to Jamestown in the second resupply ship, but he is never mentioned again. Chances are Abraham died fairly soon after his arrival, and this may be a draft inventory of his possessions made by someone trained in the law. Again, Strachey was a Gray's Inn–trained lawyer.

Left: Enhanced armorial lions above fleurs-de-lis found on the slate. *Right*:
Secretary William Strachey's coat of arms.

Some of the characters among the lines of text on side 2 do not appear
to be secretary hand letters. They seem to be a symbol using curious loops.
This raises the possibility that certain words in this message may be written
in a phonetic Algonquian script invented by the Elizabethan mathematician
and scientist Thomas Hariot.[12] He was the navigator on the first Sir Walter
Raleigh–sponsored voyage to Virginia in 1585. When that group had to
leave the following year, Hariot took two Algonquian natives, Manteo and
Wanchese, back to England. There he taught them English, and they taught
him Algonquian. From that exchange Hariot wrote an Algonquian-English
dictionary. He also created an Algonquian-English phonetic alphabet so
that Englishmen could correctly pronounce Algonquian sounds. Although
the dictionary is thought to have burned in the Great Fire of London in
1666, the phonetic alphabet signed by Hariot and dated 1585 survived, oddly
enough, among the collections of the Westminster School in London.[13] One
of the symbols appears to be similar to some of the double-looped characters in the alphabet, suggesting a possible link to the Hariot system. Of

course, one letter does not help decipher the sentences. And even if it is part of an Algonquian word, all the surviving Hariot document would tell us is how to pronounce the word. Without the dictionary, the meaning would remain unknown. But this does not rule out the possibility that the writer of the slate paragraph in the early seventeenth century may have had access to both the Hariot phonetic alphabet and the dictionary before it met its fate in the London fire over a half century later. It remains to prove a connection between Hariot and Jamestown. Henry Percy, the Earl of Northumberland, could well be the link, and Strachey again the writer.

Henry Percy became the genius Hariot's patron soon after Sir Walter Raleigh was condemned to the Tower of London in 1603. And as we know, Henry's brother George was an original colonist who became governor of Jamestown in 1609. George corresponded with Henry in 1611, asking him to buy supplies and send them with Captain Nelson, which was not his first request. An earlier wish list from George may have been granted by his brother, its contents sent with Sir Thomas Gates on the *Sea Venture* along with William Strachey in May 1609. So it is possible that a copy of Hariot's dictionary and phonetic alphabet wound up in Strachey's possession on the *Sea Venture* with Henry Percy's supplies for George. It is also likely to have survived the shipwreck, along with all the passengers and most of the cargo. Strachey, being one of the most literate of the survivors who made it to Virginia, would be the most likely person to carry the trusted texts, essential information for the new wave of settlers to communicate with the Algonquian Powhatan population. In 1616, Strachey published his own dictionary. It lists alphabetically more than a thousand English-to-Algonquian words and phrases. Most of the book is copied from other publications, and it is logical to conclude that the translation dictionary came from another source, Hariot's works. Clearly Strachey copied from Smith, but Smith only published about seventy-five translated Algonquian words and phrases. It stands to reason, then, that most of Strachey's words and phrases must have come from Hariot's dictionary.[14]

The slate uniquely raises questions about that dawn of English-Algonquian communication. Strachey may have had access to Hariot's dictionary and phonetic alphabet when he arrived in Virginia, in which case it could have been in the possession of Percy's brother George, an original settler. Although there is no direct written evidence that Hariot ever met with George before he left for Virginia, it would be foolish to think that the colonists would sail off to meet what they knew would likely be a challenging welcome from the Indians without some form of a translation diction-ary—if they knew it existed. It could follow that some of the men knew of Hariot's past work in England with the Roanoke Algonquian Indians and would arm themselves with a copy of his dictionary. Also, Smith refers to many encounters with the Virginia natives where clearly they are convers-ing openly from almost the very start.

Whether or not Strachey can be credited with some of the inscriptions on the slate, it is nonetheless clear that more than one person drew the slate pictures and wrote the texts. Obviously, there is much uncertainty and conjecture in the current "translation." More science and art may find additional meaning hidden among the scratches on this remarkable object. One thing is certain: the slate is another example of how everyday objects recovered by archaeology vividly humanize the Jamestown story.

We also found that the slate was not the only object from the Smith cellar/well with written messages about the early history of Jamestown. A num-ber of distinct Virginia-made tobacco pipe stems opened a window on the settlement's transatlantic players. Much to our surprise, some of the pipe stems were imprinted with the names of distinguished early seventeenth-century Englishmen. The lettering on the pipes spells out enough of eight individual names to identify them as high-ranking English politicians, military men, social leaders, Virginia Company officials, Virginia gover-nors, and maritime explorers. The names include Sir Charles Howard, Lord High Admiral of the English Fleet and Queen Elizabeth's closest courtier; Sir Walter Raleigh, famous New World explorer and Elizabethan court-ier; Earl of Southampton (Henry Wriothesley), Shakespeare's major patron and top Virginia Company official; Lord De La Warre (Sir Thomas West), major Virginia Company investor and first resident governor of Virginia; Captain Samuel Argall, maritime explorer and lieutenant governor of Vir-ginia; and Captain Francis Nelson, admiral of the second Virginia supply fleet. Two other pipe stems are marked: one with the initials of a Sir "W C," which likely stands for Sir Walter Cope, Virginia Company councilor and London antiquarian; and the first three letters of what must stand for "Rob-ert," likely signifying Robert Cecil, Lord Salisbury, King James's secretary of state, prime mover behind the 1604 peace treaty of London between England and Spain, and the leader of the Virginia Company of investors in 1609.

There is compelling evidence proving that these distinctive clay pipes were made at Jamestown before 1610. Remember that in 1608, Captain

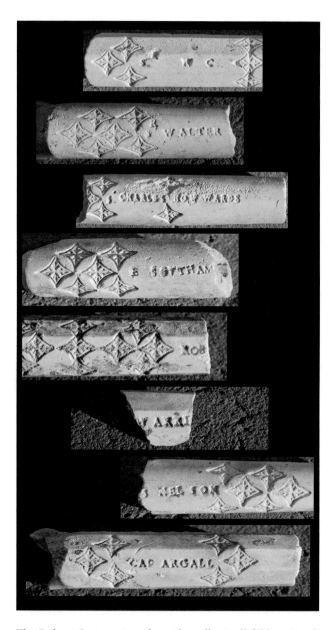

The Robert Cotton pipes from the cellar/well fill bearing the names of English colonial officials and Jamestown leaders (*top to bottom*): "SR W C" = Sir Walter Cope; "SR WALTER 1 . . ." = Sir Walter Raleigh; "SR CHARLES HOWARDE"; "E SOUTHAM . . ." = Earl of Southampton; "ROB . . ." = Robert Cecil?; ". . . WARRE" = Lord De La Warre; ". . . S NELSON" = Captain Francis Nelson; and "CAP ARGALL" = Captain Samuel Argall. (Michael Lavin)

Nelson brought 120 immigrants to Jamestown, including Robert Cotton, the "tobacco-pipe-maker" who is likely the craftsman who ultimately made and personalized his pipes. The pipes' color makes clear that they are made of native Virginia clay, which turns a bricklike reddish-orange to chocolate-brown color when fired. European pipes of the period are invariably white, made with clay from southern England. European pipes have bulbous molded bowls, whereas the Virginia bowls are distinctly trumpet-shaped like native Virginia Indian pipes. Again, there is hard evidence of the manufacturing process right at Jamestown as well. Fragments of small saggers—a type of pottery container used in kilns during the ceramic firing process—were also found with some of the Cotton pipes, along with other artifacts that can be dated to the first four years of the Jamestown settlement, 1607–10. The presence of the saggers, and the fact that they are the right size to hold the small pipes, indicates that the pipes were made and fired on-site. Also, some of the Cotton pipe stems have shaved faceted shafts, and shavings from this process have been found in early Jamestown deposits. Most of the Cotton pipes bear a distinctive impressed design obviously made by single or multiple impressions of a metal stamp of a fleur-de-lis-like cross within a diamond. These are stamps often used by bookbinders to emboss leather covers, and one similar metal stamp was also found at Jamestown. In fact, Jamestown's Robert Cotton might be a man of that name listed as a member of the Company of Stationers (a London printing monopoly) in 1602. A stationer would also likely have with him a set of printer's type that he used to spell out the names on his pipes.[15]

The Cotton pipes, and especially the Cotton pipes with names, raise two obvious questions: Why did the sponsoring Virginia Company send a pipe maker three thousand miles to ply his craft, and why was the pipe maker personalizing some of his wares with the names of such a distinguished group of courtiers, politicians, and adventurers? The first question is easier to answer than the second. By the time Jamestown was settled, smoking imported tobacco from the New World had become the rage in the Old World. This created a tremendous demand for pipes. A tobacco pipe industry soon flourished in Europe, at first centered in London, and after 1608 in Holland. The particular white clay found in Dorset, England, became the preferred material for making the pipes, and soon the Dorset miners had a monopoly on the pipe clay market. But the huge demand for pipes must have encouraged entrepreneurs like the Virginia Company investors to seek a way to beat the Dorset monopoly and share the profit of the lucra-

Top row, left to right: Lead movable type, "Jacob" printer's trademark, and two bookbinder's stamps from a James Fort soldier's pit. *Middle row:* Reversed as they would print. *Bottom row:* As they would print. (Michel Lavin, Charles Durfor, Jamie May)

tive new industry. Consequently, investors added pipe making to their list of industries that might be propagated in Virginia and sent the pipe maker, Cotton, to find the pipe clay and practice his craft at Jamestown.

Not only Europeans but also the Virginia settlers themselves would create a sizable demand for the pipes. In fact, of the 290 minimum number of the Cotton pipes found at Jamestown, about half appear to have been smoked. It is possible that the form of the Cotton pipes, so close in shape to the native Indian pipes, could also create a market in the English-Powhatan trade. In fact, it may have been Robert Cotton who took the Virginia Indian ceramic-market possibility beyond pipes. Pieces of one large pot made from pipe clay were also found with some of the Virginia-made pipes. The vessel, in its soft-clay prefired state, had been shaped inside a Virginia Indian basket, which left permanent impressions of the basket weft on the pot after it was fired. This made the final product appear in form and decoration to be an improved version of the conical cord-marked native pots of the Powhatan. The English higher-firing technique made it more durable and thus also a potential best-seller in the Indian trade. The fact that this bowl is a one-off might suggest that the idea did not appeal to the Indians.

Supply and demand certainly can explain why the company wanted to get into the tobacco pipe-making business and probably why the pipes were made, if only as a trial. But why did Cotton personalize some of the pipes, and why did he choose the names that he did? Possible answers may be found by looking closely at the relationship of the people involved in the Virginia colony who ventured their money but stayed in England, and the people who ventured their persons and actually went out to Virginia. There was obviously intense pressure on the Jamestown settlers to show the investors instant success. The colonists needed to prove that they were working tirelessly in every way possible to quickly produce fortune-making exports that would live up to the get-rich-quick expectations of the Virginia Company officials. The colonists' very lives depended on pleasing those leaders. Without the constant willingness of the Company to fund supply ships, the people left in the Virginia wilderness would lose their lifeline. Little wonder that the first boat home, which left for England just sixty days after the first landing, reportedly carried "gold"-laden soil. The settlers hoped the English assayers could find enough gold in the sample to incite a rash of new Virginia Company investments. But that hope quickly faded when no gold could be found. One of the most skeptical of the Virginia Company officials was Sir Walter Cope, who had doubted the dirt was gilded. Once he found out that his skepticism was well-founded, he concluded that the supposed gold in the cargo had "vaporized."[16]

Experimental Robert Cotton (?) clay pot retaining a clear but reverse impression of a native basket.

How does this explain the named pipes? Sir Walter Cope might be the key to an answer. Beyond being a high-ranking disgruntled official of the Virginia Company who needed an encouraging word, he was also a collector and exhibitor of exotic "Indian" objects from around the world, which he displayed in his museum in London. So creating a personalized Virginia-made tobacco pipe for him makes perfect sense for two reasons: giving him hope for a lucrative Virginia pipe-making industry in the offing, and sending him something exotic for his cabinet of curiosities.

But what about the other names on Cotton's products? Some, like Cope, were Virginia Company investors also possibly named by Cotton to hype the industrial achievements of the Virginia worker bees, assuming that, unlike the pipes found at Jamestown, some of them actually made it to England unbroken. Among these investors was the Earl of Southampton, Henry Wriothesley, an enthusiastic supporter of English colonial expansion, whom King James I appointed to the original Virginia Company Council. The naming of another colonial enthusiast—Sir Walter Raleigh—is more puzzling. Raleigh's Virginia connection went back more than two decades before the first settlement at Jamestown. His colonizing Virginia venture at Roanoke Island, North Carolina, in the period 1585–87, became the famous "Lost Colony" and cost Raleigh a considerable part of his personal fortune. To make matters worse, he fell out of favor with Queen Elizabeth, and when James became king, Raleigh was soon condemned to the Tower—from which, ironically, Southampton had emerged in 1603, after two years spent awaiting execution for his alleged part in the plot to overthrow Queen Elizabeth. Other than the fact that Southampton and Raleigh both spent some unanticipated time in the same prison at close to the same time, it is curious why Cotton and/or his employers named the downtrodden Raleigh on the Virginia-made pipes. On the other hand, Raleigh's name could be the most sensible of all. He is often credited with popularizing the recreational smoking of tobacco in England. Could this be an early use of the now-familiar marketing technique, the celebrity endorsement? Was this a marketing scheme to get Raleigh to hype the Virginia-made pipes by shipping him some with his very own name on them? True, in 1609 he was locked away and out of circulation. But during his imprisonment Raleigh became a prolific author, producing an impressive bibliography, including his million-word *History of the World*.[17] Through his writings he maintained his place in the London spotlight. Presumably, anything he could play up about Virginia would have an audience outside the prison walls. In any case, Raleigh was also connected to another London celebrity on Cotton's list of personalized souvenir pipes, a man who was second in power only to the king: Sir Charles Howard.

There is no record that Howard had any official connection with the Virginia adventure. But he certainly was a star in the Atlantic maritime world. Besides being the Lord High Admiral of the entire English fleet, he was apparently just as interested as the Virginia Company officials were in sailing west to get to the riches of China. He became a principal investor in the Northwest Passage Company, whose plan was to sail to China by discovering an ice-free route between the North American continent and the

Arctic. Howard was such an ardent proponent of English colonialism that the foremost propagandist for English colonial expansion, Richard Hakluyt, dedicated an edition of *The Principal Navigations of the English Nation* to him, commending him for his bold moves against the Spanish fleet.[18] And Howard was one of the principal negotiators bringing peace between Spain and England in 1604, a giant step toward opening up the Atlantic to English shipping and colonization in North America. Even if Howard had no official ties to Jamestown, sending him a personalized pipe might be a move to bring him into the fold. Or perhaps this pipe is the only record of Howard's more direct connection with the Virginia adventure. In any event, the named-pipe campaign at least had the ambition, if only at the pipe-trial stage, to reach into the highest of levels of the English hierarchy.

Another man of the highest political rank who appears to be named on the pipes is Robert Cecil, Earl of Salisbury, who also sat at the table with Howard and others during the negotiation of the 1604 peace treaty with Spain. In 1609 King James issued the Second Charter for the settlement of Virginia, in which he "gives, grants, and confirms" corporation status to more than 650 named individuals and companies "by the Name of The Treasurer and Company of Adventurers and Planters of the City of London, for the first Colony in Virginia."[19] The document names Robert Cecil, Earl of Salisbury, first, and Henry Wriothesley, Earl of Southampton, third among the grantees that include eight earls, fourteen lords, more than one hundred knights, and fifty-four captains. The charter also names Walter Cope and another on the named-pipe list, Lord Lawarr (De La Warre). Obviously, Cotton was catering to the Company leaders.

In fact, if the named pipes were perks for the powerful, then Lord De La Warre was an obvious choice. After all, he was Thomas West, third Baron De La Warre (1577–1618), and once the Second Charter was in hand, he was named "First Lord Governor and Captain General of Virginia for Life."[20] He was a major venture capitalist for the Virginia Company, investing 5,000 pounds, while the standard share cost 12 pounds, 10 shillings. De La Warre's appointment as governor for life, which promised to end the unworkable government structure established by the Virginia Company Council, could have been known to Cotton through news arriving with the supply ships that year.

Like De La Warre, two other men named on Cotton's pipes were later to become notable. Captain Samuel Argall could also have been known to Cotton, since he first came to Jamestown in 1609. Cotton may have been

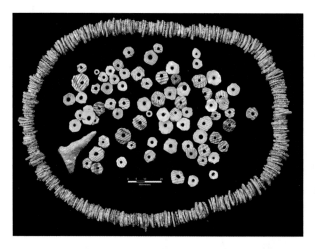

Some of the more than 2,000 mussel shell beads, a stone bead drill, and English flint arrow points from the central cellar/well are more signs of the Virginia Indian presence in James Fort.

aware of Argall's navigation accomplishments. Argall had discovered a short and fast way to sail to Jamestown from the Azores Islands by way of Bermuda, a discovery that may have led to his becoming admiral of De La Warre's rescue fleet in June 1610. In later years Argall would be appointed a lieutenant governor to rule Jamestown. Cotton would have known Captain Francis Nelson as the captain of the ship that brought Cotton to Jamestown in 1608. Nelson would become a major player in the Northwest Passage Company, ultimately dying in what would be named Nelson's Bay as he sought the elusive ice-free passage to the Orient. Perhaps Cotton recognized all-stars in the making.

These are the brief biographies of the names on the pipes. Why Cotton had to name them remains one of the most intriguing mysteries of the abandoned cellar/well finds. Like the writing slate, however, the names on the pipes are examples of some of the surprisingly literal messages left to us by Jamestown's past.

Other significant "messages" from the well surprisingly come from non-literate people in the fort who were so important to Jamestown's survival, the Powhatan Indians. More than 2,000 shell beads in the process of man-ufacture in the Indian manner and Indian arrow points made of English flint speak strongly to the presence of Virginia Indians in the fort and the mixing of the two cultures. There was indeed a nonadversarial side of Powhatan/English relations. This insight, once again, is a surprise revelation.

A "NEW PUMPE"

The colony's short-lived central cellar/well needed a quick replacement as the Jamestown population grew considerably with the inclusion of Gates's Bermuda newcomers (about 150) and then De La Warre's men (more than 200). A small initial barrel-lined well could hardly be adequate to serve so many. In 1610, Strachey refers to an "olde well and new Pumpe."[21] This sounds like he was referring to the "olde" central cellar/well first and then a new one that had a pump, and both were still in operation. A pump, probably a reused ship's bilge pump, could deliver a much greater volume of water in a shorter amount of time than the bucket-by-bucket system. To operate efficiently, the new well had to have a water reservoir much larger than a barrel. It also had to be located inside the fort, where it would be secure and readily accessible. But where did Gates's or De La Warre's men put this new and improved source? Strachey did not give a location, but a central location in the fort, like that of the first cellar/well, must have made the most sense. Yet experience had taught the men that drawing water near the brackish river was a very bad idea. So what area would meet the requirements: far enough away from the river, yet still inside the fort? It is almost certain that an enormous backfilled timber-lined well found eighty feet to the north of the central cellar/well near the north bulwark is the well of Strachey's "new Pumpe"; indeed, its location is inside the fort but as far away as possible from the river and from the brackish original well.

It took finding the half-sunken brick chimney foundation of a circa-1617 extension to the governor's rowhouse to lead to the discovery of this replacement well. The uneven surface of the brickwork hinted that it had been seated on previously unstable ground. Reason suggested that because the heavy brick chimney had been inadvertently built on top of soft soil, such as that indicating an earlier forgotten and filled-in well, it inevitably would settle down into the old shaft. That proved to be the cause of the sinking brickwork.

Excavations beneath the fireplace revealed a nine-foot-wide well shaft that extended down at that width to about eight feet below the surface. At that point the backfilled shaft morphed into a square shape, indicating

Left: The timber-lined well during excavation. *Right:* The sunken double chimney inadvertently built above the abandoned well shaft.

that the builders began building and sinking a square wood liner of some sort where the ground was still dry. The wood lining had completely disintegrated at that dry depth, but there was the strong possibility that an intact square wooden shaft might be preserved in the water below. It was. At a depth of eight feet, six inches, the soil became moist, and remnants of a timber lining appeared. Digging below that revealed more and more intact remnants of the lining until the timber was completely preserved to the bottom, fourteen feet below grade. It is significant to emphasize that the upper two feet of timber had only partially decayed. The wood below the early seventeenth-century water level remained intact because of the four-centuries-old permanently wet environment. The wood above had partially decayed, but the rising water table in recent centuries raised the well-water level gradually enough to stop the decomposition. Since the water level in wells is affected by and reflects sea level, this sequence of partially intact to totally decayed wood is evidence that there has been a two-foot rise in sea level since circa 1610. This is rare evidence from the past that may help to settle the present-day arguments among scientists about the actual yearly sea level rise in the Chesapeake area.[22]

From the original water-table line to the bottom, the well had the appearance of a vertical timber mineshaft, the inside made up of a double-walled box with horizontal boards pegged at the corners, and the outside made of vertical planks. This raises the question, Did miners actually construct the shaft? The answer might be yes: given the Company's golden hopes, they might have sent men with mining skills to the colony. Whether or not miners did build the well shaft is clearly debatable, but the water capacity of a mine-sized shaft could solve the water problem of the inflated Jamestown population. The 5' × 5', four-foot-deep box formed a reservoir that would have held at least 750 gallons of water, enough reserve to feed the "new Pumpe" and the demands of the multitude of new immigrants.

Timber-well lining made of triple-walled oak boards.

Like the brick-lined Smithfield well outside the fort, the timber-lined well stood open and serviceable long enough to catch a number of accidentally lost objects, including a number of serviceable, intact German stoneware Bartmann, or bearded man, drinking jugs. Like the various containers from the bottom of the Smithfield well, these jugs had likely been inadvertently knocked from the edge of the wellhead, then survived the fall thanks to the cushioning effect of the standing water. Obviously, they were not considered valuable enough to salvage. Other things at the bottom *were* worth rescuing but were abandoned anyway: a ceremonial battle-axe-like object known as a halberd and a very elegant pistol. The halberd was decorated with a tracery of dolphins, elements of De La Warre's coat of arms. This corroborates the date after which the timber well had to exist: June 10, 1610, when De La Warre with his halberd first set foot on Jamestown Island. In fact, Strachey mentions that a number of soldiers known as halberdiers, perhaps as many as fifty, marched in De La Warre's processions at Jamestown, probably when he arrived, and especially whenever he marched to church. But the halberd in the well appeared to be used for more than De La Warre's ceremonies. The blade had been purposely bent somewhat back onto itself, forming a hook. This may suggest why it wound up in the well. It may have been altered to become a grappling hook, then lost trying to salvage a heavy iron chain or the wooden well bucket found with it. An iron pike head found with the halberd, also bent into a hook, seems also to have been used during an aborted attempt at retrieving something.

The pistol is harder to explain. It was an expensive model almost certainly brought to Jamestown by a high-status person.[23] Surely the accidental loss of something this useful and costly would have led to a serious and successful recovery. But was it accidentally lost? Fine conservation of its

Left: Recovery of De La Warre's ceremonial halberd from the bottom of the well. *Right:* Prince Maurice with his halberdier entourage at the frozen Hofvijver, Netherlands. (Adam van Breen, 1618, Rijksmuseum, Amsterdam)

extremely corroded firing mechanism determined that it had all its parts, but the mainspring may or may not have been broken before it was lost. If it was, then it could just have been purposely thrown away. If the gun was in serviceable condition before it went into the well, it is tempting to speculate that the well was a good place to get rid of a murder weapon. In that case, there would have been no reason for the murderer ever to retrieve it. A murder weapon would almost certainly be empty when a guilty person tried to hide the evidence, but X-rays and subsequent conservation of the piece showed that it was still loaded; in fact, there were two lead balls in the barrel. A double load was often used for combat. When the gun was fired, the two balls would spread and either cause a greater wound or hit more than one enemy. But scenarios other than military combat could explain the loss. Was the weapon lost down the well during an intramural dispute that left the owner dead before he could fire his weapon? Or did a terrified wife secretly toss the loaded gun into the well to keep it away from an abusive husband?

There is, of course, no end to possible explanations for why the loaded pistol wound up in the well. But archaeological research should only deal with probabilities that require an unbroken chain of circumstantial evidence. In the case of this pistol, that chain just does not exist, so the mystery behind the lost pistol must remain. Fortunately, finding this type of gun in this James Fort well contributes to history in another way. The piece has a distinctive flint-and-steel ignition system known as a Roman lock, hereto-

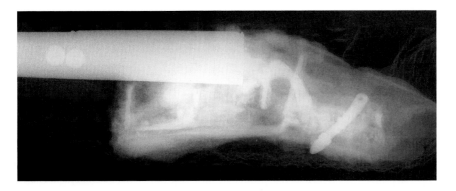

X-ray of the timber-well pistol before conservation showing its double load (*barrel left*) and the Roman lock mechanism. (Emily Williams, Colonial Williamsburg Foundation)

fore thought to have been in use on expensive guns no earlier than 1640. It is clear this Roman lock gun wound up in the well much earlier than that—sometime between 1610 (De La Warre's arrival) and circa 1617 (the date of the brick chimney). So this piece was not only still serviceable when it was lost, but it was a state-of-the-art weapon for its day, making the permanent loss of this valuable weapon even more puzzling.

Along with the halberd and pistol, a considerable collection of organic artifacts and "eco-facts" were found in the water. Shoes and shoemaker's waste leather were found to have survived in that anaerobic environment. A number of insect remains also survived, including a number of European specimens, the earliest remains of invasive species yet found in North America. Twenty-two types of beetles were among them, as well as perhaps America's first recorded bedbug.[24]

The layer of garbage and trash above the water level contained an enormous collection of butchered cow, pig, and deer bones, an abundance of oyster shells, and numerous varieties of fish bones—all evidence quite unlike the meager pulverized remains of taboo foods found in the "starving time" deposits. While the collection has not yet been thoroughly analyzed, the abundant remains of cattle and hogs paint a picture of a time when the colony was well on its feet. Interestingly, the remnants of the plants and seeds also found in the wet soil were almost all native varieties. They included maize, pumpkins, squash, blueberries, wild cherries, blackberries, and walnuts.[25] Imported plant foods were apparently lacking and perhaps unnecessary. In any case, a diet mixing domestic meat from imported

Child's shoe and a lead "Yames Towne" shipping tag (?), from the timber-lined well fill, ca. 1611.

Scarab beetle remains (*right*) and a modern example (*left*), one of the twenty-two types of European species found in the ca.-1611–17 timber well. These are the earliest evidence of European invasive insects yet found in America.

Discarded food bones from the timber-lined well, including an abundance of butchered pig and cow cuts, a stark contrast to the pulverized collection of horses, dogs, wild game, and fish found in the "starving time" layers of the central cellar/well.

European animals with the native plants is yet another instance of life in Virginia as truly a blending of two worlds.

Other artifacts found sealed in the well pin down its post–"starving time" date more precisely. More than two dozen clay tobacco pipes were found, a type dating the deposit to after 1610. But how long after 1610 is always the question. The answer seems to lie in the lowly oyster. The oyster shells turn out to be time capsules that suggest a deposition date of 1612. How? Oyster growth takes place in spurts and pauses depending on the salinity of the water. The salty period shows up as ridges on the shells. Intense study of these well-oyster growth rings indicated that the oysters were probably harvested during the Virginia drought in late 1611 or 1612, a time when the salty water was not so diluted by fresh rainwater. Since the oysters were found in the well's backfill, the oyster study suggests a relatively short life span for the well: 1610–11.[26] Another factor cutting short the life of the well was probably seeping erosion at the bottom. Archaeological excavation of the shaft had to be ended when water and silt sprang up from the bottom so fast that none of our mechanical pumps could keep up with it. Even given the two-foot rise in the water table since the well was in use, this silting must have been an immediate problem to the settlers that led to the quick demise of the well. The short life span is consistent with mention of what appears to be yet another replacement well in 1611: "a new well for the amending of the most unwholesome water which the old afforded."[27] Where was this well? It may have been the brick-lined well found just west of the fort, which appeared to date to after about 1617 and to have survived until 1625 (see pp. 111, 112). There is some reason to believe this well could have been built earlier, and quite possibly during Dale's first governorship. If so, the longer duration of this brick-lined well, as compared to the short-lived barrel- or timber-lined versions, is itself significant. This seems to be another instance where the colonists learned to adapt to the alien Virginia environment. A brick lining, they learned from experience, has staying power.

"OUR BEST COMMODITIE WAS YRON"

Our excavations south of the timber-lined well uncovered a two-room cellar containing yet another sequence of time-capsule-like strata and a pattern of deep postholes. As at Jane's kitchen, layered artifacts found in the cellar revealed an evolving use of the space: first as an early experimental metalworking shop, then as a commercial-scale bakery. The building alignment and ten-foot offset from the paralleling palisade was the first sign that this building was part of the fort plan. The postholes marked the positions of major support posts, which were sunk deep into the cellar floor, indicating that a substantial building once stood on the site. The postholes also revealed that the structure had two cellar rooms reached by earthen steps.

As the kitchen was used over time, a layered series of ash and artifact deposits built up, revealing much about the use of the space. The lowest, and therefore the earliest, surface consisted of tightly packed soil containing concentrated iron particles, waste iron, charcoal, and slag, all residue from a blacksmith's forge. Other sealed layers were composed mostly of a cinder-like waste known in the blacksmith trade as "clinker," conclusive evidence that indeed blacksmithing was the earliest use of the cellar.[28]

Here almost certainly was the site of the 1607 metalworking operation about which Captain Smith boasted: "our best commoditie was Yron which we made into little chisels."[29] Melted lead and fragments of crucibles were

Above: The Jamestown metalworking shop may have looked like this painting of the interior of a mid-seventeenth-century smithy. (*Interior of a Smithy,* Cornelis Beelt, ca. 1650–60; Frans Hals Museum, Haarlem, purchased with support of the Rembrandt Association). *Below:* The metalworking shop/bakery cellar overview showing the major structural postholes along the clay cellar walls, half-buried water barrels (*left*), the forge area (*center*), bake ovens (*upper left*), a mysterious fireplace (*upper center*), a metal finishing space (*center right*), and stairs (*lower center*).

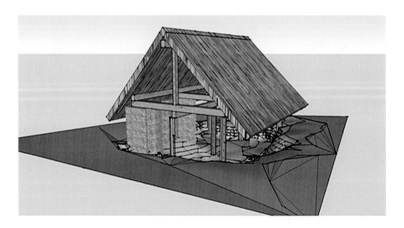

Conjectural reconstructions of the metalworking shop/bakery building. (David Givens, Jamie May)

also found embedded in the waste layers, an indication that the forge was used not only for ironworking but also for melting ore suspected of containing precious metals, and for melting lead to make bullets and shot. It is also likely that one of the ironworkers was the blacksmith James Read. He was an artisan who arrived with the first settlers and who escaped hanging for striking the governor, John Ratcliffe, at about the same time Smith reported the successful iron operation. Read's life was probably spared because his singular blacksmith's skills were so vital for the repairing of guns and armor in the cellar shop.[30]

The accumulation of debris we found on the original clay floor of the cellar indicated where the various steps in the iron manufacturing process

Blacksmith waste from the metalworking-shop levels, including (*left to right*) an apparent repaired shovel cleat; (*center*) bar iron refuse; (*right*) a broken box handle and rods for nail making. The nails indicate that smithing was taking place in the metalworking shop/bakery.

took place. For example, a change in elevation and a pattern of debris on the floor defined a line clearly marking where a partition separated processing rooms. The series of iron-rich strata in the northern room indicated where the main forge was located and where the chisels and other iron products were made. The lowest floor level in the southernmost room was embedded with only a light scatter of iron filings, suggesting that this was the space where the smith did his finishing work. Crucibles containing traces of copper and zinc were also used (and broken) in this room. Together those elements produce brass, probably the Jamestown product reported by the Spanish.[31]

In the same room an artisan seems to have made and/or dropped a sheet-copper pendant depicting a finely engraved silhouette of a Virginia Indian. Was this just decorative jewelry for the Indian trade, or was it made for another purpose? Documents suggest an answer. It was customary for the Indians and the English to require emissaries on both sides to wear something around their necks to show they were genuine officials: Indian

Copper pendant found in the metalworking shop probably depicting a Virginia Indian (Powhatan?).

shell beads to be worn by the English officials and copper pendants by the Indian spokesmen. This, then, could be an identification badge that may depict Powhatan himself, in which case this pendant is the only known image of this powerful leader.[32]

The blacksmith's floors in both rooms were eventually paved with a thick layer of clay, signifying a change in the use of the space. On that paving the workers built a rather curious structure in the corner of the south room, possibly some sort of furnace or oven. Seated on a wood foundation and then fired to a temperature high enough to turn the clay behind it brick-red, this box-like apparatus remains a mystery. Its use in some process that required such searing heat is puzzling, especially given the fact that wood was used as part of its construction. Clay must have coated the wood framing, which would offer some fire protection, but, inevitably, the wooden frame had been reduced to charcoal. The exact purpose of the feature remains enigmatic, but it clearly indicates a change in the use of the room: from iron finishing to an unknown high-heat process.

We found that five different deposits had accumulated on the charred ruins of the box and on the surrounding clay floor. Fragmented apothecary jars were found in the uppermost stratum. No residues survived in the jar fragments to reveal their original content, but the fact that these jars were made primarily for medicinal compounds may be a clue to their presence in this cellar. It is possible that an optimistic botanist, someone like the German bioscientist John Fleischer, may have been experimenting with plant residues in this structure. If so, he was working in the cellar before sometime in 1608, the year he died. His presence among the first settlers suggests that the Virginia Company investors had high hopes for discovering New World cures for Old World diseases. That may or may not be true, but the jars' possible role in producing experimental drugs and the continual change in the use of the cellar certainly prove, once again, that the early colony's specialists followed Company directions by seriously exploring all possible ways to turn a profit.

"WE DAILY FEASTED WITH GOOD BREAD"

After the two cellar rooms had gone through the blacksmithing, metallurgy, and apparent other experimental attempts at commodity production, other archaeological evidence shows that a decision was made to convert the cellar space into something that would address the major problem facing the colonists: food and its preservation. All else fails without a reliable food supply, and baked goods extended the shelf life of provisions that otherwise would quickly rot in the intense Virginia heat and humidity. Hence, the northern room was converted into a bakery. Fish, the staple at Jamestown, would spoil in a couple of days without some sort of processing. No wonder the colonists dried and powdered sturgeon for baking into fish cakes—a process obviously carried out, as we have seen, in the first kitchen: "We had more sturgeon than could be devoured by dog and man, of which the industrious by drying and pounding, mingled with caviar, sorrel, and other wholesome herbs, would make bread and good meat."[33] That great quantities of sturgeon bones were not found sealed in the oven ash in this new bakery, as they were in the first kitchen, probably reflects the fact that cornmeal and flour were more available by the time the replacement bakery was in operation. The availability of these commodities was certainly one of the "improvements" brought to the colony by new leadership under De La Warre, Gates, and Dale. Under their command, what the Indians wouldn't trade, the soldiers took by force.

We have seen that the first kitchen/bakery of 1608 wound up being abandoned and backfilled with the arrival of De La Warre. Fairly early in the Jamestown experience, it must have become apparent that making and working iron for export or finding gold and silver was unrealistic. And the grim lesson of the "starving time" was how vital a reliable source of food was. Consequently, it must have made sense to recycle the metalworking cellar into that much-needed replacement bakery.

Both the 1608 kitchen/bakery and the new bakery had some common characteristics. Both had two ovens constructed by tunneling into the clay cellar walls. The first fires in both bakeries then solidified these dome-like clay cavities and would eventually bring the space to baking temperature. Similarly, once the ovens reached the right temperature, the bakers raked out the wood ash directly onto the floors, where it accumulated over time. It appears that the baking process was identical in both structures: the bread went into the preheated oven after the ash was removed, the doors were shut, and the bread allowed to bake until done. But the new bakery differed from the old—it was not only new, but improved. The new ovens had larger baking capacities. And while the old bakery must have had only smoke holes in the roof, the newer facility had a draft hood, at first seated on wooden floor posts, then based on a substantial brick-based draft chimney. Nevertheless, the new bakers let the waste ash pile up in front of the ovens until the ever-rising working floor apparently made it too difficult to conveniently work them. To remedy this problem, some of the built-up ash, and even the original blacksmith's floor beneath, were dug away, putting the oven doors at a better working height. Ash removed from the ovens also was found piled on top of that mysterious wood firebox in the adjacent room. This is clear evidence that the larger ovens were in operation after the smaller box was abandoned. So at least we know that the puzzling smaller firebox played no role in the new large-scale baking process. In the oven room, the waste ash was also found to cover barrels that had been half buried upright in the floor along the west wall of the room, showing that they too had been used before the bakery was in operation. The barrels were probably obsolete cooling tanks left over from the earlier blacksmithing operation.

Ultimately, after the bakery went out of business, artifact-laden refuse layers filled in the abandoned cellar hole. The objects numbered in the tens of thousands and included a substantial collection of military-related finds: firearms and firearm accoutrements, edged weaponry, pike heads, and elements of armor. Many of these objects had been altered to make them more suitable for the Virginia climate and more useful in combating Indian guerrilla warfare tactics. For example, the recovery in the cellar fill of a visor mask found severed from what must have been a style of close burgonet helmet is clear evidence that the colonists had come to realize that an iron mask was of no advantage when fighting the very mobile Indians, especially in the stifling Virginia summer heat. Fifteen sword guards were also found but almost no blades. Most of the hilts appeared to have been broken away from the blades, suggesting that while a traditional combat sword was useful in European-style warfare, it was of little use in Virginia. It seems, then, that the blades were recycled into knives, which would be useful both to the English and/or as Indian trade items. Evidence of weaponry of a very different kind was also found in the cellar fill. Five deer antlers with their points sawed off with a metal saw wound up buried in the fill as well. This appears to be clear evidence that someone, either the English or Indians in the fort, was making antler arrow points. Smith wrote, "their [Indians'] ar-

Close visor section of a burgonet-type helmet (*left*), probably removed from the helmet skull by an armorer working near the abandoned metalworking shop/bakery cellar, similar to the close helmet (*right*) found at nearby Carter's Grove in a 1619–22 trash pit. (Colonial Williamsburg Foundation)

rows are made some of straight young sprigs, which they head with bone, some two or three inches long."[34] Smith's bone-tipped arrows were almost certainly headed with antler bone. In fact, examples of antler-bone tips survived in the anaerobic deposits in the timber-lined well.

Artifacts and records set the time when the blacksmith shop/bakery was in operation. If this was the site where John Smith saw the Jamestown-made chisels, then it seems safe to conclude that the blacksmith shop began its life in the fall of 1607. We already know that the arrival of De La Warre likely sets the time of the bakery conversion: after 1610. Broken pots found in the abandoned bakery cellar tend to confirm an after-1610 date for the filling of the cellar as well. Dates of artifacts, including dozens of European tobacco pipe fragments found in abundance in the cellar backfill, give a broad time range for the end of the working cellar, since pipes of this style were manufactured circa 1610–40. The latest datable artifacts found sealed in the backfilling strata—crucial to dating the fill layers—turned out to be two English coins, known as Harrington farthings, bearing the mint

Left: Swords and armor shown during their recovery from the abandoned metalworking shop/bakery cellar. *Right:* A collection of sword hilts probably discarded in the shop/bakery to convert blades into trade knives.

date of 1613. This, of course, only establishes that the new bakery went out of business sometime after 1613, but coins can circulate for years. It takes the relationship of the filled-in new bakery and the adjacent addition of Governor Argall's house to establish a more precise date for the end of the bakery. It is significant that part of the foundation of Argall's latest addition to his house was built directly on top of the post-1613 cellar fill, so the cellar probably had a ten-year life span, from 1607, based on Smith's ironworking comment, until 1617, the date of the addition.

One artifact found among the debris in the abandoned cellar fill is yet another damaged human skull. Like Jane and the trepanned skull from the southwest bulwark, it reemphasizes the dangers of life at James Fort. This cranium could be identified as the remains of a European (English) male aged approximately seventeen to twenty-one years. Forensic analysis revealed no signs of cannibalism but instead showed solid evidence of predeath blows to the head made by a dull-edged, elliptical-shaped instrument, a weapon not unlike the stone axe that apparently injured the trepanned man.[35] The trauma to this skull was almost certainly the cause of this man's death. Therefore, a case could be made that the man was killed by Indians. The disposal of this possible combat fatality (found apart from the rest of the body in a layer of trash) also needs an explanation. The most plausible scenario could be that as post–"starving time" construction took place in the fort, especially in the area of the original 1607 summer burials, an early grave that held the remains of an Indian war casualty was accidentally disturbed, the skull inadvertently removed, and then ultimately tossed into the abandoned bakery/cellar hole.

The modification of the helmet, adaptation of the swords to knives, and the fashioning of arrow points from antlers obviously did not occur in the smith's shop or the bakery, for the stratum in which these artifacts were found was an in-filling of the abandoned cellar building. It seems likely that all this reworked weaponry and armor was waste coming from an armorer's workshop, perhaps located in a structure found to have stood just west of the bakery/cellar. There we uncovered a rectangular pattern of posts and wall slots directly under a post-fort chimney foundation and a fallen mud-and-stud wall. When we removed them, we found the building's support postholes, narrow wall trenches between them, and some stains from decayed wall studs. This was an exciting find because the survival of the wall fabric with the studs showed that the actual 1607 grade both inside and outside the building was intact, and, unlike the other mud-and-stud buildings found at James Fort, the wall footing had escaped later plowing. Because of this rare happenstance, the footprint revealed the plan of the northern section of the building and, for the first time, the fabric of its walls. Gaps in the wall trench lines indicated that this building was small, twelve feet by at least twenty feet, but had at least as many as four doors.[36] This gives the impression that the structure was a small, semi-open-air workshop, but it is likely to have extended for an unknown distance south into the area where the later chimney did not shield the remains from the plow. A partition trench on the inside indicated that the building had at least two rooms, one as narrow as eight feet. In the larger room, two postholes penetrated the floor, perhaps originally holding the support posts for the armorer's bellows. Iron nodules littered the floor as well—more evidence of the armorer's work.

The question then became, Was this building used as the fort's "corps de garde" (guardhouse)? If so, then any objects found on the floor ought to be military in nature. In fact, more than two dozen lead shots, bullet-making waste, a bandolier (powder cartridge), a gunflint, two jack plates (vest armor), a cannon primer, a falconet cannonball, a dagger blade, and a rapier

Rare surviving mud-and-stud wall remnants between major structural postholes found at the site of an armorer's shop (corps de garde?).

sword hilt were recovered in these rooms. Recovery of a 1602 silver coin, an English half groat, is evidence that this building was likely built very early in the life of the fort. In that case, it was standing by 1610, when Strachey listed it among the buildings in the "middest" of the fort. Clearly this armorer's workshop could double as a small guardhouse.

JAMESTOWN "MANSIONS"

After 1610, the building of new living quarters and the razing of others seem to reflect a shift in the Virginia Company's thinking from their first concept of Jamestown as a mere military trading post to visions of creating a permanent English town. As we have seen, the fort town plan changed dramatically after the arrival of De La Warre. The "middest" of the fort became a permanent "town center," while dwellings for soldiers and settlers were moved outside the triangle. The mud-and-stud building walls were leveled and pushed into cellars, while the more public Virginia Company structures like the church, the storehouse, and the corps de garde were left standing in the center of the fort. Then the more permanent cobble-based rowhouses for the governors and councilors were constructed just west of the fort center (see illustration on p. 102).

During De La Warre's urban-renewal campaign, his men likely leveled a well-built structure that was located along the south wall of the fort that may have been the president's house. A fifty-foot-long straight line of structural postholes, spaced precisely ten feet apart, was found near the southwest bulwark, marking the north wall line of this short-lived structure. Unfortunately for archaeologists, it had been built on some of the ground that was eventually swept away by nineteenth-century river shore erosion, which presumably took the south side of the posthole building site with it. Nonetheless, the one surviving line of postholes was, surprisingly, enough evidence to determine the building's overall size, and even its quality. First, its size. Its location relative to the projected fort wall line reveals its overall dimensions. How so? Remember that all the fort buildings found along the palisade lines were offset ten feet from the palisades, leaving space for the fort streets that are described in documents.[37] In all likelihood, the missing south wall bordered the ten-foot-wide street, and the single posthole wall line was parallel with and thirty-four feet north of the projected south palisade wall line. It follows that the missing south wall once existed twenty-four feet from the northern wall line (thirty-four feet minus ten feet). This math defines a sizable $24' \times 50'$ structure. Second, quality plaster was found in some of the postmold fill—the soil that could accumulate only after the post either was removed or decayed. In other words, the plaster only had a chance to get into the open posthole after the building ceased to exist, probably when the building was being razed. As the walls came tumbling down, fine wall plaster would likely wind up in the holes left from the removed posts. This in turn suggests that this sizable structure with finished plaster walls was almost certainly a step up in quality from the mud-and-stud "castles in the air" to which Smith so mockingly referred. But even more revealing of quality is the fact that, as in the church, the precise alignment and spacing of the posts indicates the use of formal joinery in the building frame. All the other postholes of the early fort-period earthfast building frames were almost random in spacing and haphazardly aligned, a sure indication that they were not formally framed up. The plaster and the formal framing are then signs that this early house was meant for a high-status person, possibly the president of the council.

A Robert Cotton pipe was found in one of the postholes, which proves that the probable president's house was built sometime after the fall of 1608, when, as we know, Cotton arrived at Jamestown. That chronology would fit with the time period when George Percy was president of the colony, from May 1609 until Sir Thomas Gates arrived from Bermuda a year later. Percy did have a house, and a house of quality. In his account of the events of 1609–10 he mentions that one day he "stepped out of my house with my sword drawn."[38] Later he wrote that he kept a "continual and daily table for gentlemen of fashion." By the time he wrote this, in 1611, these entertainments in the new governor's house probably continued a tradition he had started in his earlier house.[39] That first upscale house could well be our six-posthole structure, a house that did not stand for long and indeed was razed by De La Warre to accommodate the erection of the more elaborate governmental half-timber rowhouses nearby. It follows that the earlier president's house must have set a precedent for reserving the western side of the fort for the Company officials.

The timber-framed rowhouse foundations, likely built by Gates in 1611 and described by Ralph Hamor as "two faire rows of houses, all of framed Timber, two stories," were defined archaeologically by their surviving foundations (see p. 102). The northernmost building was probably for the governor. Its footings suggested that this house had eight rooms, enough space to accommodate most of the leaders who lived there. But the house was not big enough for Governor Samuel Argall, who expanded it in 1617. The Company records state: "Such were built [rowhouses] wherein the governor always dwelt [with] an addition being made thereto in the time of Captain Samuel Argoll."[40] Why did Argall need more space? Was it a political move? Did the house need to be a more powerful symbol than it was during the administrations of its builder, Sir Thomas Gates, and the residence of the stern Sir Thomas Dale? They were all governors when the fort was ruled by strict martial law. The same laws were in effect when Argall ruled the colony, 1617–18, and he used his privileged position to assign Jamestown workmen, at Company expense, the task of making the house larger and more formal.

Signs in the ground of Argall's personal improvements to the governor's house certainly suggest that they had a formal design, although eighteenth- and nineteenth-century plowing destroyed parts of the addition's footprint, and earthmoving for the 1861 Civil War fort gouged away much of the north foundation. Under that earthwork, however, the earlier archaeological evidence, as piecemeal as it may seem, remained. Bits and pieces of surviving fragments of the foundations were remarkably revealing. They showed that the basic addition added two rooms on the ground floor, a massive double-hearth brick fireplace between rooms, and a three-sided "tower" on the east. The double-hearth brick fireplace was partially built on the site of the abandoned timber-lined well, very unstable ground. That proved to be a big problem for Argall and those who followed.

Workmen were either unaware that the timber-lined, backfilled well once stood on the site they chose, or they thought the heavy foundation would somehow bridge the unstable ground. The latter might explain the configuration of the footing found there: a foundation of mortared brick or brickwork that was based on a bed of cobble, mortared English flint, or Bermuda limestone. Regardless of intent, however, these heavy footings nonetheless failed to solve the instability problem, as part of the addi-

Excavation of Samuel Argall's addition to the governor's house (*center*) showing the brick tower or bay window foundation (*center foreground*) and the sunken brick chimney base (*right center background*).

tion's double-hearth brick fireplace sank into the soft soil of the abandoned timber-lined well shaft. This was not a good thing for the governor's new quarters, but it turned out to be fortuitous for the archaeology. As much as five feet of the chimney foundation sank into the well, where it was protected from the later disturbances.

Once we totally exposed the remarkably intact chimney block, it had much to reveal about the nature of Argall's addition. It indicated that the building was as fashionable as one would expect of a governor's house. A thick formal plaster stucco survived on a hearth section, which would probably mean the southernmost room was pretentious. Brick tile paving in front of that fireplace also indicated that this was an ornate room, possibly where Governor Argall would meet and impress visitors with his high rank. That might partially explain efforts to hide the fact that the chimney and hearth were sinking. We also found clear signs of a face-lifting process in which a mason leveled up the sinking firebox floor and added a buttress to support a leaning chimney.

The two-story building was very likely of half-timber construction like the original section of the governor's residence that Hamor described. But

Argall added an unexpected design element to the south facade. A half-hexagonal brick foundation two bricks thick was found attached to the southernmost room, which suggests that either a bay window in each of the two stories or a two-story balcony was once included in the governor's house design. If it was a balcony, the footing would have supported a commanding position from which Argall could address his subjects and keep an eye on the masses as they went about their business in the rest of the fort. Argall may have even kept a gun in that elevated position to remind the people that martial law prevailed and that he meant to enforce it. Ruling by force must have aroused security concerns in Argall's mind, which may explain another brick foundation built onto the south wall of the original section of the house, a footing that could have been for a small guard booth.

Clay tobacco pipe fragments associated with some of the building repair deposits, as well as deposits made directly on the brickwork after the house was dismantled, date the life span of the addition. The pipes were a style popular in 1610–30, so they could date to Argall's governorship. The numerous repairs to the chimney also suggest a lengthy life for the building as a residence for Argall's successors: Nathaniel Powell in 1619; George Yeardley in 1619–21; and perhaps for a time even Francis Wyatt in 1621–26.[41]

At some later time, yet another addition was made to the original 1617 extension, built partially upon a mortared flint-stone footing, and partially upon yet more unstable ground: the adjacent backfilled metalworking shop/bakery. Curiously, the apparent masonry foundation morphed into a wall supported by ground-set posts heading to the south. Uniquely for James Fort buildings, a section of a plastered mud-and-stud base survived between posts. This construction seems to be a particularly "slight built" extension of the more substantial half-timber house, suggesting it may have been a lean-to, possibly to be used for drying the tobacco that was reportedly growing in the streets of the fort as early as 1610. By 1623, the palisade wall, or what was left of it, could have evolved from a barrier defending the town from Indians to becoming just a fence keeping the hogs out of the tobacco crop. At that time, even a small yield of tobacco in the then-tumbledown, one-acre fort would have turned a sizable profit. Such was the rather inglorious end to James Fort and its governor's mansion. But of course the glorious success of the tobacco plantations that sprang up along the James would live on to make Virginia the richest English colony in America.

EPILOGUE

Since *Jamestown, the Buried Truth* was published, I have heard people say time and time again, "You have rewritten the Jamestown story." I am not naïve enough to agree. Long before we put a shovel in the ground, the basic Jamestown "creation" story had been told and retold from historical documents alone—written accounts that supply the narrative context for our archaeological *discoveries*.

But exactly what does the word "discover" mean? By the "age of discovery" in the fifteenth century, the word had evolved to mean the act of revealing something to someone, as we archaeologists do with our shovels and trowels. That definition fits. To put it simply, our archaeological act of discovery makes the unknown known to the unknowing. For example, Columbus in his first expedition *discovered* six islands in the Western Hemisphere, a geographic fact that ultimately made a "New World" known to an unknowing "Old World." By the same token, George Percy's vivid 1607 narrative *Observations* chronicles his revelations of bountiful Virginia that he passes on to a heretofore unknowing English nation. In reality, however, four centuries later, our Jamestown archaeological discoveries are more than just *discoveries;* rather, they are *rediscoveries* of what men like Percy *discovered.* What are our *rediscoveries?*

Overall, adding a powerful third dimension and concrete physical reality to what we thought we already knew about Jamestown is certainly no small accomplishment. Our unearthing of objects last touched four centuries ago by characters known only from their written words transforms, in a very real sense, our understanding of who they were and what they did. To me, that process comes as close as one can get to time travel. Bare facts come alive—an empathetic process that reveals daily life at James Fort for the English and for the Powhatan.

Beyond lending that powerful sense of reality to the age-old Jamestown story, our rediscoveries have, indeed, added remarkable new perspectives to early American history. We have seen that the "lazy gentlemen" label for all the early colonists does not entirely jibe with the archaeological evidence. Clearly some of them had to build the fort and its buildings, and others, specialists, scientifically experimented with ways to capitalize on the natural resources of Virginia. It is also now clear that the Indians were on both sides of the palisade, as evidenced by the things they were making in the traditional Indian fashion in the fort. Poor "Jane" finally solves the enigma of the stories of cannibalism and powerfully shows how close Jamestown came to complete failure. The size and location of the first substantive church and the chancel burials emphasize that religion was not just a side issue for the Virginia Company, nor was the Jamestown Protestant church without Catholic influences.

Living on the far-flung reaches of the Virginia frontier did not seem to affect the English hierarchy. The real beginning of the great leveling of colonial society had to wait until 1616–19, when the Virginia Company began giving land to individual immigrants who paid for their own passage or to pay off apprentices. Representative government followed. The monumental policy shift from the strictest limitation of individual freedom of all except the well-born during the first ten years of the settlement (1607–17) to the rudimentary elements of representative democracy in the colony by 1619 had to happen before the idea of America could really begin to take form.

The first edition of this book began with the suggestion that the American Dream was born at Jamestown in 1607. Now, based on more recent archaeological discoveries, it seems more accurate to say that English America was all but stillborn, the growing pains excruciating, and the Company town atmosphere stifling. Yet the hard times taught the English that a successful life in America was possible only if everyone could get a piece of the action. The land itself turned out to be the gold, the tobacco republic was born, and Virginia would become the first permanent English settlement in North America. Then the American dream could begin.

As this book goes to press, more truths lie buried. While we can now know the development of James Fort and its town center, it remains to rediscover a much larger "James town." Already traces of an expanded defensive perimeter give tantalizing hints of what remains to be revealed. There is every reason to suspect that the original fortified area encompassed the entire twenty-plus acres on the western end of Jamestown Island. And sea level rises, and bones will turn to dust. The Jamestown Rediscovery journey across four centuries must continue.

Notes

Introduction

1. Edmund S. Morgan, *American Slavery, American Freedom* (New York, 1975), 56.

2. David A. Price, *Love and Hate in Jamestown* (New York, 2003).

3. Alison Wangsness Clement, "Rewriting American History: Does the Grade School American History Curriculum Reflect the Native American Experience?" (master's thesis, Georgetown University, 1997), chap. 1.

4. William M. Kelso, Nicholas M. Luccketti, and Beverly A. Straube, "A Re-evaluation of the Archaeological Evidence Produced by Project 100: The Search for James Fort," Colonial National Historical Park MS, 1990, Jamestown Rediscovery Center (hereafter JRC), Jamestown, Va.

1. Reimagining Jamestown

1. George Percy, *Observations Gathered out of "A Discourse of the Plantation of the Southern Colony in Virginia by the English, 1606" written by the honorable gentleman, Master George Percy,* ed. David B. Quinn (Charlottesville, Va., 1967), 15.

2. Philip L. Barbour, *The Jamestown Voyages under the First Charter, 1606–1609* (London, 1969), 1:49–54.

3. Ibid., 1:16.

4. Dennis Blanton, personal communication, 1996.

5. John Smith, *The Complete Works of Captain John Smith, 1580–1631,* ed. Philip L. Barbour (London, 1986), 1:29.

6. When Newport returned to England in July 1607, one hundred were listed as alive, as three had died between the May landing and that time. I am indebted to Nancy Egloff for the math on the numbers.

7. Smith, *Complete Works,* 2:38.

8. Percy, *Observations,* 16.

9. Ibid., 17.

10. Ibid., 18–19.

11. Gabriel Archer, "A Relatyon . . . written . . . by a gent. Of ye Colony," in Barbour, *Jamestown Voyages*, 1:95.

12. Ibid.

13. Percy, *Observations*, 22.

14. Louis B. Wright, *A Voyage to Virginia in 1609: Two Narratives: Strachey's "True Reportory" and Jourdain's Discovery of the Bermudas* (Charlottesville, Va., 1964), 63–64.

15. Smith, *Complete Works*, 2:142–43.

16. Percy, *Observations*, 27.

17. Smith, *Complete Works*, 2:143.

18. Percy, *Observations*, 27; Smith, *Complete Works*, 2:144, 145.

19. Smith, *Complete Works*, 2:153–54, 157.

20. Ibid., 2:169, 180, 325.

21. Ibid., 2:180–81.

22. Ibid., 2:187.

23. Ibid., 2:208, 212.

24. Ibid., 2:213, 223.

25. Ibid., 2:225.

26. Ibid.

27. Fred Fausz, "England's First Indian War, 1609–1614," *Virginia Magazine of History and Biography* 98, no. 1 (Jan. 1990): 3–56.

28. Smith, *Complete Works*, 2:232–33; Nancy Egloff, personal communication, May 1997.

29. William Strachey, in Wright, *Voyage to Virginia*, 63–64, 76.

30. "Thomas West to Lord Salisbury, September 1610," in *Jamestown Narratives: Eyewitness Accounts of the Virginia Colony: The First Decade, 1607–1617*, ed. Edward Wright Haile (Champlain, Va., 1998), 465.

31. Strachey, in Wright, *Voyage to Virginia*, 79–81.

32. Ralph Hamor, *A True Discourse of the Present Estate of Virginia, and the successe of the Affaires there till the 18 of June, 1615* (Richmond, Va., 1957). Compare Smith, *Complete Works*, 2:242.

33. Susan Myra Kingsbury, ed., *The Records of the Virginia Company of London* (Washington, D.C., 1906–35), 3:101–2.

34. Don Diego de Molina to Don Alonso de Velasco, May 28, 1613, in *Jamestown Narratives*, ed. Haile, 749.

35. Smith, *Complete Works*, 2:262.

36. Samuel H. Yonge, *The Site of Old James Towne, 1607–1698* (Richmond, Va., 1903), 65.

37. Gravenhage Colectie Leupe Supplement Algemeenrijksarchief, The Hague, Velh 619.89. Michael Jarvis brought this chart to my attention, and Jeroen van Driel gave valuable references.

38. Smith, *Complete Works*, 2:242; Hamor, *A True Discourse of the Present Estate of Virginia*, 40, 45.

39. Smith, *Complete Works*, 2:138, 1:35.

40. Strachey, in Wright, *Voyage to Virginia,* 79–82.

41. Ibid.

42. Smith, *Complete Works,* 2:225, 262, 324; Ivor Noël Hume, *The Virginia Adventure* (New York, 1994), 274.

43. Kingsbury, ed., *Records of the Virginia Company of London,* 4:259.

44. "A Brief Declaration of the Plantation of Virginia during the first twelve years, when Sir Thomas Smith was governor of the Company, and down to this present time. By the Ancient Planters now remaining in Virginia, 1623," in *Jamestown Narratives,* ed. Haile, 893–901.

45. Smith, *Complete Works,* 2:136.

46. Rosemary Taylor, *Blackwall, the Brunswick and Whitebait Dinners* (Blackwall, England, 1991). I am indebted to Ms. Taylor for providing a copy of this booklet.

47. I am indebted to Daniel Brown for alerting me to the exact numbers.

48. Alexander Brown, *The Genesis of the United States* (Boston, 1890), 2:943–44, 977–78, 904, 1006–10, 1055; Jocelyn R. Wingfield, *Virginia's True Founder: Edward-Maria Wingfield and His Times, 1550–c. 1614* (Athens, Ga., 1993); Samuel Merrifield Bemiss, *Ancient Adventurers: A Collection of Essays* (Richmond, Va., 1964); Warner F. Gookin, "Who Was Bartholomew Gosnold?," *William and Mary Quarterly* 6, no. 3, 3d. ser. (1949): 401.

49. Mary Abbott, *Life Cycles in England, 1560–1720: Cradle to Grave* (London, 1996), 135.

50. Catherine Correll-Walls, Jamestown Biographies database project, JRC, 2004. This is a database of biographical information gathered from traditional sources such as firsthand accounts, scholarly publications, and British and Irish manuscript collections. These age estimates are based on the Correll-Walls database.

51. Ibid.

52. Nell Marion Nugent, *Cavaliers and Pioneers* (Baltimore, 1974), xxi.

53. Correll-Walls, Jamestown Biographies database, passim.

54. That Martin does eventually get by grant ten shares (1,000 acres) of choice land in 1616 and stays in Virginia may mean his English prospects were not major. Brown, *Genesis of the United States,* 2:943.

55. Correll-Walls, Jamestown Biographies database.

56. Gookin, "Who Was Bartholomew Gosnold?," 401.

57. Ibid. The author is indebted to Nicholas Hagger, past owner of Otley Hall, the Gosnold mansion, for suggesting sources for Gosnold's biography.

58. Smith, *Complete Works,* 1:203.

59. Percy, *Observations,* 24.

60. Correll-Walls, Jamestown Biographies database.

61. Smith, *Complete Works,* 2:140–42, 160–63, 190–91.

62. Federal Emergency Management Agency Flood Insurance Study and Flood Rate Map, Jamestown Island, Virginia, 1991.

63. Strachey, in Wright, *Voyage to Virginia,* 37.

64. Edward Arber, ed., *Captain John Smith's Works, 1608–1637* (Westminster, 1895), xcv.

65. William Strachey, "The Historie of Travell into Virginia Britania" (1612), in *Jamestown Narratives,* ed. Haile, 58.

66. Frederic W. Gleach, *Powhatan's World and Colonial Virginia: A Conflict of Cultures* (Lincoln, Neb., 1997), 91.

67. Smith, *Complete Works*, 1:173.

68. Correll-Walls, Jamestown Biographies database.

69. Helen C. Rountree, *The Powhatan Indians of Virginia: Their Traditional Culture* (Norman, Okla., 1989), 184–94.

70. Strachey, "Historie of Travell," 619.

71. Smith, *Complete Works*, 2:258, 260–61.

72. Survey Report no. 01538, PRO, Class SP14/90, State Papers, Domestic, James I, Letters and Papers, 1611–1618, pp. 421–56, Virginia Colonial Records Project, Library of Virginia, Richmond.

73. Smith, *Complete Works*, 2:262.

74. Strachey, "Historie of Travell," 622; Percy, "A True Relation of the procedings and occurrents of moment which have hap'ned in Virginia from the time Sir Thomas Gates was shipwrack'd upon the Bermudes, anno 1609, until my departure out the country, which was in anno Domini 1612," in *Jamestown Narratives*, ed. Haile, 509.

75. Hamor, *A True Discourse of the Present Estate of Virginia*, 40, 45; Smith, *Complete Works*, 1:63, 73.

76. Strachey, "Historie of Travell," 622; copy of deciphered letter of the Marquess of Flores to the King of Spain, August 1, 1612, vol. 2589, folio 61, General Archives of Simancas, Department of State, in Brown, *Genesis of the United States*, 2:572.

77. Strachey, in Wright, *Voyage to Virginia*, 64.

78. Arber, ed., *Captain John Smith's Works*, xcv.

79. Pedro de Zúñiga to Philip III [February 23] March 15, 1609, in Barbour, *Jamestown Voyages*, 2:255.

80. Strachey, in Wright, *Voyage to Virginia*, 63.

81. Virginia M. Meyer and John Frederick Dorman, *Adventures of Purse and Person*, 3d ed. (Richmond, Va., 1987), 71.

82. Brown, *Genesis of the United States*, 2:895.

83. Douglas W. Owsley, Parvene Hamzavi, and Karin L. Bruwelheide, "1997 Analysis of the APVA Skeletal Collection, Jamestown, Virginia," MS, JRC, January 1997.

84. "Thomas West to Lord Salisbury, September 1610," 466.

85. Brown, *Genesis of the United States*, 1:116, 393.

86. Ibid., 116, 121–22, 125–27, 141, 143–45.

87. Ibid., 243.

88. Frank Hancock, *Jamestown Revisited: A Medical Proposal with Circumstantial Considerations* (Burlington, N.C., 1998); Percy, *Observations*, 24–27.

89. Smith, *Complete Works*, 2:223–24.

90. Brown, *Genesis of the United States*, 1:311.

2. Rediscovering Jamestown

1. Haile, ed., *Jamestown Narratives*, 891–915.

2. Smith, *Complete Works*, 1:234.

3. Richard Randolph, "Island of Jamestown," *Southern Literary Messenger* 3 (1837): 303; John L. Cotter, *Archeological Excavations at Jamestown, Virginia* (Washington, D.C., 1958), 17; Thad Tate, "Early Jamestown History," volunteer training lecture, Yeardley House, Jamestown Island, February 1994.

4. William M. Kelso, Jamestown Rediscovery Archaeological Project: The Search for the Site of James Fort (1607), Master Plan, Association for the Preservation of Virginia Antiquities (APVA), Richmond, 1993.

5. Strachey, in Wright, *Voyage to Virginia,* 63–64.

6. Ivor Noël Hume, conversation at Jamestown Island, March 1994.

7. Smith, *Complete Works,* 2:212.

8. Cotter, *Archeological Excavations at Jamestown,* 17.

9. Ivor Noël Hume, *Here Lies Virginia* (New York, 1963), 46; Ivor Noël Hume, "Thinking the Unthinkable," keynote address delivered at the Society for Historical Archaeology Conference, Williamsburg, Va., 1984; Virginia A. Harrington, "Theories and Evidence for the Location of James Fort," *Virginia Magazine of History and Biography* 93 (January 1985): 36–53.

10. Kelso, Luccketti, and Straube, "Re-Evaluation of the Archaeological Evidence Produced by Project 100," 42.

11. Strachey, in Wright, *Voyage to Virginia,* 63–64.

12. Ivor Noël Hume, Fort Raleigh National Historic Site, 1991 Archaeological Investigation, MS, National Park Service Southeastern Archaeological Center, copy at JRC, 25–26.

13. Smith, *Complete Works,* 2:187.

14. Ransome True, ed., "Seventeenth Century Patents from the State Land Office, Richmond, Virginia," MS. no. 83, JRC.

15. Percy, *Observations,* 22.

16. Strachey, in Wright, *Voyage to Virginia,* 81.

17. Smith, *Complete Works,* 2:157.

18. See chap. 1, p. 48.

19. Smith, *Complete Works,* 2:180–81, 324.

20. Strachey, in Wright, *Voyage to Virginia,* 79–81.

21. Hamor, *A True Discourse of the Present Estate of Virginia,* 33.

22. Mary Jeffery Galt, "Report to the Jamestown Committee," n.d., in Cotter, *Archeological Excavations at Jamestown,* 222.

23. Smith, *Complete Works,* 3:295.

24. I am indebted to the research and master's thesis of Eric Deetz for the "discovery" of the mud-and-stud tradition at early Jamestown and his direction of the fieldwork at Building 165 (Eric Deetz, "Architecture of Early Virginia: An Analysis of the Origins of Earthfast Tradition" [master's thesis, University of Leicester, England, 2001]). See also Rodney Cousins, *Lincolnshire Buildings in the Mud and Stud Tradition* (Lincolnshire, England, 2000).

25. Correll-Walls, Jamestown Biographies database.

26. Strachey, in Wright, *Voyage to Virginia,* 79.

27. Jeffery P. Brain, "Fort St. George VI," privately printed archaeological report, Pea-

body Essex Museum, Salem, Mass., 2001, 8; Ivor Noël Hume, *Shipwreck! History from the Bermuda Reefs* (Hamilton, Bermuda, 1995), 16.

28. I am always indebted to the unique and precise expertise of Bly Straube, Jamestown Rediscovery senior curator, for the identification and dating of the artifacts discussed in this book.

29. Joann Bowen, "The Starving Time at Jamestown," MS report, JRC, 1999.

30. Smith, *Complete Works,* 2:232.

31. Nancy Egloff, "Report on the Starving Time Population Figures," MS, Jamestown-Yorktown Foundation, Jamestown, Va., 1990; Correll-Walls, Jamestown Biographies database.

32. Strachey, in Wright, *Voyage to Virginia,* 71.

33. "Thomas West to Lord Salisbury, September 1610," 466.

34. Smith, *Complete Works,* 1:259.

35. Smith's Map of Virginia, 1612, detail ibid., 2:140–41; Scott Weidensail, "Tracking America's First Dog," *Smithsonian Magazine* (March 1999): 45–57.

36. This is a preliminary identification by veterinarians at Virginia Polytechnical and State University, Blacksburg. Thanks especially to Dr. Thomas Chamberlain.

37. Percy, "A True Relation," in *Jamestown Narratives,* ed. Haile, 505.

38. Copy of deciphered letter of the Marquess of Flores to the King of Spain, August 1, 1612, vol. 2589, folio 61, General Archives of Simancas, Department of State, in Brown, *Genesis of the United States,* 2:572.

39. "Brief Declaration of the Plantation of Virginia," 894.

40. Smith, *Complete Works,* 2:317–18.

41. "Lord De La Warre to Virginia Company of London, July 7, 1610," in *Jamestown Narratives,* ed. Haile, 466.

42. Strachey, in Wright, *Voyage to Virginia,* 81.2

43. Ibid., 64.

44. Smith, *Complete Works,* passim.

45. Beverly Straube, personal communication, 2003.

46. Timothy Easton, personal communication, 2004.

47. Strachey, in Wright, *Voyage to Virginia,* 56.

48. Barbour, *Jamestown Voyages,* 52.

49. Hamor, *A True Discourse of the Present Estate of Virginia,* 45; Kingsbury, ed., *Records of the Virginia Company of London,* 4:101–2.

50. "Brief Declaration of the Plantation of Virginia," 912.

51. Thanks to John Schofield and Chris Elmers of the Museum of London for showing me London parallels.

52. Engraving entitled *Van Dun's Almshouses in Petty France,* in John Thomas Smith, *Antiquities of London* (London, 1791).

53. I am indebted to Dennis Blanton, past director of the Center for Archaeological Research, College of William and Mary, for assessing the collection.

54. Archer, "A Relatyon . . . written . . . by a gent," 96.

55. I am grateful for the advice of Jamestown Rediscovery staff archaeologist David Givens regarding projectile-point manufacture.

56. Smith, *Complete Works,* 2:175. I am grateful to Jamestown Rediscovery conservator Michael Lavin for an explanation of why copper preserves organic material.

57. Archer, "A Relatyon . . . written . . . by a gent," 96, 98. I am indebted to Dennis Blanton for assessing the collection.

58. Strachey, in Wright, *Voyage to Virginia,* 99.

59. John G. Hurst, David S. Neal, and H. J. E. van Beuningen, *Pottery Produced and Traded in North-west Europe, 1350–1650,* Rotterdam Papers 6 (Rotterdam, 1986), 63.

60. William M. Kelso, *Jamestown Rediscovery, 1994–2004,* with Beverly Straube (Jamestown, Va., 2004), 133; Strachey, in Wright, *Voyage to Virginia,* 82.

61. Brown, *Genesis of the United States,* 1:492.

62. Smith, *Complete Works,* 3:262.

63. I am indebted to archaeologist Danny Schimdt, who spent six weeks in the well shaft, half-submerged at times, to reveal its secrets, and for his summary of the results: D. Schimdt, "Excavations Results and Interpretation STR170 at Jamestown," MS, JRC, 2003. I am also indebted for the arduous months of conservation of the well artifacts by Michael Lavin and Dan Gamble.

64. Kelso with Straube, *Jamestown Rediscovery,* 137, 140.

65. William M. Kelso, *Kingsmill Plantations, 1619–1800* (San Francisco, 1984), 55, 56.

66. Kelso with Straube, *Jamestown Rediscovery,* 132.

3. Recovering Jamestownians

1. Tonia Deetz Rock, "Report on Burial 1046 at Jamestown, Virginia," unpublished report, JRC, 2003.

2. Strachey, in Wright, *Voyage to Virginia,* 76.

3. Warner F. Gookin and Philip L. Barbour, *Bartholomew Gosnold: Discoverer and Planter* (London, 1963), 49–177.

4. Haile, ed., *Jamestown Narrative,* 185.

5. This important artifact was identified by the combined efforts of senior curator Bly Straube, conservator Michael Lavin, Professor James Lavin, and arms expert Claude Blair.

6. *Drill Postures,* an engraving by T. Cockson, 1615–20, The British Museum.

7. Smith, *Complete Works,* 1:206.

8. I am indebted to Dr. Ashley McKeown, who, with a generous grant from the crime novelist Patricia Cornwell, and under the direction of Dr. Douglas Owsley, Smithsonian Institution, spent two years in residence at Jamestown during the burial study and taught us all some of the science and art of forensic anthropology and skeletal biology.

9. I am grateful for the skillful research of Edward and Joanna Martin of Hitcham, Suffolk.

10. W. C. Metcalfe, *The Visitations of Suffolk 1561, 1577 and 1612* (Exeter, 1882), 170: Tylney.

11. British Public Record Office: PROB/11/136 and PROB/11/199; Higham St. Mary parish register, Suffolk Record Office (Ipswich, England).

12. GC17:755, vol. III, *f.* 178, Suffolk Record Office (Ipswich, England).

13. The original Davy manuscripts are in the British Library (Add. MS 19105), but there are microfilms in the Suffolk Record Office. The Shelley visit is on *ff.* 96r–99v.

14. Death date given in W. Copinger, *Manors of Suffolk* (1910), 6:81.

15. W. H. Rylands, *Heralds' Visitation of Suffolk 1664–1668* (London, 1910): Blackerby of Shackerland Hall.

16. Public Record Office: PROB/11/396.

17. British Library Add. MS 19,133, *ff.* 9v–12r.

18. Public Record Office PROB/11/396.

19. A. G. H. Hollingsworth (vicar of Stowmarket, 1837–59), *The History of Stowmarket* (Ipswich, 1844), 207.

20. *White's Directory of Suffolk* (1855), 418.

21. Julian Litten, *The English Way of Death* (London, 1992), 106. This critical dating evidence was confirmed by Mr. Litten in a cell-phone call with the Council for the Care of Churches archaeologist Joe Elders, directly from the Stowmarket vault site.

22. Dr. Terry Melton, memo to Dr. William M. Kelso, Re: Skeletal Remains JR10456B, Skeletal Remains Shelley Church, Mitotyping Technologies Case no. 2477, August 22, 2005.

23. Edward Martin, "Evidence for the Burial Places of Two Maternal-Line Relatives of Capt. Bartholomew Gosnold of Virginia," Rediscovery Center, Jamestown, 2005, n.p.; Mary Abbott, *Life Cycles in England 1550–1720* (London and New York, 1996), 96.

24. Dr. Terry Melton, memo to Dr. William M. Kelso, Re: Skeletal Remains JR10456B, Skeletal Remains Shelley Church, Mitotyping Technologies Case no. 2477, August 22, 2005.

25. Douglas Owsley and Karin Bruwelheide, "Mitochondrial DNA Sampling at Shelley Church, Suffolk County, England, October 6, 2005," 6, appendix I, "Report provided by Dr. Sam Stout, Department of Anthropology, The Ohio State University."

26. Advisory Panel on the Archaeology of Christian Burials in England (APACBE), "Comments on the Report: 'Mitochondrial DNA Sampling at Shelley Church by Douglas Owsley and Karin Bruwelheide'" (November 14, 2005), Rediscovery Center, Jamestown.

27. For a summary of these aging tests, see Margaret Cox, *Life and Death in Spitalfields* (York, England, 1996), 93.

28. Geochron Laboratories, "Radiocarbon Determination of Age, GX-32317, 10/06/2005, JRC." I am indebted to Catherine Correll-Walls, who found the very generous architectural historian Philip Aiken, who in turn connected me with the owner of Shelley Manor, Andrew Scott, who then led me to Shelley Church.

29. Smith, *Complete Works*, 1:xxix.

30. Haile, ed., *Jamestown Narratives*, 25.

31. Peter Wilson Coldham, ed., "The Voyage of the *Neptune* to Virginia, 1618–1619, and the Disposition of Its Cargo," *Virginia Magazine of History and Biography* 87, no. 1 (1979):

32. I am indebted to Martha McCarthy for bringing this reference to my attention.

32. Percy, *Observations*, 24–27.

33. Douglas Owsley, personal communication, October 6, 2005.

34. Smith, *Complete Works*, 2:142.

35. I am indebted to Dr. Ashley H. McKeown and Dr. Douglas W. Owsley for this analysis.

4. Reanimating Jamestown

1. Smith, *Complete Works,* 2:225.

2. Barbour, *Jamestown Voyages,* 49–54.

3. Edward S. Neill, *History of the Virginia Company of London* (Albany, N.Y., 1869), 8–14.

4. Wherever soil layers survived under the 1607 fort deposits, they contained a type of Virginia Indian pottery known as "Townsend series," made and used by late Woodland-period people, who cleared and farmed in Virginia into the late sixteenth century.

5. I am indebted to Daniel W. Brown for our discussions about palisade construction and engineering.

6. Unless otherwise noted, the references for the facts about the Jamestown "medical men" and other activities illustrated by the Rediscovery finds come from the fine research of Beverly Straube, Jamestown Rediscovery senior curator, much of which appears in chap. 4 of Kelso with Straube, *Jamestown Rediscovery, 1994–2004.*

7. Smith, *Complete Works,* 2:294.

8. Percy, *Observations,* 22.

9. David W. Stahle et al., "The Lost Colony and Jamestown Droughts," *Science,* n.s., 280, no. 5363 (April 24, 1998): 564–67.

10. I am indebted to Beverly Straube for her meticulous research that identified most of the artifacts discussed throughout the remainder of this chapter.

11. Smith, *Complete Works,* 2:138.

12. Carter C. Hudgins, "Articles of Exchange or Ingredients of New World Metallurgy?," *Early American Studies* 3, no. 1 (2005): 32–64.

13. Brown, *Genesis of the United States,* 110.

14. J. C. Harrington, *A Tryal of Glasse* (Richmond, Va., 1980), 10.

15. David Higgins, *Devon Archaeological Society Proceedings, no. 54, 1996* (1998): 245.

16. Warren Billings, *Jamestown and the Founding of the Nation* (Gettysburg, Pa., n.d.), 46.

17. Kelso with Straube, *Jamestown Rediscovery, 1994–2004.*

18. Thomas Davidson to Beverly Straube, personal communication.

19. Although this cut stone has yet to be specifically identified, it is likely from the banks of the Thames, still littered with similar ancient stones to this day.

20. Daniel Schmidt, "The Role of Fishing in Sustenance of the Early Jamestown Colony: The First Decade" (master's thesis, Royal Holloway, University of London, 2004), 7.

21. Joanne Bowen and Susan Trevarthen Andrews, "The Starving Time at Jamestown," report submitted to JRC, December 1999, 2.

22. Smith, *Complete Works,* 2:189.

23. Ibid., 1:219, 2:212.

24. Ibid., 2:187.

5. Holy Ground

1. Bill Warder, "Capture, Courting, Conversion, and Conjugality: Pocahontas, John Rolfe, A Pretty Chapel, and Archaeology at Jamestown Shed Light on an Unresolved Mystery," MS, Colonial National Historical Park, Historic Jamestown.

2. Edward Maria Wingfield, "A Discourse of Virginia," in *Jamestown Narratives,* ed. Haile, 196.

3. Smith, *Complete Works,* 1:218.

4. Strachey, in Wright, *Voyage to Virginia,* 80.

5. Tom McLaughlin, "The 1611 Church at Henricus," Henricus Foundation, 2011, p. 22; Carl Lounsbury, personal communication; Joe Elder, personal communication.

6. The "Laws Martial and Moral" of 1610 required strict church attendance, twice a day (Strachey, in Wright, *Voyage to Virginia,* 80).

7. William Graham, *The Jamestown Church 1608,* drawing, Department of Architectural Research, Colonial Williamsburg Foundation, 2012.

8. Correll-Walls, Jamestown Biographies database; Martha McCartney, *Virginia Immigrants and Adventurers, 1607–1635: A Biographical Dictionary* (Baltimore, 2007), 88, 408, 738, 770; description of Wynne in Public Record Office, State Papers, 14/8 fo. 164r (no. 81), in Paul E. J. Hammer, "A Welshman Abroad: Captain Peter Wynn of Jamestown," *Parergon* 16, no. 1 (July 1998): 60–64. Jamestown Rediscovery staff archaeologist Mary Anna Richardson kindly brought this article to my attention.

9. Douglas Owsley and Kari Bruwelheide, Smithsonian, personal communication.

10. "Captain William West," manuscript report by Ancestry.com, Smithsonian National Museum of Natural History.

11. Emily Williams, Colonial Williamsburg chief conservator, generously provided the powerful X-rays and the XRF analysis; Tim Sledz and Benjamin Ache of Microphotonics, Inc., kindly provided the box scan.

12. Once the microphotonic scan was read, Michael Lavin, senior conservator, and David Givens, senior archaeologist, alerted me to this possibility. See also S. Tarlow. "Reformation and Transformation: What Happened to Catholic Things in a Protestant World," in *The Archaeology of Reformation,* ed. David R. M. Gaimster and Roberta Gilchrist (Leeds, England, 2003), 108–21.

13. Scot Whitaker, Smithsonian National Museum of Natural History, provided the microscopic analysis.

14. Michael Lavin, personal communication.

15. "Captain Gabriel Archer," manuscript report by Ancestry.com, Smithsonian National Museum of Natural History.

16. Reverend Msgr. Timothy Keeney, St Bede's Catholic church, personal communication.

17. Gary Vikan, former director of the Walters Museum, Baltimore, Md., personal communication.

18. Reverend Chris Epperson, Bruton Parish, personal communication.

19. Hammer, "A Welshman Abroad," 60–64.

20. "Reverend Robert Hunt," Ancestry.com.

21. Strachey, in Wright, *Voyage to Virginia,* 80.

22. Owsley, Smithsonian National Museum of Natural History, personal communication.

23. Strachey, in Wright, *Voyage to Virginia,* 80.

24. Tarlow, "Reformation and Transformation," 113–14.

6. Jane

1. The study of Jane is described in detail in James Horn, William Kelso, Douglas Owsley, and Beverly Straube, *Jane: Starvation, Cannibalism, and Endurance at Jamestown* (Colonial Williamsburg Foundation, Preservation Virginia, 2013). The details of the forensic analysis are excerpted from various passages on pages 17–28.

2. Percy, "A True Relation," in *Jamestown Narratives,* ed. Haile, 505.

3. John Smith, *The General History* (London, 1624), in *Complete Works,* 2:232.

4. Ancient Planters, "A Breife Declaration of the Plantation of Virginia," by Francis Wyatt, George Sandis, John Pott, John Powntis, Roger Smith, Raphe Hamer, William Tucker, and William Peerce (1624), in *Journals of the House of Burgesses 1619–1658–59,* ed. H. R. McIlwaine (Richmond, 1915), 29.

5. *A True Declaration of the estate of the Colonie in Virginia, 1610,* and *The Tragical Relation of the Virginia Assembly, 1624,* in *Tracts and Other Papers,* ed. Peter Force, 4 vols. (Washington, D.C., 1836–46), 3:16.

6. Brown, *Genesis of the United States,* 1:392.

7. Dan Boyd Smith pointed out these possibilities. Sir Edward Coke, *The Institutes of the Lawes of England II, 1628–1644,* 7 vols. (London: E. & R. Brooke, 1794), note 43.

8. Percy, "A True Relation," in *Jamestown Narratives,* ed. Haile, passim; Virginia M. Meyer and John Frederick Dorman, *Adventures of Purse and Person,* Order of the First Families of Virginia (Richmond, 1987), 7–71.

9. Douglas Owsley, personal communication.

10. Dan Boyd Smith, digital English parish records, FamilySearch.org, database of the Church of Jesus Christ of Latter-day Saints; Coke, *The Institutes of the Lawes of England II, 1628–1644,* note 43.

11. Strachey, in Wright, *Voyage to Virginia,* 3–58.

12. Smith, *Complete Works,* 2:219–20.

13. Ibid., 1:211.

14. Edmund S. Morgan, *American Slavery, American Freedom* (New York, 1975), 73.

15. Percy, *Observations,* in *Jamestown Narratives,* ed. Haile, 99; Smith, *Complete Works,* 2:225; "A Brief Declaration of the Plantation in Virginia during the first twelve years when Sir Thomas Smith was governor of the Company and down to this present time. By the Ancient Planters now remaining alive in Virginia," in *Jamestown Narratives,* ed. Haile, 895.

16. Smith, *Complete Works,* 2:223–24.

17. Percy, "A True Relation," in *Jamestown Narratives,* ed. Haile, 504.

18. Ibid., 505.

19. Smith, *Complete Works,* 2:218.

20. Strachey, in Wright, *Voyage to Virginia,* 64.

21. Ibid., 71.

22. Smith, *Complete Works,* 2:213.

23. Stahle et al., "The Lost Colony and Jamestown Droughts," 564–67.

24. Matthew T. Balazik, personal communication.

25. Smith, *Complete Works,* 2:125.

26. Strachey, in Wright, *Voyage to Virginia,* 71.

27. Horn, Kelso, Owsley, and Straube, *Jane,* 30.

28. Percy, "A True Relation," in *Jamestown Narratives,* ed. Haile, 499.

29. Woodbury Lowery, *The Spanish Settlements within the Present Limits of the United States* (New York, 1911), 343.

30. John T. McGrath, *The French in Early Florida: In the Eye of the Hurricane* (Gainesville, Fla., 2000), 55.

31. Henry Norwood, *A Voyage to Virginia,* in *Tracts and Other Papers,* ed. Force, 4:10.

32. James Horn, *A Land as God Made It* (New York, 2005), 289–90.

33. Noël Hume, *The Virginia Adventure,* 185.

34. Smith, *Complete Works,* 2:157.

7. Company Town

1. Ralph Hamor, *A True Discourse of the Present Estate of Virginia,* London 1615, in *Jamestown Narratives,* ed. Haile, 827.

2. Smith, *Complete Works,* 2:142–43.

3. Dr. Greg Hancock, professor of geology, College of William and Mary, personal communication.

4. The enhancing was accomplished by hours of skillful work by Jamie May, senior staff archaeologist, and Michael Lavin, conservator, Jamestown Rediscovery Project.

5. National Aeronautics and Space Administration (NASA) officials at Langley Air Force Base, Hampton, Virginia, conducted these tests.

6. Dr. Melvin Wachowiak, senior conservator; Jeff Speakman, head of technical studies; and Dr. Robert J. Koestler, director, Smithsonian Museum Conservation Center, kindly performed this analysis.

7. These tests were conducted by researchers at the Federal Bureau of Investigation, Quantico, Virginia.

8. Heather Wolfe, curator of collections at the Folger Shakespeare Library, Washington, D.C., kindly deciphered some of the text.

9. These articles of clothing were identified by Jamestown Rediscovery senior curator Bly Straube.

10. Archaeologist Audrey Horning alerted me to this practice.

11. Ivor Noël Hume, *Wreck and Redemption: William Strachey's Saga of the "Sea Venture" and the Birth of Bermuda in a Newly Discovered Manuscript* (Hampton, Va., 2009); William Strachey, "Commonplace Book, 1615–1628," untitled MS, Accession #1123, Albert and Shirley Small Special Collections Library, University of Virginia, Charlottesville.

12. Joe Marenghi and Aleck Loker alerted me to this possibility.

13. Rita Boswell, consultant archivist of Westminster School, London, graciously found

and copied the manuscript of the Hariot phonetic alphabet. Vivian Salmon makes a strong argument that Strachey had use of Hariot's dictionaries (Vivian Salmon, "Thomas Harriot and the English Original of the Algonkian Language," The Durham Thomas Harriot Seminar, Occasional Paper 8, pp. 1–23, Rockefeller Library, Colonial Williamsburg, 1993).

14. William Strachey, *The Historie of Travaile into Virginia Britannia; expressing the Cosmographie and Comodities of the Country, together with the Manners and Customes of the People. Gathered and observed as well by those who went first thither as collected by William Strachey, Gent., the first Secretary of the Colony and "A Dictionarie of the Indian Language"* (London, 1849). Strachey admits in the title that he got some of his information from earlier travelers to Virginia.

15. Jamie May, Jamestown Rediscovery senior archaeologist, personal communication.

16. Noël Hume, *The Virginia Adventure,* 166.

17. Sir Walter Raleigh, *History of the World* (London, 1614).

18. Richard Hakluyt, *The Principal Navigations of the English Nation* (London, 1589–1600).

19. Samuel M. Bemiss, ed., *The Three Charters of the Virginia Company of London, with Seven Related Documents, 1606–1621,* Jamestown 350th Anniversary Historical Booklet no. 4 (Williamsburg, Va., 1957), 42.

20. Ibid., 27.

21. William Strachey, *For the Colony in Virginea Britannia: Lawes Divine, Morall and Martiall, &c* (1611), 15.

22. For example, see A. J. Longa, N. L. M. Barlow, W. R. Gehrels, M. H. Saher, P. L. Woodworth, R. G. Scaife, M. J. Brain, and N. Cahill, "Contrasting Records of Sea-Level Change in the Eastern and Western North Atlantic during the Last 300 Years," *Earth and Planetary Science Letters* 388 (2014): 110–22.

23. Beverly Straube, personal communication.

24. Gary Andrew King, Allison Bain, and Frédéric Dussault, "Assessment of Insect Remains from a Colonial Well (JR2158; Structure 177) at James Fort, Jamestown, Va., Laboratoire d'archéologie environnementale, CELAT, Université Laval, Québec.

25. Steven N. Archer. "Jamestown 1611 Well Archaeobotanical Analysis," report prepared for Historic Jamestowne, MS 2014, Jamestown Rediscovery Center, Jamestown.

26. Juliana M. Harding, Howard J. Spero, Roger Mann, Gregory S. Herbert, and Jennifer L. Sliko, "Reconstructing Early 17th Century Estuarine Drought Conditions from Jamestown Oysters," *Proceedings of the National Academy of Sciences* 107, no. 23 (June 8, 2010): 10549–54.

27. Thomas Dale to the Council of Virginia, May 25, 1611, in *Jamestown Narratives,* ed. Haile, 523.

28. Shelby Browder and Steve Mankowski, Colonial Williamsburg blacksmiths, personal communication.

29. Smith, *Complete Works,* 2:35.

30. Noël Hume, *The Virginia Adventure,* 162.

31. Carter Christian Hudgins, "Chemistry in the New World: Jamestown Reconsidered," *Chemical Heritage* 25, no. 2 (Summer 2007): 20–26, Beverly Straube. "Surprises from the

Soil: Archaeological Discoveries from England's First Successful Transatlantic Colony," *Post-Medieval Archaeology* 47, no. 2 (2013): 266; Emily Williams, personal communication.

32. Bly Straube, "In Praise or Damning Caricature: An Early Seventeenth-Century Identification Badge," *Colonial Williamsburg Journal* (Winter 2010): 49–53.

33. Smith, *Complete Works*, 2:117.

34. Ibid.

35. Douglas Owsley and Kari Bruwelheide, personal communication.

36. Mary Anna Richardson, Draft Report Structure 186, MS, Jamestown Rediscovery Center.

37. Strachey, in Wright, *Voyage to Virginia*, 79–82.

38. Percy, "A True Relation," in *Jamestown Narratives*, ed. Haile, 506.

39. George Percy to Northumberland, August 17, 1611, in *Jamestown Narratives*, ed. Haile, 558, 559.

40. Kingsbury, ed., *Records of the Virginia Company of London*, 4:101–2.

41. William W. Abbot. *A Virginia Chronology, 1585–1783* (Charlottesville, Va., 1957), 74.

Index

Page numbers in italics refer to illustrations.

Calthrope, Stephen, 35–36
cannibalism. *See* Jane; survival cannibalism
Cape Cod (Massachusetts), 120
Capper, John, *33*
captain's burial (Bartholomew Gosnold?), 118–31; alternative colonists proposed for, 136; artist's reconstruction of burial, *119*; bone chemistry analyses, 135; circumstantial evidence indicating burial is Gosnold's, 136; death of Gosnold and, 20, 36, 120; discovery and dating, 118–20; DNA comparisons with relatives of Gosnold, 122–38, *123*, *129–31*, *133*; full-body reconstruction of Gosnold, *137*; leading staff or half pike, *119*, 120–21, *121*, 136, 175–76; location of, 118–19, 136, 148
captain's leading staffs: in captain's burial (Gosnold?), *119*, 120–21, *121*, 136, 175–76; in church burial C (Archer?), 172, *174*, *175*, 175–76
Carew, Lord, 40
carpenters and carpentry, 159, *161*
Cassen, George, Thomas, and William, *33*
casting counters (jettons), *59*, 84, 98, *99*–100, 106, 152
Catholicism and Catholic artifacts, 38, 43, 44, 161, *163*, 168, 176–80, *177*, 183, 250
Cawsey, Thomasine, 42
Cecil, Robert, Lord Salisbury, 219, *220*, 225
cellars/pits: of barracks, 80, 83–88; circular pit inside south bulwark, 63–64, *64*; of factory, *80*, 92–98, 100; fill layers, 79–80, *80*; Jane, cellar/kitchen fill containing, 185–88, *186–88*, 202–3, 239; north of factory, 106–10; of quarter, 89, 90–92, *91*; as trash deposits, 96–100
ceramics. *See* pottery artifacts
Charles Fort (Virginia), 27, 88
Charles II (king of England), *198*
Chiconamians (tribal group), 40
children: child's shoe found in well, 116, *233*; as colonists, 41, 197, *198*; infant's coral teether and silver whistle, *198*
Christ Church, East London (England), 134–35
church attendance requirements, 262n6
Church of England (Anglican Church), 2, 128, 168, 178, 179, 183

church structures, 8, 167–84; under Argall's administration, 27, 76, 77, 136, 167, 168, 184; artifacts from, 170, 172; belfry, *169*, 169–70; burials inside or near, 136, 168, 171–76, *173–75*, *177*, 180–82; chancel plan and layout, 182; commemorative fence, 89; construction methods, 168–71, *171*; construction process for 1608 building, 168–71, *171*; dismantling of, 50; documentary evidence for, 21, *47*; excavations of, 52–53, 168–71, *169*, *171*, 183–84; original building of, 21, 167; quarter building and, 89–90; rebuilding/reconstruction of, 3, 22, 53, 89, 162, 167, 171; relocation of, 53, 75, 76–77, 184; as Statehouse, 184; surviving brick church tower, 27, 52, *53*, 56, 76, *90*; transfer of English social hierarchy to Virginia and, 182–84; Virginia Company instructions and, 161, 250
Civil War earthwork: archaeological display at, 3–5; church and, 168; construction of, 50, 66, 89, 101–3, 106, 204, 246; in determining fort site, 54, 55, 56, 67; excavations of, *5*, 54, 68, *69*, 70–72; graves under, 118; walls under, 68, *69*; wells under, 70, *71*, 111, 117, 208
clay tobacco pipes: captain's burial and, 119; Cotton pipes, 157, *158*, 208, 210, 219–26, *220*, *222*, 245; date ranges determined from, 83–84, *84*; from factory, 98; from governor's rowhouse, 248; from "new pump," 233; from rowhouses, *103*, 113, 119, 157, *158*; from Smithfield well, 113; from south palisade, 59; Virginia Company business plan and, 157
climate, impacts of, 1, 20, 21, 116, 143–44, 240
clinkers, 159, 234
Clovill, Eustace, *33*, 109
coins and currency, 63, *79*, 84, 98, 100, 106, 208, 209–10, *210*, 241–42
Collier, Samuel, 140
colonists: age, circumstances, and place of origin, 31–34, *33*; children, 41, 197, *198*; De La Warre, accompanying, 24, 42–43, 76, 88, 201, 227; first arrivals, 15–18, 30–36; Gates, accompanying, 23–24, 85–87, 199, 216, 227; intermarriages with

colonists (*continued*)

Virginia Indians, 40–41, 90; laziness/ incompetence of, 2, *3*, 8, 22, 23, 144, 164, 197–98, 250; moving to Falls of the James or Nansemond River, 22; non-English, 22, 155–57; reasons for coming to America, 32–34; shipwrecked in Bermuda, 23, 216; Spain, relations with, 16, 26, 30, 37, 43–45, 194; Virginia Indians, relations with, 1, 16, 20–21, 23, 36–41, 94, 97–98, 101, 109–10, 121, 151–52, 198–99, 210, 250; women arrivals, 22, 41–42, 198

commercial trade, economy, and manufacturing artifacts, 146, 152–60, *153, 154, 156, 158, 160, 161*

Confederate earthwork. *See* Civil War earthwork

construction methods: box-frame, 101; church, 168–71, *171;* "mud and stud," 81–82, *82, 83,* 91–92, 95–96, *97,* 101, 243, *244;* for wells, *111,* 111–13, *112,* 227–29

Cooke, Roger, *33*

Cope, Sir Walter, 219, *220,* 223, 225

copper, 21, 96, 106, 108, 152, *153,* 155, *156,* 237

costrels (handled jugs), 113

Cotton, Robert, 113, 157, *158,* 210, *220,* 221–26, *223,* 245

Council for the Care of Churches (England), 128

Cowper, Thomas, *33*

cratchets, 81, 95

Crofts, Richard, *33*

crucibles: from barracks, 85; from churchyard, 53–54, *54, 55,* 56, *58;* from factory, 98; metallurgy and glassmaking, 155–57, *156, 158,* 208, 234–36, 237; from south palisade, 59; from well, 208

CT (micro-computed tomographic) scans, 176, 212

cucurbit, 98, *99,* 155

cultivation, 21, 22; garden plots, *17, 18,* 68, 152; plowing and archaeological evidence, 50–52, *51,* 100; tobacco, 2, 26–27, 83, 157, *158,* 248; Virginia Company instructions on, 146, 152

Cuttyhunk colony (near Cape Cod, Massachusetts), 34

Dale, Sir Thomas, 25, 26, 40, 113–14, 234, 239, 246

Davis, Captain, 199

Davy, David Elisha, 124, 125, 126, 127

De La Warre, Thomas West, Third Lord: Argall and, 226; arrival of, 24, 42–43, 76, 88, 201, 227; ceremonial halberd of, 229, *230;* Cotton clay tobacco pipe imprinted with name of, 219, *220,* 225; death and burial of, 136, 171; departure of, 24; leader's chair in church for, 182; painting of, 25; relatives buried at Jamestown, 171–75, 180, 182; renovations by, 65, 76–77, 96–97, 98, 113–14, 167, 185, 203, 208–10, 239, 244, 245

de Passe, Simon, *14, 41*

Delft ware, 96, *106,* 151

Deliverance (ship), 23, 42

dendrochronological (tree ring) dating, 9, 152

Devereux, Robert, Earl of Essex, 34

diet. *See* cultivation; food supplies and diet; "starving time"

distilling operations, 98–99, *99,* 155

Dixon, Richard, *33*

DNA testing, 122–38, *123, 129–31, 133*

documentary evidence, 8, 13–45; of evacuation of James Fort, 23–24, 42–43; eyewitness accounts, 13, 48, 162; on first settlers, 30–36; for James Fort, 15–29, 46–49; scarcity and ambiguity of, 1–2; Spain, relations with, 16, 26, 30, 37, 43–45; of "starving time," 15, 23, 190–95; Virginia Company instructions to colonists, 15–16, 104, 121, 143–48; Virginia Company official reports, 161–62, 193–94; on Virginia Indians, 36–41; for wells, 22, 110, 113–14, 227; on women colonists, 41–42; writers of, 14–15

Dods, John, *33*

dogs, 88–89, *89,* 109, 185, 193, 208, *209,* 233

Don Luis, 38

droughts, 1, *152,* 197, 199–200, 208, 233

drug jars (albarellos or apothecary jars), 106, 150–51, *151,* 238

economy, trade, and manufacturing artifacts, 146, 152–60, *153, 154, 156, 158, 160, 161*

47 (*see also* Zúñiga map); marketplace, 26, 208–9; metalworking shop/bakery, 8, 234–43, *235, 236*; north bulwark, 67–70, *69*; quarter building in, 79, 89–92, *90*; rebuilding/renovation of, 21, 24, 29, 64–65; rowhouses in, 25, 79, 101–6, *102, 104, 105*, 138–40, *139*, 244–48, *247*; site of, 4–6, *6, 7*, 15–17, 24, 49–57, *56*; south bulwark, 59–65, *60, 63*, 74; south palisade, 57–59, *58, 60*; storehouse, 8, 21, 100, 101, *105*, 204–6, *207*; transition from fort to town, 26–29, 74–77, 244; west bulwark, 21, 25, *73*, 74, 96, 109, 111, 140, *141*, 150, *154*, 242; west wall, 70–74, *73*, 103, 119. *See also* artifacts; cellars/pits; kitchens; wells

Jamestown, 1–9, 249–51; abandonment of, 50; anniversary excavations/celebrations, 3, *5*, 6, 49; daily life in, 162–64; documentary evidence for, 1–2, 8; excavation of, 3–8, *4–7*; failure, portrayal as, 2, *3*, 8, 144, 164, 250; growth and expansion of, 162; population of, 36, 86–87, 88, 201, 227; representative government and, 184, 250; transition from fort to town, 26–29, 74–77, 244; White (John) building in, 62–63, *63*. *See also* artifacts; burials; documentary evidence; James Fort; Jane; *specific structures*

Jamestown Biographies database project, 255n50

Jamestown Island, 16–18, *18*, 24, 27, 36–37, *51*

Jamestown Rediscovery Project, *6, 57*, 71, 106, 110, 118, 120, *144, 149, 177*, 251

Jane, 8, 185–203; age, social status, and background, 189–90, *191*; artifacts found in fill with, 185, *187, 198*; excavation of, 185–88, *186–88*; facial reconstruction of, *202*; forensic examination and analysis, 188–90, *189–91*; identification of, 195–96; "starving time" and, 185, 186, *189*, 192–200; survival cannibalism of, 186, 188–96, *189–91*, 200–202, 250

Jansen, C., *25*

Jesuits, 38

jettons (casting counters), *59*, 84, 98, 99–100, 106, 152

Joones, Elizabeth, 42

Jordan's Point (Virginia), 116

Kelso, William M., 2–8

Kemps, 22, 40

Kendall, George, 19, 31, *33*, 43

Keyence, 212

Kinistone (Kingston), Ellis, *33*

kitchens: cellar/kitchen (with fill containing remains of Jane), 185–88, *186–88*, 202–3, 239; metalworking shop/bakery, 8, 234–43, *235, 236*; in quarter building's cellar, 90–92

Kocoum, 40

Krauwinckel, Hans, 100

Laxton, William, *33*, 82

Laydon, John, 22

lead cloth seals, 85, 160

lead levels, in bone, 141–42, 181–82, 196

lead shipping tag, *232*

lead tokens, 85

leading staffs. *See* captain's leading staffs

lean-to structures, 77–79, *78*, 83, *102, 104*, 248

literacy artifacts, 161–62, *163*, 194–95, 210–19, *211, 214, 217*, 226

Litten, Julian, 259n21

London rowhouses, *104*, 105

Love, William, *33*

Luccketti, Nicholas, 5

Machumps, 40

Manteo, 217

Mantiuas (Nantaquawis), *39*, 40

manufacturing artifacts, trade, and economy, 146, 152–60, *153, 154, 156, 158, 160, 161*

maps: of Blackwall (England), *31*; James Fort, 15, *16, 17*, 24, 46–48, *47* (*see also* Zúñiga map); Tindall map (1608), *17*, 24, 46; Vingboons chart (1617–20), 15, 27, *28*, 47–48; Virginia, John Smith's map of, 15, *38*, 46

marketplace in James Fort, 26, 208–9

marriages: between colonists and Virginia Indians, 40–41, 90; Laydon, John, and Anne Burras, 22; Pocahontas and John Rolfe, 40–41, 167, 168

Martha's Vineyard, 120

martial law period, 113, 246, 248

Martin, Edward, *133*

description of Virginia by, 13, 15; on first days of settlement, 14–15; governance of settlement and, 22, 87, 179, 198, 245; painting of, *14*; at Point Comfort, 42, 88; rowhouse of, 245; on siting of settlement, 14–15; "starving time" and, 15, 89, 192, 194, 195, 200–201; Strachey's account based on, 15; on West, William, 175

Percy, Henry, Earl of Northumberland, 218

pewter ware, 100, 114, *116*, 141–42, 181, 196, 216

Philip III (king of Spain), 15, *43*, 43–45

Phipson, R. M., 126

Pickayes, Drew, *33*

Pierce, Richard and Elizabeth, 114

pipes. *See* clay tobacco pipes

Pising, Edward, *33*

pit sawing, *154*

pits. *See* cellars/pits

plowing and archaeological evidence, 50–52, *51*, 100

Plymouth (Massachusetts), 1, 50

Pocahontas, 1, 20, *39*, 40–41, *41*, 167, 168

Pocahontas statue, *3*, 55

Point Comfort (Virginia), 27, 42, 43

pottery artifacts: from barracks, 85–86, *86*; from bulwarks, *61*; from burials, 119, 139; Cotton(?) clay pot with impression of native basket, 222, *223*; cross-mending of, 96, 209; from distilling operations, 98–99, *99*, *156*; from factory, 98, *99*, 100; Jane, cellar/kitchen fill containing, 185, *187*; medical-related, 106, 150, *151*; from metalworking shop/bakery, 241; from pit north of factory, 106, *107*; from rowhouses, *106*, *107*; from south palisade, 59; from wells, 113, 114–15, 208, 229. *See also specific types*

powder magazines, *64*, *71*

Powell, Nathaniel, 248

Powhatan (Wahunsonacock; chief), 20, 36–40, *38*, *39*, 44, 109, 153, *153*, 198–99

Powhatans (tribal group), 37, 87, 94, 179, 218

precious and semiprecious stones, 155

precious metals, 1, 15, 32, 98, *99*, 154–55, 162, 223, 239

president's house, 9, 244–46

printers' trademarks, 221, *222*

prisons and jails, 94–95, 101, 224

Project 100, 54–56

projectile points, 106–8, *108*, 140, *226*, 240–41

quarter building, 79, 89–92, *90*

quilt method of excavation, 52

Raleigh, Sir Walter, and Sir Walter Raleigh house (Blackwall, England), 30, *32*, 218, 219, *220*, 224

Randolph, William, 49

Ransacke, Abraham, 216

Ratcliffe, John, 19, 31, 178, 179, 199, 236

Read, James, *33*, 238

reed matting, 106, 108–9, *109*

Reflectance Transformation Imaging (RTI), 212

religious artifacts, 161, *163*, 176–80, *177*, 183

reliquary box, 176–80, *177*, 183

representative government in Virginia, 184, 250

road construction, nineteenth-century, 67, 68, 89–90

Roanoke Island (North Carolina), 224

Roe, Sir Thomas, 40

Rolfe, John, 2, 26–27, 40–41, 167

Roman lock pistol mechanism, 229–31, *231*

Roods, William, *33*

rowhouses (Governor's Row), 25, 79, 101–6, *102*, *104*, *105*, 138–40, *139*, 244–48, *247*

RTI (Reflectance Transformation Imaging), 212

saggers, 157, *158*, 221

Salisbury, Robert Cecil, Lord, 219, *220*, 225

Salmon, Vivian, 265n13

Sands, Thomas, *33*

Santa Lucia (Florida), 201

sassafras root, 150, 162

saw pit, *154*

Sawtell, Barnaby, 125

Sawtell, Francis, 125, 126

Scot, Nicholas, *33*

Sea Venture (ship), 23, 84, 86, 87, 199, 216, 218

sea-level rise, wells indicating, 228

Shakespeare, William, *163*, 219

shell beads, 107, 109, 151, 208, *226*, 238

shoes, 114, 116, 231

Simmons, Richard, *33*

skeletal evidence. *See* burials

slate tablet, 194–95, 210–19, *211, 214, 217,* 226

Smethes, William, *33*

Smith, Herbert Luther, *14*

Smith, John: accounts written by, 1, 14, 15; age, social status, circumstances, and place of origin, 14, 31–32, *33*; Algonquian dictionary published by Strachey and, 218; alleged mutiny of, 1, 35–36; building of houses and, 20, 77, 82; on church, 81, 167, 168; construction/design of settlement and, 16–17, 21, 48, 74–76; on deaths of colonists, 21, 36; "dungeon" story, 108; on fire (1608), 21; on first days of settlement, 17–18; on food supplies, 22, 199–200; on Gosnold, 34, 120; governance of settlement and, 20–23, 31, 179; Hunt and, 172; injury of, 22, 179, 198; interior explorations by, 21, 36; on laziness/incompetence of colonists, 22, 23, 144, 197–98; map of Virginia by, 15, *38*, 46; on metalworking shop, 234, 241; painting of, *14*; planning of Virginia venture and, 31, 35; return to England by, 22; "starving time" and, 15, 86, 192, 197, 200; statue of, 3; Virginia Indians and, 39, 40, 44, 94, *95*, 108, 109, 151, 198, 219, 240–41; on wells dug for settlement, 22, 110, 113, 114, 116–17, 206

Smithfield (west of fort), 21, *71*, 111

Smithfield well, *71, 84, 111,* 111–17, *112, 115, 116,* 229

Smythe, Sir Thomas, 15, 34, 48, 105

snaphaunce pistol lock, *59*

Somers, Sir George, 199

Somerset House Conference (1604), *45*

South Carolina, French settlement in, 201

Southampton, Henry Wriothesley, Earl of, 34, 219, *220*, 224, 225

Spain and Spanish in America, 16, 26, 30, 37, 43–45, 194, 200–201, 219, 225

spatula mundani, 63, *65*, 150

stable isotope testing, 135, 138, 181–82, 189–90, *191*, 196

"starving time" (1609–10), 8, 196–200; deaths and burials from, 54, 86–87, 135, 179 (*see also* Jane); documentary evidence for, 15, 23, 190–95; droughts and, 1, *152*, 197, 199–200, 208, 233; food supplies and diet during, 41, 85–88, 208, *209*; relations with Virginia Indians during, 41, 198–99, 200, 210; social hierarchy and, 183, 195, 201–2; survival cannibalism during, 23, 89, 183, 186, 188–96, *189–91*, 200–202, 250; water supply and, 110, 207

Statehouse: burials under, 42; church serving as, 184

Steen, Jan, *Skittle Players outside an Inn* (painting, ca. 1660–63), *3*

Stevenson, John, *33*

St. Georges Church, Gravesend (England), 40

storehouse, 8, 21, 100, 101, *105*, 204–6, *207*

St. Peters and St. Marys Church, Stowmarket (England), 122, *123*, 126–27, *129*, 130–33, *131*

Strachey, William: account written by, 15, 23, 162, 216, 265n13; Algonquian dictionary published by, 218; arrival in Virginia, 23–24, 199; on Bermuda shipwreck, 216; biographical information, 15, *163*; buildings described by, 28, 79, 82–83, 105; on church, 52, 76, 167, 168, 169, 183; on De La Warre's renovations, 76, 77, 96–97; family crest and coat of arms, 162, *163, 217*; on food stores brought from Bermuda, 89; on halberdiers, 229; on James Fort, 23, 24, 48, 64, 66–68, 70–73, 97; on marketplace in James Fort, 26, 208–9; on Powhatan, 39; signet ring and, 162, *163*; slate tablet and, 216, 218–19, 265n13; on "starving time," 89, 199; on transition from fort to town, 74–76; on Virginia Indians, 37; on wells dug at James Fort, 110, 113, 116–17, 206–7, 227; on West, William, 175

Straube, Bly, 5

sturgeon, 22, *186*, 199–200, 203, 239

support industries, 157–58, 162

survival cannibalism, 23, 89, 183, 186, 188–96, *189–91*, 200–202, 250